Finding Karen Black

Finding Karen Black

Roots Become Wings

A Memoir

By Diane Bay

Roots
to Wings
Press LLC

Finding Karen Black
Roots Become Wings

A Memoir
© 2022 by Diane Bay

ISBN 978-0-578-37371-3 (pbk.)

Library of Congress Control Number: 2022905698

BIO026000   BIOGRAPHY & AUTOBIOGRAPHY /
Personal Memoirs
BIO005000   BIOGRAPHY & AUTOBIOGRAPHY /
Entertainment & Performing Arts
FAM004000   FAMILY & RELATIONSHIPS /
Adoption & Fostering

Internet: www.findingkarenblack.com

Cover photo and design by Diane Bay
Interior design by Jackie Saunders
and Diane Bay

To my birth father Beny Benedetti and his wife Joan:
Thank you for your love and encouragement.

This book is based on my memories and journals and on various photos and videos of the included events. All events actually occurred but are filtered through the lenses of memory and time, and may contain details that others remember differently.

CONTENTS

Acknowledgments

So many people have helped me on this trek. My will alone was not enough to keep me on the path: if these folks hadn't been there, I would have turned back and abandoned my goal long ago.

Closest to my heart first: to my husband, Rich, who shared my moments of discovery and endured my years of toil.

To Karen, for the courage to begin.

To my birth father Beny, for his willingness to accept me into his family and to have our story be told; and his wife Joan, whose active help in editing has been essential.

To my fellow travelers in the online writing community, Scribophile, to which I belonged for a few crucial years. Especially to Bonnie Skiles Rost and the memoir critique group who helped me learn to *show* not *tell*.

To authors whose books were integral to my learning process: William Zinsser, *On Writing Well;* Bill Roorbach, *Writing Life Stories;* Dani Shapiro, *Inheritance.*

To those who helped me finish strong: my editor Grace Wynter and my book designer Jackie Saunders.

To these and more, a million thanks. I'm forever in your debt.

—Diane, April 2022

To love someone is to make them feel seen.
— Karen Black

PROLOGUE

Summer 2012

A LIFETIME OF LONGING had come down to this one moment. Standing in the shade beside our country mailbox, I stared at the envelope in my trembling hands. The return address read *Illinois Secretary of State, Records Department.* Time slowed. Blood throbbed in my ears. I prayed for strength to handle whatever I found inside.

Then I unfolded my original birth certificate:

Mother: *Karen Blanche Black.*

Age at birth: *nineteen.*

Tears rimmed my eyes as I gazed at the name of the woman who had given me up for adoption fifty-three years ago. The woman whose name I was only now able to see, thanks to a law that opened Illinois' adoption records.

I clutched the certificate to my chest as I strode to my home office. Now would begin the arduous, long hoped-for process of searching for my birth mother. I mentally prepared myself for long hours searching the internet, for near-misses and disappointing failures.

But that's not the way it happened at all. When I typed my mother's name in a Google search, the first link led to a Wikipedia page: Karen Black, an actress. Could my mother be a Hollywood actress? Her photo looked familiar, yet nothing like me. And anyway, this

Karen Black was famous. What were the chances of that? I scanned the details just to dismiss the idea.

"Karen Black (born July 1, 1939) is an American actress, screenwriter, singer, and songwriter."[1] I did the math in my head. She would have been nineteen on my birth date. "Black was born as Karen Blanche Ziegler in Park Ridge, Illinois." She was from the Chicago area, same as me. I clicked back to Google and stared at the page. All the other entries were about this same person. A tingle ran up my spine.

I did an image search and started finding photos of Ms. Black at a younger age. There were striking similarities between us. Stunned into silence, unable to believe what I saw on the screen, I pushed back in my chair and looked out the window at the woods beyond our yard. Could this really be happening? People don't find their birth mothers in two clicks and ten seconds!

Five minutes later, I was outside walking our dogs to clear my head. I called my husband, Rich, and told him all about it. "So, she really could be my mother," I said. "What do you think I should do? How should I contact her? Maybe try to find her address and send a letter?"

"Well," he replied with a grin in his voice, "is she on Facebook?"

I turned around right then and hurried home. Of course, she would be on Facebook. I was sure of it. Five minutes later, I found her fan page and typed a brief message:

Hi Karen. Illinois has recently allowed adoptees like me to access their original birth certificates. I just received mine today. I was born on March 4, 1959 at Cook County Hospital, and the name listed for my mother is Karen Blanche Black. Would this happen to be you? I realize this is not your everyday question. I promise I will not make anything public. PS I don't want your money, just want to know if you are my mom.

PROLOGUE

I pressed enter.

And then nothing. No reply. Silent days dragged on. Waves of worry engulfed me, and a tide of longing swept me into the past.

PART ONE

LIFE APART

CHAPTER 1

1963–1965

MORNING SUN PEEKED THROUGH the eyelets of our lace kitchen curtains and made my crayons glow. Jazz music drifted into the kitchen from Dad's Hi-Fi. Mom busied herself baking chocolate chip cookies behind me, and the oven door creaked as she drew out one batch and put in another. Their warm aroma filled the room.

I turned around, peeking over the chair back. "Can I have one?" I asked.

"Not yet," Mom said, distracted.

"I'm making a picture of Daddy." I held it up for her to see.

"Mm-hmm," she mumbled. She pushed the cookies off the baking sheet and didn't look up. The sunlight showed off her curly hairdo, gingham dress, and freckled arms.

I turned back to my artwork. It looked like Daddy all right, with brown hair on the sides of his head, and none on top. Just then, he walked in from the living room wearing his ever-present dress shirt and pocket protector. "I'm drawing your picture," I told him. "Look, here's your glasses and there's your pocket."

"Can I hang it in my office?" He smiled. "Come outside with me, DiDi. I want to talk to you." He took my hand, and I hopped off the chair. Mom watched us leave while she wiped her hands on her apron.

Outside, Dad and I sat on the cool cement of our suburban stoop. I snuggled in next to him and looked out at our street. The house straight across matched ours, a modest brick cape cod with dormer windows. Rows of elm trees stood soldier straight, two guarding each home. Near the corner, friends played hopscotch on the sidewalk.

Daddy looked up at the trees for a long while. I fidgeted, curious what he would say. I counted the polka-dots on my new pedal-pushers. At last my father pressed his glasses up on his nose and cleared his throat. He smoothed my silky dark hair.

Our brown eyes met, and his sparkled with a secret. "DiDi, you're a big girl now."

I smiled and held up four fingers.

"Right." He gave me a squeeze. "Your mommy and I want you to know, next week we're bringing home a baby sister for you."

My eyes widened in wonder. Dad took a deep breath and let it out slowly. Then he smiled. "We're adopting her like we adopted you."

"Adopted?" I frowned up at him, trying the new word.

"Adopted means we chose you," Dad said. "You have another mother, your birth mother. She loves you, but she couldn't keep you, so we got the chance to bring you home to live with us."

"I have another mommy?" I asked, absorbing this amazing news without knowing its implications. I didn't wonder why Mom was still in the kitchen, wasn't with us. She was not part of the us that was my daddy and me.

"Yes, the Stork brought you to her, and then she gave you to us," he answered.

I knew about the long-neck bird that flew with his bundles. "Did the Stork bring my baby sister, too?"

"Yes. She's downtown in Chicago now, at the Foundlings Home, with nurses caring for her."

"What's her name?" I asked, a smile tugging at my lips.

"We named her Denise."

"Denise starts with D, like Diane."

"You are so smart." He ruffled my hair. "Let's get cookies."

That night, I had trouble falling asleep. The word *adopted* rang in my mind with the idea I had another mommy somewhere: someone I'd never met but who loved me none the less. My heart sang with this news. Plus I had a baby sister. How would I wait a whole week to meet her?

Six long days later, Dad drove our yellow '55 Chevy down the new Eisenhower Expressway, chatting with Mom. I was in the back seat, feeling fancy in my blue velvet dress, sitting up straight so I could see the big city of Chicago ahead. We took an off-ramp onto a busy street, then stopped by a tall brick building with lots of windows.

Daddy pointed and said, "This is it, the Foundlings Home. Denise is in there."

I bounded out of the car. Dad took my hand, and the three of us walked through a courtyard into an echoing lobby to sit on a long wooden bench and wait. Mom's foot tapped the tile floor. Dad fiddled with his fedora. Where was my sister?

Soon a man in a black suit stood before us. "Don and Jodie Koehnemann? Follow me." A hallway led to a silent gray office, where the grown-ups sat at a black desk and shuffled papers. I wandered around and investigated, finding a door with a window in it. Curious, I walked over and stretched up on my toes to peek through the glass.

A large room with rows of white cribs met my eyes. Rectangles of bright light cast a winter glow as nurses moved among the beds. Their dresses and caps were white, and their shoes clacked on the tile floor while the babies cried. I didn't want my sister to be in that eerie place. I sank back on my heels, crept away from the door, and ran back to Daddy. He put his arm around me when I leaned against him. I did not know yet that I, too, had lived in that room for the first nine weeks of my life.

My dad and mom stood up. The man shook hands with each of them and smiled at me. The window-door opened, and a nurse stepped out holding a bundle wrapped in a blanket. She bent to show me my sister's tiny face, then placed Denise into my mother's arms. Mom gazed down at our new baby with tears in her eyes. Daddy picked me up. My sister's tiny pink cheeks were soft and warm under my fingers. My chest swelled with happiness, and I skipped all the way back to our car.

At home, I bounced baby Neecy in her red sling seat and helped Mom give her a bottle. I snuggled with her in our parents' bed and rocked her bassinet. In her innocent eyes, I felt a kinship. She was my sister, and I would help take care of her.

Our life was sunny when Denise was a baby. Our mom stayed home with us, and sometimes she let me help her in the kitchen. I loved when she hooked the hand-crank meat grinder to the back of a chair, and I used my muscles to turn the handle. We'd smile while I cranked and she pressed cubes of beef into the hopper. Chunky hamburger meat squeezed out like Play-Doh.

But these good times were rare. Mom focused on keeping the house, and I have no memories of playing with her. I learned early to amuse myself.

When Dad came home from work, on the other hand, he showered us with attention. He bounced my sister on his knee while she giggled. One afternoon he built a boat for me from a cardboard box. We decorated it with white paint and red swirls and named it "The Good Ship Lollipop" after a Shirley Temple song. Another time he came home with a rope swing. We chose a sturdy branch of our crabapple tree; he tied the rope tight and pushed me high into the sky. At bedtime I cuddled on his lap for a book. I leaned against his chest and ran my fingers through the soft hair of his forearm, and he read to me in his deep calming voice.

As months went by, my mom stopped humming while she worked and started muttering instead. She gave me a lot of housework. My hardest new job was putting away the twisty vacuum cord that refused to untangle. One day I threw it and cried in frustration, "I hate housework!"

My mother stomped into the hallway and grabbed me by the ear. She'd never done that before. It caught me up short, and I gasped as she yelled and yanked me to the floor. Kicks jolted me, and I curled into myself on the rug, hands cradling my face, eyes shut.

Dad's footsteps hurried near us. "Jodie! What's come over you?"

He bent down and wiped my face. Then he hugged me until my sobs subsided. "Finish wrapping up the cord now, DiDi." He took Mom into their bedroom and shut the door. Their harsh muted voices made my head buzz as I cleaned up. Denise stood in the hall doorway in her diaper, eyes haunted, staring at me and sucking her thumb.

On a dreary winter day soon after that, we drove to Grandma Ringling's apartment in South Bend, Indiana. I stood in the bedroom doorway watching my elegant grandmother comfort my distraught mother. They were sitting on the bed, talking and crying together.

"It'll be all right, Jodie," Grandma said. "We'll get you help."

Dad shooed me out into the hallway. I wandered into the green sitting room and stole M&Ms from a glass dish. Then I climbed on the Victorian couch to have a closer look at Grandma's large painting of a sailing ship. I touched the water; it looked wet, and the sky was angry, but a sunset shining through the clouds colored one wave aqua. The masts glowed with sun, too. I wanted to be on the deck, traveling the ocean.

The bedroom door creaked open. I jumped off the sofa and trotted over, then stopped, confused. Dad shrugged on his overcoat, then held Mom's pea coat for her. Ridges wrinkled his forehead. He picked up Denise and started down the stairs in silence. I hugged Grandma and followed them out, chin tucked, wondering what had happened.

We drove through town to a tall building with stacks of windows. Dad didn't explain what was going on, but I sensed the tension and kept quiet, nervously following my parents along hallways with my head down. My next memory is of driving away without my mom. I searched the building's windows for her face, feeling betrayed. Was she so mad at me she wanted to stay behind without us?

"Why isn't Mom coming home?" I asked, afraid to hear the answer.

"She's sick and has to stay in the hospital, Diane." Dad was curt, keeping his troubled eyes straight ahead. His voice sounded scratchy. "We'll come back and get her next week."

A deep unsettled heaviness pinned me to the seat, like there was a stone in my stomach. On some level I knew there was more to this than he was telling me, but I couldn't risk asking too many questions. At least Dad was still with us. But what if he left too?

The farther down the highway we drove, the more my stomach hurt. I reached for Denise, but she had her thumb in her mouth. Her vacant eyes stared at the rain, while the windshield wipers swished a rhythm like waves on a shore. Confused and helpless, I floated alone in my grandma's ocean painting, looking up at that angry sky while the tall ship sailed away.

We did not go get Mom the next week, or the next. Instead, she became a patient in the psychiatric ward of St. Luke Hospital in Chicago.

As the months went by, I adjusted to her absence. My bond with my father had been the stronger tie all along, and the three of us settled into a new routine. On Sundays, he took us to the Lutheran Church in our neighborhood where we sat in a wooden pew under shining stained glass windows. I had no trouble accepting the idea of a spirit world; I imagined God all around us, invisible as air and warm as sunlight. At home, a little painting of Jesus hung on the wall above my bed, and I touched it each morning when I woke up.

The summer after kindergarten was filled with activity. The baby boom had filled our block to brimming, and the sidewalks teemed with youngsters jumping rope and riding metal scooters. A dozen of us played tag, red-light-green-light, and Mother, May I, with no electronics distracting us from the business of childhood society.

One morning, high in the branches of an apple tree, a friend and I surveyed our kingdom of kids. We were pirates on the sea, climbing to the crow's nest at the very top of the ship. Up there we spied all the way down the gravel alley to the end of our realm. To my six-year-old self, clinging to a branch as thin as my arm and swaying in the breeze was heady and delightful stuff.

My dad had the summers off since he taught speech at a grammar school. At lunchtime, he made me peanut butter and jelly sandwiches and fed Denise in her wooden highchair. Then, like every day, he packed us into our new Chevy Bonneville, and we drove downtown to see Mom. My stomach hurt as soon as the hospital came into view. Our short visit loomed ahead like a monster ready to pounce.

We met with her for the designated half an hour in a tiny, closet-size room. The air smelled like the brown iodine Dad put on our scraped knees. He put Denise on Mom's lap, but I sat on the tile floor, hugged myself, and rocked. Mom cried. So much of what they said I didn't understand, words like *depression* and *psychiatrist*. Why did she look at us with empty eyes? As we walked away down a long hall, my chest felt hollow.

Back at home that evening, Dad served us TV dinners, and I missed my mother's cooking. I cleaned the few dishes, and then we enjoyed playtime in the living room. Denise climbed on my back, and I was her horsey while Dad set up our cardboard puppet theater. Then I gave a puppet show starring Lamb Chop and Charlie Horse. After Dad tucked my sister into bed, I curled up on his lap and listened to his tenor voice read *Ozma of Oz*.

"What happens next, Dad?" I asked, keen to go on with the story.

"Tune in tomorrow night for another chapter. Time for bed."

Upstairs, alone in my room, my thoughts stuck on Mom. *What's wrong with her? Why doesn't she hug me? Maybe she doesn't love us anymore.*

I don't remember telling my dad these worries; they often floated below the surface of my awareness. But in the darkness of my room they haunted me. I escaped into daydreams of my birth mother, the one who loved me but couldn't keep me. I hoped she lived close by. Maybe I'd see her at the grocery store, and of course we'd know each other right away. Then we could have adventures together. On and on my mind mused, yearning for maternal connection.

———•••———

But this was not to be: I would never meet my birth mother at a local store. In fact, during my preschool years, Karen Black lived 800 miles away in New York City, struggling to make ends meet. In pursuit of an acting career on Broadway, she endured life in little cold-water flats: no stove, just a hot plate to cook on; shared bathrooms; windows that looked out on other rundown brownstone apartment buildings. She worked as a part-time secretary so she could pay for rent and groceries while she focused on auditions and rehearsals off-Broadway, always with an eye on the future.

In 1965, Karen landed her Broadway debut as Judy in *The Playroom*. The critical acclaim she received led to a role in Francis Ford Coppola's UCLA thesis project *You're a Big Boy Now* which recharted the course of her career from theater to cinema and from New York to Hollywood.

CHAPTER 2

1965–1970

IN 1965, WHEN MY BIRTH MOTHER walked on stage for her Broadway debut, I walked into my first-grade classroom and found my place in one of the neat rows of wooden desks. The windows let in a breeze and framed the golden trees along the street. Our teacher stood in front of the chalkboard, reading a giant *Dick and Jane* book, using a red pointer to tap each word as she pronounced it.

"Look, Jane, Look," she read.

I looked. And a new world opened wide. I mouthed the word, heard it in my mind as the sounds conflated into meaning: *L-oo-k*. The moment imprinted on me; I can still sense the thrill in my throat, the yearning to jump out of my little chair and shout. But I stayed put at my desk until that last bell rang. Then I ran the seven blocks to our house, crunching leaves with my PF Flyers.

"I can read!" I announced, bursting in the front door. My father was thrilled.

For the next couple of years, Dad took Denise and me to the library each week. While he sat in a rocking chair reading to my sister, I checked out every children's science book on each subject that interested me, from dinosaurs to outer space. At home, he created brain teasers on mimeographed pages of squares. He'd fill each one with a word riddle and then listen to my guesses. Even after I could read well, he still took the time to read aloud: we'd devour *Tom Sawyer* or *Huck Finn,* and his calm voice soothed me. I did my best in school to please him, and *smart daughter* became my first identity.

The leaves were sprouting on our elm trees in the spring of my ninth year, 1968. I was admiring them through our picture window when an old car, gray and rusty, pulled up in front of our house. My mother stepped out of the passenger's side and started toward the house. I gasped and stared. She should have been in the Madden Mental Health Center.

"Dad! Dad! Mom is here!" I yelled down the hall as I swung the front door open wide.

Mom was on the stoop wearing a thin print dress over her fragile frame. She hadn't been home for three years. When she opened the screen door and stepped in, I was shocked to see I was as tall as her. I hadn't realized what a small woman she was. I gave her a tentative hug. She didn't hug me back. I shied away, a lump forming in my throat.

"Where's your father?" She asked, sounding sleepy. Her eyes looked past me to the empty living room. Then my Dad's hurried footfalls sounded in the hall. He looked large as he filled the room in a rush, concern on his face. I stood there, mute.

"Jodie, what are you doing? How did you get here?" He said, his hands on her shoulders.

"I ran away, Don, and I'm not going back," she said, looking up at him and standing straighter. "I hitchhiked home to stay here with you and the girls."

Dad looked as stunned as I felt. His voice was harsh. "Hitchhiked? That was so dangerous!"

When I heard this, I burst with pride for my mom, imagining the guts it took to sneak out of the locked facility. Surely she was better now and would want to spend time with me. But my buoyancy was short-lived. My mother would sit on the couch all day in tears. I'd sit by her, consoling her, holding her hand. She gained weight and became morose: sobbing, clacking away with her knitting needles, and chain-smoking.

Dad assured me Mom would get "all the way well," but I had trouble believing him. She wasn't the same sunny, bustling mother I remembered. During those three institutionalized years, she had endured electroshock therapy that wiped away months of her memory. She became dependent on powerful antipsychotic drugs—Stelazine and Thorazine—that made her listless and uninterested in our lives.

To add to our troubles, four-year-old Denise languished in her crib for days. One night I crept in to see her, and when I touched her, my hand burned as if she were on fire. I ran, frightened, to tell Dad and found my parents arguing about whether to take Denise to the ER. Dad took her to the doctor the next morning, and they admitted her right away. A spinal tap showed she had viral encephalitis. We spent evenings at West Suburban Hospital for several weeks that March. When my sister came home, her legs were weak. She finally walked on her own again on her fifth birthday, May 2, 1968.

The elm trees on our block started dying later that year. Their leaves fell weeping to the ground as they succumbed to the Dutch Elm disease that swept the nation. I mourned when workmen cut ours down and chopped them up. What was left of my happiness died too, because that was when my Mom suddenly changed for the worse.

She weaned herself cold turkey from the numbing medications. What a month that was, with her outbursts of rage and confusion. Our home was in turmoil. My heart pounded each time her strange ravings rang through the walls. But we survived, and she joined a self-help group called Recovery. The members followed the teachings of Dr. Abraham Lowe's book, *Mental Health Through Will-Training*, which advocated taking charge of your own mind. My mother no longer lay sobbing on the sofa.

But it seemed to me, as I listened to her recite Dr. Lowe's words day after day, that she was going too far. She took charge of every-thing about our lives, and not in a nice way. She became nasty and bossy, controlling my every move. She woke me early every Saturday morning to do a series of chores in an exact way. At dinner, I couldn't eat the food on my plate the way I wanted to: I'd get yelled at for mixing my peas into my mashed potatoes. In the evenings, we could only watch what she wanted, and we only had one TV. If I expressed annoyance at her rules, she rebuked and belittled me, accusing me of not loving her the way a daughter should. I learned to keep my face expressionless and my voice quiet while I wrestled with guilt and anger. She deflated me, and I had no one to fill me up again.

My dad wasn't around much anymore. Our close relationship withered as he withdrew into his world of reel-to-reel tapes in the basement. He spent most of his time, when he wasn't working two jobs, immersed in his hobby of collecting old radio shows. Our wonder-filled world of learning had collapsed with the falling elm trees.

I had two sanctuaries: my climbing tree—the aging crabapple in the backyard—and my upstairs bedroom where I could be myself. Mom had polio as a child, so stairs were hard for her, and she never came up. In my room, I was free. The slanted pink walls displayed my creations: a drawing of Denise, woven God's Eyes, and colorful marker designs. My dormer window opened to the fresh air and outdoor sounds I loved.

One morning the following summer, when I was ten, I sat cross-legged on my old hooked rug with my new Saturn V rocket model spread out on newspaper. I was lost in memories of the moon landing: *One small step for man, one giant leap for mankind.*[2] Constructing the tiny lunar module was absorbing my attention as I dreamed of being an astronaut.

My mother's muffled voice from downstairs pierced my reverie. "Di-yan! Come bring me my Pepsi and cigarettes!"

I cringed, and my peace dissipated. My legs unfolded and carried me to the top of the stairs, and my feet trudged to the door at the bottom. My chest tightened as I turned the knob. The stale tobacco air, chilled by her window air conditioner, crashed over me.

"What are you doing up there, Diane?" She said, her tone accusatory.

I hung my head. "My new model, Mom. You should see how detailed—"

Her hand swept away my words. "It's already ten o'clock. You're supposed to be mopping the kitchen floor! I'm tired of begging you every week. You're a total discredit to this household! Now come here and take my glass."

Her sunken corner of the couch was next to a growing pile of misshapen knitted pieces. Her big metal needles lay on her lumpy lap.

She frowned up at me, makeup crooked, pushing her lipstick-stained glass into my hand.

I took it and suggested, "Why don't you make Denise another sweater, Mom? You have enough pieces—"

"Just get me my drink and cigarettes, Diane. Don't tell me what to do."

The once-sunny kitchen was now dull, curtains yellowed, wallpaper sagging, no cookies baking. Nothing like the happy place of my preschool years. The faded linoleum floor taunted me as I plodded back with her Pepsi and a pack of unfiltered Old Golds.

"Mom, no matter how hard I scrub, that floor never gets clean. Maybe we could try something besides Spic and Span?"

"You're always making excuses. Just get in there and get to work before I call your father!" She spat the words as she lit a cigarette.

Dad was working his second job, so I had to endure her alone. While I was in the bathroom filling the bucket, I watched Denise blissfully stacking blocks in her bedroom. She was always quiet and cheerful and oblivious.

As the mop trailed gray water over the kitchen linoleum, I lamented my fate as only an adopted child can: *I am not like HER. I bet I'm like my birth mom: I bet SHE loves to learn and read and create like me. I will do something with my life, become an astronaut or an artist. Or maybe I'll run away and live in the woods.*

As soon as I finished, I escaped upstairs and stood in my room, breathing hard. Instead of going back to my model, I opened my sketchpad and drew a picture of my fist.

But drawing that fist was as rebellious as I ever got. My frustrations rarely boiled over into anger; instead there were times I was bullied. One classmate made me carry her books home from school every day. I took it without complaint for weeks before finally throwing them on the ground and marching away. Confrontation was hard for me because I had little self-worth.

Another year passed, and spring finally came again. On a cool sunlit day, I knelt in jeans and bare feet weeding my garden at the side of the house. Sitting back on the warm flagstones, I watered my young plants with our hose, pressing my thumb to the end to make a spray, watching the rainbow appear in the sunlight. I took a cool drink, the refreshing taste of hose water quenching my thirst, droplets wetting my face, dripping on my tie-dye T-shirt.

When I'd asked if I could grow my own flowers, Dad had bought me zinnia seeds. I nurtured them, and now the first flower buds were appearing. Gardening satisfied me in the same way drawing did, creating breathing space in my mind, allowing inner freedom to emerge. I was finding seeds of my true self, as well, but I had no native soil to plant them in. Closed adoption had kept me from the context of kin I needed to nourish my budding identity.

My dad came out to empty the trash, and on his way back from the alley, stopped to watch me. "Your garden looks nice, Diane."

"Thanks, Dad." I looked up at him, shielding my eyes from the sun. He was a big man. His old work cap sat on his bald head, and beads of sweat trickled down his temples. Under his gray work shirt I could see his ever-present pocket protector and pens. He had on slacks and dress shoes, and I realized that my father didn't even own a pair of jeans. He did all the work around our house dressed like this.

He tried so hard. I stood up and wrapped my slender arms around his great girth. "I love you, Dad," I said and held his gaze.

"I love you too, honey."

"Mom's been mean," I ventured. "She bosses me around and never listens." I searched his face, hoping he would advocate for me.

He looked at the ground. "Your mom's sick. She's doing her best. We have to give her the benefit of the doubt." He shook his head and walked away. His shoulders slumped like my heart. Maybe he felt trapped, too, wishing Mom was back to normal but unable to help her change. I looked toward the backyard, fighting off tears, and saw that my crabapple tree had bloomed.

The bright blossoms cheered me up, and I trotted back toward the alley, wiping my eyes. I touched the smooth bark and gazed upward, climbing to my favorite spot in the branches, a dozen feet in the air. The blooms' fragrance was intoxicating here. I picked a small sprig and held the pink petals to my nose.

In the midst of my sadness, a familiar sweetness filled me, a blend of peace and strangely soothing emptiness. I had just learned the word *melancholy*. I knew it meant *sad*, but also had something to do with beauty. I embraced the word to describe this mysterious warm longing that became a persistent part of my personality, a comfort in quiet moments. Nearly half a century would pass before I'd know the source of this poignant melancholy.

During this season, while I was struggling to bloom despite a lack of watering, my birth mother's career blossomed. In 1966 she moved to LA and began to win guest appearances in TV series. Karen was swept into the New Hollywood cinema movement with a role in Dennis Hopper's *Easy Rider*. By 1970 she was poised to become an A-list actress when she garnered an Oscar nomination for her portrayal of Rayette in the drama *Five Easy Pieces*. She had striven for years to cultivate a successful acting career, and her tenacity was bearing fruit.

Chapter 3

1970–1974

On a blustery winter afternoon, Dad drove us downtown to a specialist's office for Denise. My sister had become less attentive, less able to interact with us. When she ate, her fork trembled in her hand, and her eyes shuddered. I was scared for her.

Now she sat with a doctor at a child-sized table in the next room, while we watched through a one-way mirror. The doctor spread his arms and touched his nose with his fingers. Then Denise tried and missed her nose.

After more tests, he burst into our room and rushed up to us. "Don, Jodie, you need to get her to Children's Memorial right away! I'll call ahead and inform the neurosurgeon you're coming." He pulled my alarmed father aside and whispered to him before we hurried out, tugging our coats on as we walked.

At the door, Dad hung back and touched my shoulder. "This is very serious, Diane. We need to be strong." His eyes locked on mine in a moment of candor. He seldom showed emotion, but I glimpsed fear in his eyes that night.

Denise's first neurosurgery took place hours later. She would have died if my parents had waited any longer. She had hydrocephalus, known as water on the brain: her ventricles couldn't drain their fluid. Most children who have this condition were born with it, but the doctors said Denise may have developed it from the viral encephalitis she'd had when she was four.

And so began three years of daily trips to Chicago's Children's Memorial Hospital. My sister had ten brain surgeries by the time she was ten years old. They tried to put in shunt after shunt, but none lasted. Dad, Mom, and I lived on cafeteria food. I did homework in the hallway, spent my allowance at the gift shop, and drank Red Cream Soda from the pop machine.

Mom was too preoccupied to be angry at me, and spent her evenings in the waiting room, knitting and smoking. So Denise and I had fun during the times she was well enough to get out of bed. At the end of the hallway was a wide, elevated landing with a play area. There at the top of the ramp, I helped my half-bald sister into her wheelchair. We giggled and shouted, "Time for takeoff!" Then I leaned my weight into a launch. We zipped down the slope, zoomed by smiling nurses at their station, rolled past the smoky waiting room, and lurched around a corner into the east wing to visit our friend John. With his head wrapped in white bandages, he drove a wooden cot on wheels like a race car. There were other friends there, too, with half-shaved heads. They smiled and laughed and joked, and although I couldn't express it at the time, I learned from them that happiness was a choice.

One day I sat in the east wing hallway in front of a pane glass window watching my sister, with a group of other post-op kids, play together in the physical therapy room. They took turns pouncing onto a three-foot red ball and giggling as they slid off onto a floor mat. I realized that I had been choosing to let my mother decide my mood. If these kids could be happy despite their challenges, then I should be able to, as well.

I was learning to take charge of my own internal state. As my teen years went by, although I never rebelled against my mom's overly strict rules, I wasn't stuck feeling sorry for myself, either. I could slough her insults off my back. This was about the time I stopped getting bullied, too, and I started writing poetry and thinking about spiritual matters.

The feelings of melancholy and isolation still plagued me, but I began to find my own center. This would stand me in good stead in future rocky times.

One day during the winter when I was a freshman in high school, the classroom door opened during algebra. A girl came in and walked up to the teacher. As we watched from our desks with curiosity, our teacher read the note she'd handed him, and then looked straight at me.

"Diane, you need to follow this young lady. Your father is here."

Startled, I gathered my things. A quick stop for my jacket at my locker and we hurried to the office, where my dad stood with his gray overcoat buttoned, his fedora in his fidgeting hands.

"What's wrong, Dad?" I asked, worried for my sister, who was in the hospital again.

"Denise had emergency surgery this morning, and she didn't wake up afterward," he said, opening the door to the hallway. He looked at me as we walked, weary concern and doom in his eyes. "She's in a coma."

Breath stuck in my throat, and I didn't know how to respond, except to quicken my pace. We opened the school doors into a blustery winter wind and hastened into the car where Mom waited, a lit cigarette in hand. The drive felt like one of the longest rides of my life. It would be the first of many.

For the next nine weeks, we drove downtown every evening to Children's Memorial. My dad sat beside Denise's bed, reading to her motionless form. He had learned that people in comas could hear you, so he kept faithful vigil while I studied, and my mother knitted in the waiting room. I walked back and forth between them after I did my homework. Mom was taciturn, closing herself off as her way, I guess, of dealing with the stress. I have no memories of her sitting with Denise.

A few weeks later, on a rainy day, my parents met with Denise's doctors. I had to wait in a row of plastic chairs outside a closed door. When it opened, Mom came out crying. Dad looked stern. He shuffled over and sat next to me, folding his hands in his lap. I tucked my legs up and wrapped my arms around them, waiting for dismal news.

"The doctors say Denise may never wake up," he said. His lower lip trembled. Then he straightened and smacked his thigh with his fist. "I refuse to believe it." He got up, touched my shoulder, and put his arm around my mother, then led her to Denise's room.

Alone in the silent east wing hall, I gazed out a tall window as rain trailed like tears on the glass. Our friend John's wooden cart stood empty nearby. Had he gone home or—?

The previous weekend, my Sunday School teacher had encouraged us talk to the Lord when we had a problem. So, for the first time, I told God my worries, and not for the last time I felt resolve rise in my heart. I walked down the hall to Denise's bedside where Dad was reading her favorite story, *Little Toot*.

"May I have a turn?" I asked. He handed me the book, and I read. I wouldn't give up on her, either.

More weeks crawled by. Then one day, while my dad was at his post by the bed, he called my name with delight. I dropped my textbook and ran to him.

"Diane, go get your mother. Denise smiled!"

I dashed through the hall and slid to a halt at the waiting room. "Mom, Denise smiled!"

She hurried after me. Nurses' shoes clacked behind us. The news shot around the floor, and soon the room was crowded with congratulations. I'd never seen my parents so elated. We hooted and laughed, and the staff joined us. My sister had been in a coma for nine weeks.

Days later, we celebrated when she opened her eyes. And then, with her bed surrounded by doctors and nurses, she spoke her first halting words, a family joke. "Dad, you have ants in your pants!" Everyone clapped and cheered and cried. Our elation made the room feel like a hot-air balloon rising into the sky.

Our next celebration was the day Denise stood up from her wheelchair and walked across our living room floor. A tutor, Miss

Michelle, helped her in our home for a few months, and then a bus took her to special education at Longfellow School in another district. I was overjoyed to have Denise back, to know I would have a sister to grow up with. But as I matured into my teen years, Denise stayed a little girl. She always would.

⋯

Despite our family's challenges, my dad provided a bright spot in our life by making sure we took a vacation almost every summer. My mother's love of the lakefront was his motivation, and I'm thankful to both of them for the good memories we had there. For one week each August we rented a cottage in Fish Creek, a tiny harbor village nestled between bluffs and bay in Door County, the Cape Cod of the Midwest.

Halfway through the six-hour trip north from the Chicago suburbs, we'd drive through the tiny village of Manitowoc. Every year, the neighborhood rolled by and I sighed, inexplicably drawn to this small town. I was unable to fathom why I loved the place so much. It just felt so familiar, like the memory of a dream.

"Dad, can we stop here this year, please?" I'd ask.

"No, we ate an hour ago. We're not stopping now."

As we turned north along the lake and Manitowoc faded in the rear window, disappointment filled me. Like my sweet melancholy, Manitowoc's allure was another mystery that would be solved decades later.

The year I was fifteen, we arrived at Fish Creek and our usual resort, Dun Rovin. Cottage Seven had pink siding and a low stone wall around the yard.

That year my sister's doctor finally gave her the green light to travel. She trailed behind me with a wig perched off-kilter on her bald head as we climbed the wooden steps at the back of our cottage. I plunked our suitcases on our bed, helped her unpack, and walked to the screen porch facing the road. I stepped out into the fresh Wisconsin air and listened to the cry of gulls drifting in from the lake.

To my surprise, displayed on the lawn next door were rows of watercolor paintings on wooden easels. I sauntered among them, lingering at each one. In the front window of Cottage Six, a woman painted at a wooden table cluttered with jars of brushes, tubes of paints, and piles of papers. A tall older gentleman in a splattered smock carried new artwork to an empty easel.

"Excuse me, sir," I greeted him. "I'm Diane. We're your neighbors this week." I pointed to number Seven.

He dipped his white-crowned head. "I'm William. My wife, Lydia, is in the cabin. Interested in art, are you?"

"Yes, I'm—kind of—an artist, too," I couldn't claim the title after seeing their skillful work.

"Would you like to see our studio?" He asked, in his quaking elderly voice.

My heart skipped a beat. I'd never seen a real art studio. I nodded, shoved my hands into my jean pockets and followed him.

Inside, he introduced me to Lydia. "We have an aspiring artist here this week."

Her smile was genuine and made wrinkles at the corners of her eyes. She offered her hand. "Look around. Can I get you something to drink?"

"No thanks. Just being in here is great." I took in everything: paints, brushes, paper, mats, and framing tools. Sunlight lent a glow to the rich tones of worktables and stools. Two tall brass lamps lit the space where Lydia worked. And the smell was heavenly. The sawdust from the fresh-cut wood frames transported me to a pine forest.

William took a seat on a stool next to his wife, taping a large sheet of watercolor paper to the table. I walked over to them.

"May I watch a while?" I asked.

"Sure." Lydia said. She pulled up a stool for me.

William's hands made music as he swept paint onto the dappled paper with deft strokes. A sunset appeared as if by magic. He used each brush a different way: a large flat one to blend the sky, a small pointed one to create trees and sailboats. I was keen to try it myself.

Back in my bedroom later that day, I counted the allowance money I'd brought. With the change jingling in my pocket, I walked to the General store, and found a blue tin of Prang watercolors and a sketchpad.

The next day's morning light shone through the east window above my bed. I dressed in silence, to not wake my family, then I stole out into the cool air and chose a group of birch saplings as a subject. At a wrought iron table nearby, I opened my paint tin and picked up the included brush.

Half an hour later I held my first watercolor painting as I ran to show it off to my friend Debby, who'd be fishing on the dock. She and I met every year; her family vacationed the same week we did. I arrived by her side, out of breath, and held up my treasure for her to see. But before she looked up, the wind grabbed it from my fingers and carried it away, flipping like litter out onto the water. My painting floated face down, bleeding. Deflated, I vowed never to brag again.

I hung my head as I told my new artist friends of my loss. They consoled me with encouragement, two paintbrushes, and a sheet of real watercolor paper. I thanked them, walked back to my birches, and began again. As I painted, enjoying the textured surface and supple brushes, I noticed everything: the whir of bird wings as they flitted by, the far-off clang of ship bells in the harbor. The painting was much better, but humble from my lesson in pride, I showed no one.

"Did you try again?" Lydia asked, as I browsed through their yard. When I nodded, she wanted to see my work, so I brought it to her.

"William, come and look," she said. He walked outside, drying his hands on a chamois.

His face became serious as he held my piece. "You have talent. Are your parents artists?"

"I'm adopted," I said.

"Hmm, I imagine someone in your birth family has ability, young lady. You're a natural. You've captured the texture of the bark and the color of the shadows. Well done."

Lydia agreed, and I blushed under their praise. I could tell they meant it.

I never saw them again, but those folks helped me see another piece of who I was: an artist, for real.

At the end of the day, Sunset Park beckoned villagers and tourists to watch the sun descend over the bay. We walked the three blocks from our cottage to the shore in a way that mirrored our life as a family: Mom, Dad, and Denise strolled along the asphalt with the crowd, while I enjoyed the path less taken in the woods beside the road. Immersed in the soft hues of twilight, I twirled, breathing in the pine scent, basking in the birdsong all around. Where did I get this spirit of wonder? Certainly not from my humdrum parents. Although Dad hung my drawings in his office, he also made it clear that art was not a serious study like math or science. And Mom berated me for my "flights of fancy."

I glanced their way and saw her frowning face. Why couldn't she just let me be me? The thought propelled me into a run, and I raced up stone steps onto the park lawn where townsfolk were silhouetted in sunset beams. Kids skipped stones, grown-ups chatted, and we all watched a sailboat swing lazily back and forth in the golden waves. When the last sliver of orange sun slipped below the horizon, the crowd applauded. God was the best artist. Maybe my birth mother was an artist too.

If I had only known how true that was. By then Karen had made her mark on the '70s cinematic culture. She had starred in a dozen hit films including *The Great Gatsby*, as Myrtle, and *Airport 75*, as Nancy Prior, the stewardess who flew the plane. In August 1974, as I watched the sunset in Wisconsin, she was in Tennessee on the set of the movie *Nashville*. This film showcased the breadth of her talent, as she not only played a country music star but also wrote and sang her own original songs for the role.

By the summer of 1975, Karen's iconic good looks and acting prowess had made her a well known name. When Roger Ebert interviewed her that June in the upscale Polo Lounge of the Beverly Hills Hotel, a hush fell over the room when Ms. Black entered, and all eyes followed her to the center table. This was the height of her fame.

CHAPTER 4

1975–2000

I TURNED SIXTEEN on March 4, 1975 and started my first job at the local suburban McDonald's, where the sign with the Golden Arches boasted *19 Billion Served*. I buttoned the scratchy brown-and-white uniform and stood behind the counter taking orders and making shakes.

The tedium of repeating, "Welcome to McDonald's. How can I help you?" was broken by unexpected comments from my customers. Every few days someone would say, "You look so familiar," or "Where do I know you from?" This happened so often there were only two choices in my mind: either I had a twin nearby, a thrilling possibility, or I was a Plain Jane, a depressing probability. My features might have been so generic, I resembled any other brown-haired girl.

The problem was that closed adoption took away anyone who shared my features, or moved with my gestures, or thought in my way. I wasn't able to see myself in others, and I didn't know whether I was pretty or plain. Only three things were sure about my identity: I was smart, artistic, and *adopted*. That last word banished me from myself, obscuring me, inside and out. I lived on a shrouded island off the coast of humanity, as lost as if I'd grown up in a foreign country where I couldn't learn the language or culture. That was how I felt in my adoptive family, and this aloneness became pervasive: I didn't fit in anywhere.

So to have strangers keep telling me they recognized me was bewildering at best. I would never have dreamed that my birth mother was a famous actress, and that our looks were strikingly similar. In fact, on my sixteenth birthday, the made-for-television horror anthology Trilogy of Terror aired. Karen starred as all four protagonists. I never saw the movie as a teen, but I bet a lot of McDonald's customers did.

Fast forward to the next spring. I started noticing a cute guy flipping burgers on the grill. Rich Bay had shoulder-length blonde hair and boyish green eyes that sparkled when he smiled at me. He was a year older, a mature senior.

Rich and I clicked in a way I'd never experienced before. We talked about anything easily, spending hours facing each other with our legs entwined in the front seat of his rusty Buick LeSabre. That's where I told him I was adopted.

His eyes registered surprise. "So those aren't your real parents? Denise isn't your real sister? No wonder you don't look like them!"

"They are my real family, I'm just not related to them," I explained.

"Do you know who your birth parents are?"

"No, adoption agencies hide all that stuff. And my parents don't know, either."

"But you must wonder about them?" Rich asked.

I sighed. "I think about my birth mother all the time. But my birth father? I guess I assume he walked out on her and didn't want me. But who knows? There could be lots of reasons they gave me up."

"Yeah, that's true," Rich agreed. "Do you want to find them?"

"I read a book of adoption reunion stories, and it was split: half happy and half sad. So I don't know, I mean I do want to know who my birth parents are, and whether I have brothers and sisters, but I am afraid of what I might find. People always say I remind them of someone, so that makes me curious. Maybe I have siblings nearby, who knows? I think if I get a chance, I should go for it."

After that I looked forward to sending for my birth certificate. Someone had told me I could get it when I turned eighteen, so the day after my birthday in 1977, I flopped on my bed with a notebook and a pen in my hand. Seals & Crofts' album *Summer Breeze* was on my record player as I began a letter to my birth mother.

Dear Mom,

Hi! I'm your happy, intelligent, Christian, going steady, 18-year-old daughter, who has no idea who you are.

If I find you, I will tell you how happy and how grateful I am to you for my life. Don't kick yourself for having me, because I love being alive. I'm writing this now in case I can never get to talk to you. Well let's see…

I have a good family, so you don't have to worry. I have an adopted little sister too. She's thirteen and in special education and she's very lovable.

I have a steady boyfriend named Rich Bay and we are thinking of getting married. He is not-too-cute but cute-to-me, which is the best way for a guy to be, because then they are not conceited and are very devoted.

The letter told her more about my relationship with Rich, my life at home, my faith, and my fears. My teenage heart poured out to her. I ended by giving her my address and saying:

If I send you pictures of me, can you send a picture of you? I always wondered how you look! I hope you write back so much. At least just to say, I got your letter, Okay? I love you!

Your Daughter, Diane

I folded the five pages and put them in an envelope addressed To Mom. Then I found photos to send, working up courage to take this big step.

A week later, waitressing at a small neighborhood restaurant, I chatted with two regulars with a coffee pot in my hand.

"I'm adopted," I related, smiling, "and since I'm eighteen, I'm sending for my birth certificate to find out who my birth mom is!"

"Were you adopted in Illinois?" The husband asked. They exchanged a glance.

"Yes, why?"

Their faces fell. "We're sorry to tell you this," said the wife, "but Illinois sealed their adoption records, even to adult adoptees."

"What do you mean?" I asked, afraid to find out.

The man saw my confusion. "You won't be able to access your records."

"Are you sure?" I blinked back tears. They nodded. I shook my head, walked away stunned, and plopped in the booth at the waitress table. Was this true or were they wrong?

It was true. One phone call to a state office confirmed it. In my naivety I had gotten my hopes up without checking facts. Disappointed, I packed the letter in a box with other keepsakes.

It was only a year and a half later that Rich and I married. I was grateful for the support my family was able to provide: My mom helped me choose my white lace wedding dress, my sister was a bridesmaid, and my father walked me down the aisle. Both my parents had tears in their eyes as Dad placed my hand in Rich's. We made our vows surrounded by our wedding party, the girls in yellow chiffon and the guys in white tuxes. At our reception, our friends bought us a band that played the traditional songs—hokey pokey, chicken dance, polkas, and waltzes. We tallied up the gifts and found that the total covered our costs. It was the best free party we ever gave.

We were kids: nineteen and twenty years old. Rich had claimed me as his own from the start. With him there was security and freedom. Besides, we had fun together, a welcome change from my stifling home life.

In March 1983, our first child was born. During my pregnancy, the movement of life inside my body mesmerized me. This tiny being was flesh of my flesh, with my blood coursing through him. And after Matthew was born, I memorized his face, ran my fingers over his supple skin, and drifted in an ocean of love. I was fiercely protective.

And I was plain terrified. I'd never held a newborn, never helped an aunt or friend care for a baby. I had no playbook at all. The maternity ward nurse who gave me her phone number probably regretted it. One time I called to find out how to take a shower. Since I was so anxious, she told me to put the baby in his car seat in the bathroom with me.

But at better moments, I had a genuine sense of being one with nature. This life of ours was as it should be. Having a baby was so fulfilling that we did it again and had another son only twenty months later.

In 1984, with our two little boys, we moved from an apartment into the brick duplex right across the alley from Rich's grandma Thelma, our *GG*. Those were wonderful years, sharing our life with her. She was a quiet soul who helped with the kids and taught me how to cook and sew.

During that time Rich began his career at the Bellwood Fire Department while I stayed home with our preschoolers. But a one-salary income was just above the poverty level. Fortunately, good friends in our church met our needs with shared clothing and food. Thelma let me borrow her car for appointments, and a discount grocery store was in walking distance. We got by. Our third son, Ricky Jr., was born in June 1988; our family was complete and we weren't quite thirty years old.

My inner void persisted, though, and I feared it was a weakness within me—a neediness I had to hide. The old melancholy haunted me. I sought myself in the faces of my children, the only people I knew who shared my genes. Matt, our take-charge oldest, and Ricky, our head-strong youngest, had the Bay family's green eyes and fair complexion. But our quiet middle child, Mike, had my olive skin and brown eyes, and that felt good in a quiet, satisfying way.

Years flew past us. Once the kids were all in school, I enrolled in Community College and graduated with an Associate of Arts, becoming a freelance graphic designer. Rich accumulated days off at the firehouse, so we took adventurous summer vacations as a family. Sometimes we roamed the country—we camped at KOAs all over—out east on the Outer Banks, and out west near Yellowstone and Arches National Parks. Often we stayed at Kentucky Lake and spent days on the water in a small fishing boat just big enough for the five of us. Rich dreamed of becoming a fishing guide someday, and we chatted about moving to the lake when he retired.

My biological mother stayed on my mind all through our kids' teen years. I signed up for the national and state adoption registries, hoping she would want to reunite. But neither registry service ever called to say there was a match.

Karen Black had a good reason for never adding her name to those lists: opportunists had tried to masquerade as a long-lost child. She'd been pregnant once before me, but she'd had a miscarriage. Gold-diggers found out about that first pregnancy and pretended to be her child. So Karen was wary to put her name and the correct birth date on a public record. But, of course, I didn't know this. Whenever I felt the sting of unwantedness, I'd tell myself that my birth mother simply did not know about the registries.

Even though Karen's fame waned, her acting career lasted. She gave herself fully to each part she played. After *Trilogy of Terror*, she gained a second celebrity as a cult horror icon. She also became known as a hard-working character actor who brought her signature spark of believability to any role.

CHAPTER 5

2001–2009

By the new millennium, my adoptive parents were elderly. Denise lived in a group home and stayed with them on weekends. The time was coming when Rich and I would need to take over responsibility for her care.

My mother, Jodie, who had survived polio as a toddler, developed post-polio syndrome in her seventies and needed a wheelchair in her last decade. Lung cancer claimed her life. Her mental illness continued to cloud her mind until the end: her self-centeredness even prevented her from enjoying her grandchildren. Filled with fear, she mistrusted everyone, including my father who spent his energy caring for her. My grief was mixed with relief when she passed in 2001.

After mourning her, my dad enjoyed a time of renaissance. Don remembered his Jodie before her nervous breakdown as if the intervening years had never happened. He took Denise each weekend; they attended the Lutheran Church of my childhood, and he wrote a column for the church newsletter. He enjoyed time with our boys, who learned to appreciate old-time jazz by listening to their Grandpa K's vinyl records. Boxes filled with three-ring binders multiplied around his house, as my pack-rat dad organized mementos and family portraits. He was proud of his heritage. When we visited, he'd sit with me and flip through the photos he captioned. Although I was interested, the faded sepia folks were not my blood. My own people were out there somewhere.

Six years sailed past like fall leaves in the wind, and then in November 2006, Dad suffered a major stroke. Lingering in a nearby nursing center, he couldn't talk, write, move his limbs, or even answer yes-and-no questions. He had aphasia. We saw love in his eyes, nothing more. The irony was, he had worked as a speech therapist for stroke patients with this condition and now was living through it. We hoped he'd recover and record his experience.

Bright snow sagged the pine tree outside my dad's room at DuPage Convalescent Center. Propped up in a wheelchair, where two nurses placed him each day, Daddy wore his dress clothes like a lumpy rag doll. I sat on the edge of his bed, with my laptop on the rolling tray, working on a book illustration. *Jazz with Dick Buckley* crooned from the radio.

As I crafted a picture of heaven for a children's Bible, my dad's minister arrived to bring him communion. The tweed-suited clergyman unzipped his leather communion kit, lifted out small glass cups, a tiny bottle of grape juice, and a silver pill box of wafers. With quiet words, he ministered to my dad. But my father's face showed no signs of acknowledgment. My body sagged at his empty stare.

Afterward, I walked the pastor to the elevators. "Your dad didn't respond today. He wasn't with us," he said.

"In the last few days he's withdrawing." My breath caught as I spoke.

"I have to tell you what a touching scene it was, seeing you with him, creating a picture of heaven. Your dad is blessed to have a daughter like you."

On the way back down the hall, I followed the tile lines on the floor, willing my heavy feet to keep trudging. I visited every day and never saw my dad complain. And he was a favorite here: the workers loved Mr. Don. His quiet faith shone during these months. I learned so much from his patient smiles as staff cared for him. Without a word, he taught me dignity, how to face outward, thinking of the feelings of others instead of letting pain or fear rule his reactions.

I was blessed to have him as a father. As I sat by his side again, I took his hand and told him, "Daddy, even though you can't speak, you're teaching me so much." And he smiled, for one of the last times. He passed away in the spring of 2007.

Over the four months of his decline, Rich, Denise, and I had become our own little family. Our boys were men: our eldest, Matt, had married. He and his wife Becca moved into my dad's house and fixed it up to sell. Then they packed their Jeep Cherokee to overflowing and moved to Seattle where Matt had taken a new job. Mike shared an apartment with friends in a Chicago suburb; Ricky, nineteen, still lived at home in our finished basement. We fixed up a bedroom with ocean decor to please my dolphin-loving sister, and we picked her up from her group home every Saturday morning.

When Rich's retirement drew near, we put our house on the market for our long-awaited move to Kentucky. Our son Ricky found a place to live in a nearby suburb with friends.

But we had a dilemma: should we bring Denise, take her away from the daily routine she knew, her apartment and her job? Or should we leave her behind, secure in her surroundings and pattern of living, but 400 miles away? We told her about our moving plans and asked what she wanted to do. She took several weeks to decide, asking trusted staff for advice before choosing to come with us.

We began our search for a house with an attached apartment. Months passed with no luck, and then our realtor sent us a link to a one-story ranch in the woods, with a quaint living space for Denise. Could we afford so nice a place? With my inheritance, and help from Rich's parents, we did. It became our home in January 2009.

Karen continued her career into these later years. Her acting was celebrated at film festivals, and her writing won a place at the Sundance Screenwriters Lab in 1986, with a screenplay entitled *Deep Purple.*

She also became a mother to a son, Hunter Carson, born in 1975. Although her marriage to his father, L.M. Kit Carson, fell apart, she found lasting love with Stephen Eckelberry in the early eighties. They married and adopted a daughter, Celine Eckelberry, in 1987. Karen lived through the many uncertainties of being a show business mother, and she came through it with an appreciation of life's blessings.

Then, in 2009, she was diagnosed with a rare form of cancer.

Getting On

Wandering along this great long year
I sense the lights are dimmer
than they once were.

The straight tall knowing structures waver
in the lessening light, they seem
taller than I can own

like great alien skeletons whose bones
have lost the chance to bear
their burdens, they can't atone

for failures to be strong; their sides give out
or just begin to bow
beginning to give me doubt

about the distance, the measurement from top
down to the earth, or grave.
Is it a shorter drop?

Though well remembered friends in passing greet me,
now I notice death
is rising up to meet me.

PART TWO

TIME TOGETHER

Chapter 6

Spring & Summer 2012

My breath made bright little clouds in the cool sunlight as I padded barefoot down the driveway. The tiny puffs of air shimmered for a moment as they faded. Maybe I should have sensed magic in their fleeting beauty, seen an omen of the future in their brevity, but I had no hint of what waited in my mailbox.

I tugged out a stack of mail and strolled back to our house, tearing open an unexpected letter from my mother-in-law. A note wrapped a folded newspaper clipping:

Found this in the Chicago Sun Times. Guessed you would want to see it.

I unfolded the article. The headline announced, "Adoption Law Gets It Right." After reading a few sentences, my heart leaped and I hugged the paper to my chest. Illinois had opened their adoption records—after fifty years of yearning, I could finally search for my birth mother.

While I did dishes that afternoon, Denise's bus arrived from the adult daycare center in town. After a minute, I heard her footsteps in the hall that led from her apartment to our kitchen.

"I have something to show you, Diane," she said, holding out a colorful drawing. "Here's what I did today."

"Wow, that's great. Let me see," I said, drying my hands. I held up the wrinkled paper and acted impressed. She smiled up at me with the pride of a preschooler. She was chubby, four-foot-ten, and about to turn fifty years old.

The picture was the same as usual: dolphins and marine life. "These three fish are colorful," I said, locating a difference from yesterday's creation and complimenting it.

"Those are lionfish," she explained. Denise was an encyclopedia of sea life.

"You should show the ladies at Art Guild. They'll love it." Each Thursday Denise and I spent the day painting with the Marshall County Art Guild, a group of local women artists.

I handed her artwork back. "Hey, Neecy, I actually have something to show you today!" I trotted to my office for the article and brought it to the kitchen. "Mrs. Bay sent this. It says we can get our original birth certificates and try to find our birth mothers."

She took the article and read the title out loud. Reading was essential to her remarkably independent life; it enabled her to pick out her own groceries and cook her own meals. As we grew up, our dad took pains to teach her to read, a kindness not always extended to disabled people at the time.

As she read, Denise frowned. "I don't want to find my birth mother. She abandoned me." She expressed this whenever I mentioned the subject.

"We don't know why our mothers put us up for adoption," I said gently, hoping for the millionth time to change her mind. "I've always been glad mine gave me life, whatever else may have happened along the way." I didn't remember ever feeling my birth mom had abandoned me.

There was a short pause. "I have a headache today." She held her hand to her forehead. Denise was a sweetheart, but her world was small and very concrete.

I sighed and dropped the subject. "Have you taken Tylenol for it?" I asked. She nodded, and that was the end of the conversation. She ambled back down the hall to her apartment to watch Animal Planet.

My sister had many endearing qualities—she was kindhearted, laughed often, and celebrated small successes. But at times like this, when other sisters might share a deeper connection, she couldn't. I sank into a quiet sadness. If only I had other siblings. Now I might be able to find out if I did.

Rich came home from the bait shop as a gold sunset shone through the silhouette of trees beyond the yard. "Nice night for a fire," he suggested, and busied himself arranging wood in our fireplace. The dancing flames highlighted the wrinkles around his eyes and the gray white of his hair. "Randy was at the bait shop today talking about the pontoon," he said, smiling. "I told him I'd take the job."

A local guide had asked him to be the captain of a new fishing boat. Before we moved to the lake, we had brainstormed guiding options. Rich wanted to cater to families instead of seasoned fishermen. A pontoon would be perfect.

"Your dream is coming true!" I said. But as happy as I was for him, my mind was far from fishing this evening. I fidgeted and decided to just come right out with it. "Hey, guess what? Your mom sent me an article today. It says Illinois changed the adoption law, so I can order my birth certificate."

As I spoke, the impact hit me—this was a life-altering decision—and fear crept in to douse my fire. My face crinkled in worry.

"That was nice of her," he began, then noticed my expression. "What's wrong?"

"Well, what if my birth mom is dead by now? Plus, she never put her name on the registries. I might… open an old wound, or something."

"She might not have known about the registries, Di. You don't know why she gave you up. This is your opportunity to find her."

So, I found the forms I needed on the Illinois website and printed them. But I couldn't bring myself to send them. Did I have the nerve to take this life-changing step?

I'd wanted to find her ever since I was four years old when my dad told me I was adopted. and I found out about my unknown birth mother. I'd always had a warm affection toward her, an expectation of connection, and I assumed she felt the same toward me. Now I saw the thinness of this notion, and I wrestled with reluctance.

One crisp morning a few weeks later, I sipped my coffee on my front porch swing, wrapped in a blanket. Wind whispered in the bare March trees. Each day, I spent quiet moments here, enjoying nature and reading scripture. Today my mind was on those unsent forms on my desk. My eagerness to find my birth mother had flagged; days passed as I pushed the thought away. I had to get past this mental block.

Dread surfaced, whispering my biggest fear: *What if she didn't love me?* Denise might be right. Our biological moms could have abandoned us. Maybe the reality was, she'd moved on, not just in her life but in her heart. I had been a burden, unwanted and unloved.

No. That isn't true, I assured myself. But I faced the fact she might rebuff my attempt to reconnect: the fear of rejection was the reason behind my hesitance.

So, since I'd confronted my fear, could I face reality too? It was the *possibility* of finding my birth mother that had been important to me all along: she was a shining fictional figure in my mind, someone who never forgot me, who might look up at the moon at the same time I did and remember me with affection. Dare I shatter the comfort of my imagination and find out the truth?

Taking a deep breath, I prayed for the courage I needed and settled into silence, letting my eyes wander over the woods across the road. Swift cloud shadows floated over the forest in waves of shade and light. A low thrum of wind in distant branches drew closer and louder until the nearer trees swayed as air rolled over them like ocean breakers. Treetops blushed with the green of fresh new leaves. I smiled at this first sign of the coming spring.

Newness, I thought, and remembered a Bible verse I'd come across several times over the last months. I'd commented in my journal, wondering why it came up so often. The passage was in Isaiah 43:

> *Behold, I will do something new, now it will spring forth; will you not be aware of it? I will even make a roadway in the wilderness, rivers in the desert.*[3]

Now the greening trees were echoing the theme. This was a new road to follow, a once-in-a-lifetime chance to explore my long-hidden identity. Even if my birth mother didn't want to connect, the birth certificate itself might be a wellspring of clues opening the way into the landscape of my own unknown story.

Later that day, I filled out the forms, walked down the driveway, and put them in the same mailbox that had brought me this opportunity.

Weeks of waiting for my birth certificate became two months. In May, an envelope from Illinois arrived. I opened it with excitement but met disappointment. An official letter said one or more of my parents' names did not appear. Did I still want my records? I checked yes, signed and mailed the form, and sighed, steeling myself for a letdown.

Another two months crept past before the day that changed my life.

As I stood next to our mailbox holding my birth certificate for the first time, a flood of memories and emotions rolled over me. My dad's big news on the front stoop when I was four and the thrill of hearing I had another mommy; my adoptive mother's harshness and the sting of her words; my first-born son in my arms and the heart-deep connection to my own flesh and blood. What would this document bring me? I strode inside the house and sat down at my computer.

Then came my two-second Google search; Karen Black's Wikipedia page; my stunned incredulity as I stared in disbelief at our matching facts. Goose bumps ran up my arms. Was it possible this famous actress was my mother?

I took a few deep breaths to calm my nerves and read my birth certificate more carefully. My birth father's name was missing, the space for it was blank. I briefly wondered why but was so shocked by my discovery that I could only focus on my mother. I turned back to my keyboard. In an image search, I found Karen's younger self, at the height of her fame, and gasped. Her face and lanky build were so similar to mine. I leaned back and ran my hand through my hair. Could this really be happening?

I needed to get outside to breathe. My hands put leashes on our dogs, Brandi and Bristol. My feet found their way to our road, but my head was elsewhere, pondering what I had learned. Had I discovered my biological mom in mere moments? What should I do now?

I called Rich and told him what happened in one long, shaky breath, and wondered aloud how to get ahold of her.

His response was quick and lighthearted. "Is she on Facebook?"

Of course. I turned around, hurried home, and typed my message, ending with the big question: *Are you my mom?*

And then, days of silence.

Anxiety replaced the joy of discovery. Each morning I opened my computer and checked for a reply to find none. The rejection I feared seemed to be coming true. After the first few days of dwelling on the past, I tried to keep my spirits up by exploring her career.

I scoured through images and videos of Ms. Black to quell lingering doubts that she was actually my mother. I took my laptop to the bathroom mirror, staring from her photos to myself in a surreal dream.

She made her Broadway debut in 1965, in *The Playroom*, when I was in first grade. While the world had unfolded for me in books, opportunities in the acting world had opened for Karen.

As I scanned through images of her early career, I stumbled on a closeup of young Karen with her face in profile. Awestruck, I remembered a photo in my closet. I brought out the old album and flipped through the pages. There: twenty-year-old me, virtually her twin. Chills ran to the tips of my fingers. I was certain now; this actress was my mother.

In 1970, while I had dreamed of flying to the stars as an astronaut, my birth mother became a star. Her portrayal of Rayette, opposite Jack Nicholson in *Five Easy Pieces*, won her an Oscar nomination.

I rewatched the 1974 *Great Gatsby*, which I'd seen at a theater as a teen. Her character, Myrtle, sauntered down a dreary stairwell. For a moment, her form in a doorway: just like my own young, slender silhouette. In another scene, Karen held a puppy, and her voice and gestures were mine.

Synchronicity had happened on my sixteenth birthday when *Trilogy of Terror* first aired. My mind flashed back to the McDonald's customers who recognized me that same spring. My face had been any-thing but plain—it had echoed the features of my iconic birth mother.

When Karen hosted *Saturday Night Live* in '77, she held a baby in her arms. I had another sibling! Hunter Carson was born to Karen and her third husband, L. M. Kit Carson. This made me wonder about other relatives.

Impatient to learn more about my roots, I joined Ancestry.com. While I had read about Karen's career, I had learned her first husband was named Charlie Black. Maybe he was my birth father? But no details for any Charlie Black matched my records.

I searched for my maternal ancestors. Typing in Karen's infor-mation revealed long threads of history leading back to the 1700s. In minutes I stared into the faces of my grandparents. These images were a solace to my soul. When most people looked in the mirror, they could take their family resemblance for granted. I never experienced this natural belonging. I had been like a discarded skein of yarn, never knitted into the fabric of humanity. Here was the cloth where I belonged.

Most of our ancestors were from Bohemia—modern day Czechia. I had not known I was Eastern European. I searched "Bohemian faces," and brought the laptop to the mirror, comparing their features with my same high cheekbones, rounded nose, full eyebrows, smooth hair. I recognized myself.

My grandmother, Elsie Reif Ziegler, had been a writer, and I ordered three of her books. She wrote historical fiction about young people grappling with life's hard realities. I stayed up late each night reading, woke early to check Facebook for a reply to my message, and built my family tree on Ancestry.

I inundated our boys with photos. When Matt called from Seattle and heard the excitement in my voice, he cautioned me. "Ma, when something is too good to be true…"

"I know, I know, I'm getting too invested."

Two weeks crawled by, and Karen Black did not reply. It seemed she had spurned me entirely, and my mood tottered from delight to dread.

CHAPTER 7

August 2012

ON THE MORNING OF AUGUST 8, 2012, Rich and I sipped our coffee on the front porch, our laptops on a table between us. I opened Facebook with a glum sigh, something that had become automatic.

My heart jumped.

"There's a message from her!" I reached for Rich's hand.

He put down his cup, and sheltering my hand in both of his, he prayed. "Heavenly Father, please help Diane deal with whatever she finds here."

I held on tightly to his hand and clicked.

The private message box opened, and I read the best reply I could have imagined to my question, *Are you my mother?*

I am. Been a long time. I hated leaving you behind, turbulent waves of sorrow. Thank you for making this possible Diane. (Her phone number and email address were here.) Your father is still a good friend, a genius, a professor, a television producer. You will love him. We will all love each other. I'm kinda stunned.

I was stunned myself, swathed in a brand-new kind of peace, vaguely aware of my husband crying next to me, still squeezing my hand. The entire world spun silent and suspended as I turned to Rich in slow motion and smiled.

Tears wet his cheeks, and relief shone from his eyes. "Oh, Di, I was so worried you'd get your heart broken." He wiped tears from my face, and then from his own as we laughed together.

I wrote a simple reply to Karen, thanking her and giving my phone and email. I was almost mute with amazement. Happy was not a good description, even joy, while closer, wasn't expansive enough. I was a ghost who'd come alive; a black and white sketch bursting with colorful paint; Dorothy stepping into Oz. I'd become three-dimensional. All that day, my heartbeat was a lullaby and breathing was a pleasure. I wanted to dance and sing and float. I hoped this lovely peace would melt into my bones and last forever.

On the second day of this new life, Rich and I had finished lunch when my cell phone rang. I pulled it from my pocket and bobbled it when Karen's number appeared. My throat tightened. Rich met my eyes, and I nodded, unable to speak.

"I need to take it outside," I whispered.

"Good luck, baby." He opened the door for me.

On our back deck, I plopped down in a patio chair and took in a deep breath. Exhaling, I pressed talk and brought the phone to my cheek. "Hello," I answered, trembling.

"Hello, dear," said a husky voice.

A smile burst from my heart. "Hi… Mom!"

"Hi, Daughter!" Karen replied, sounding as excited as me. "It is so wonderful to hear you!"

I twisted in my chair so my legs were hanging over the arm, bouncing. "I can hardly believe this is happening!"

"So where are you, right now? What does it look like?"

She wants to picture me talking to her. "Well, I'm outside on my deck, sitting in a green patio chair under a tan canopy. It's sunny and warm out, and birds are singing in the woods past our yard."

"Sounds lovely! I miss the woods in the Midwest. There are no good trees here in Southern California. I've never felt at home here, but this is where the work is."

We both love trees. Should I talk about that? My mind buzzed with panic and delight, but Karen didn't seem to notice the pause.

"Thank you so much for this, Diane! You've done a great thing by contacting me. I always wondered about you. My brother, Peter, helped me try to find you, but we…we couldn't." Her voice dropped to silence, so I spoke up.

"I wondered if you tried. I signed up for two adoption registries, the International Soundex and an Illinois list. If you had joined, they would've connected us. Did you ever hear of them?"

"Yes, Peter talked about that, but I had two bad experiences with people contacting me saying I was their mother, which shook me up, you can imagine. My husband, Stephen, and I decided not to put my name out there."

"Oh, okay," I said, and sighed in relief. She'd just been protecting herself. "So how did you decide I was your real daughter?"

"Because you had the date right! March 4, 1959. Those others had different dates. It's scary being an actor, being famous, because people can treat you very badly if they like. And I've always been awfully gullible. It's how I lost my fortune, being too trusting. We really have no money at all now. But anyway, we didn't join the registries, so you've done a wonderful thing for me, Diane, by reaching out and making this possible."

"Well, your being famous did make it super easy for me to find you. And I've always wanted to meet you—"

"Oh! But how were you able to feel that way?" Karen cut in with passion in her voice. "You didn't have hard feelings about it?"

"No, never! I don't know why, but I only ever wanted to thank you for giving me life. So… thank you! I love life!" I stood up and paced around the deck, running my hand through my hair in joyful disbelief.

"Well, I don't know what to say to that, but thank you. What a great attitude! It was the hardest thing I ever did to give you up."

She paused, then her voice took on a more somber tone. "Diane, it's quite unnatural for a mother to be separated from her newborn. I remember sitting in a fetal position on my bed, rolling along the wall, unable to control my sobbing. They didn't let me hold you. If they had I would never have let you go. I got to see you one time; a kind nurse led me to a window. I peered through the glass. You were in distress! You had scratched your face with your little fingernails. It was all so much to bear."

At that moment, I wished she had held me, that she had kept me. Her openness was amazing. "Thank you for sharing that." The words came out in a whisper. I was barely able to breathe as the revelation of my mother's love washed over me.

After a pause, she asked, "What else do you want to talk about?"

It took a minute to come back to earth. "Well, here's another thing I want to ask: Why did it take you two weeks to respond to my message?" I had to learn the reason.

"What? No, I answered you right away!"

"I didn't get a message for two weeks, I thought maybe…"

"Oh, darling, I had no idea it'd been that long! You know, Stephen doesn't check my fan page very often. I am so sorry! That must've been so disconcerting for you!"

Relief flooded me. "So, you… answered right away?"

"Yes, of course! We were in the middle of a photo shoot in our living room when Stephen came rushing in. 'Karen!' He said, with intensity, 'Karen! Nina just messaged you on Facebook!' I was flabbergasted! I sat down at his computer and typed my message back to you right then, darling."

My eyes lit up at her use of such a familiar term. I wanted to hold her but all I could do was hug myself. After we got that straightened out, our conversation jumped from one subject to another, covering random topics as we craved to know more about each other. She mentioned a screenplay she had written, which I said I'd love to read, and she promised to email it.

"So, you have two other kids, right? I saw you have a son, Hunter Carson, and then a daughter, Celine?"

"Yes, my son is the light of my life. He's so smart and sensitive and funny! And Celine, well she was full of light as a child, but then she grew into a teenager, and we didn't know what to do—she was like a different person. And oh, do you know that we adopted her?"

That caught me up short. She'd given me up only to adopt a child, and a daughter at that? "Why?" I blurted out, feeling almost betrayed. But Karen didn't seem to notice the emotion behind the question.

"Stephen wanted a baby," she went on, "and I was 45 when we married, Diane. I went through menopause early, like my mother. Did you?"

"Um, no, I was 51."

"Well it did create a problem for us, but Stephen said we can just adopt, like it was the most natural solution in the world. We chose an open adoption. Celine knows her birth mother and met her little brother when she was eleven."

"Wow, that's the way it should be. I hope I get to meet her sometime," I said. My initial feeling of betrayal faded. It made sense for them to adopt. Karen was at a totally different stage of life from when she had me. I was happy for her and was sorry for my hurt reaction.

The call ended with a back and forth about tentative plans. Karen thought she might come here to Kentucky in the fall with Stephen and Celine. She wanted me to meet the rest of the family, too; Hunter, of course, and Diane's sister and brother were excited we connected.

It felt natural to converse with her, as if we'd known each other forever. The last thing she said was, "Talk to you tomorrow, dear."

I bounded back inside to find Rich at his computer, tears in his eyes. "I was just emailing my family to say you were on the phone with your birth mother!" He said. He reached out to squeeze my hand. "How did it go?"

"So great! I'm comfortable with her already. I even called her Mom! She told me it was hard to give me up, and she always wanted to find me but couldn't..."

I related the conversation as best I could, not able to remember everything word for word but animated as I recounted how interested Karen had seemed in me, how much she shared about her life. "...And then she said, talk to you tomorrow!"

Rich got up and hugged me, neither of us caring that we were crying on each other. These were tears of joy.

The next day I opened my Gmail and found her screenplay, *Deep Purple,* in my inbox. I opened the file and after the first few paragraphs I pushed my chair away from my desk and fought the urge to cry again. The story was about a woman searching for the daughter she'd given up for adoption, and Karen had wanted me to read it. This was proof that my birth mother had never forgotten me.

I was into the fourth page when Karen rang my phone. Would talking to her feel as comfortable as yesterday? Butterflies fluttered in my stomach again, but as soon as she spoke, I was right at home. "I love your screenplay, Mom. Your writing is powerful."

"Thank you, darling. Have you read it already?"

"Started it," I said.

"It's based on our story, you know," she confided.

"I guessed that. I'm honored to read it." More tears pressed out of my too-full heart.

After a few minutes I asked a question that had me dying of curiosity. "My father's name wasn't on my birth certificate. Would you tell me about my dad?"

"His name is Robert Benedetti, Beny for short. I can't imagine why his name wasn't there, but it was all a blur. You know a man came to ask me a string of questions while I was in labor? How is that supposed to be all right? Anyhow, your father and I, we've never lost touch. We're still friends. He's gentle and easy going, a brilliant television producer and writer. He is full northern Italian, and very tall, six-foot four I think."

"That explains why our three boys are so tall. Matt is six-seven!"

"I can't imagine! Oh, I got the picture you sent of them. It was awfully much for me to take in, suddenly having three adult grandsons, but did they have to be so handsome!" We laughed, then she added, "Beny and I named you Nina, you know. Do you like it?"

"I love it, Mom. Have you told him yet that I found you?"

"I did, and he will definitely contact you. He is different from me, Diane, at this time in our lives. I'm still working in my garden, continuing to create and do new things. Beny is sitting and enjoying his garden now."

I smiled, enjoying the expansive way she talked, the metaphors she used. "That's an interesting way to put it, Mom."

When I got off the phone, I Googled my father. The top of his website said Producer/Director/Writer/Teacher/Consultant. His list of achievements was staggering and spanned a fifty-year career in the arts. His accomplishments were intimidating. He'd won three Emmy awards and more; he'd been the president of Ted Danson's production company. He was obviously an intellectual, having also been Chairman or Dean at several universities. He authored lots of books, mostly about acting. One intrigued me, *The Long Italian Goodbye*, about a young Italian boy growing up in Chicago. The description made me wonder if it might give me insight into his upbringing. If so, it could be a treasure. I was both eager and abashed to meet him.

Several days later, Beny's first message appeared in my inbox. I paused before clicking on it, hoping he would be as accepting as Karen. Nervousness made me fidget as if I were going into a job interview.

Hello! This is a strange email to be writing, but this address Karen gave me is the only contact I have for you. As you may guess, I am your biological father. Karen and I lived together for several years in college and have remained dear friends ever since. We are both glad to have connected with you; Karen tried a few times before you were able to contact her. The lovely communication you sent her touched me. You are obviously a wonderful person. I saw your picture on Facebook, and Karen is right, you do look like both of us!

His easy way of expressing himself relieved my anxiety. He seemed down-to-earth as he described himself and his family. I actually had two more biological siblings and a stepsister. As these words unfolded, thankfulness enfolded me. My brother Ben and sister Nina—my eyes went wide when I read her name—were a decade younger than me, and they each had adult sons. Their stepsister, Kirsten, was my age. Then I read something that astonished me: my father told his kids about me when they were teenagers, and they were just as excited to meet me as he was. He hoped it was okay that he'd given them my Facebook address.

I read his message twice and sat blinking at my screen with wet eyes, chin quivering. Somewhere in the back of my mind I had always assumed my birth father had abandoned my mother. I guess that's why I didn't wonder much about him. Maybe, too, it was because I had a good relationship with my adopted dad, who I'd been missing terribly since he passed. And now Beny was here, giving me a chance to have a paternal figure in my life again. And not just a role model—someone who shared my DNA. Someone who loved Karen and had never forgotten me. Someone who'd told his other kids about me. Gratitude brought me to tears once again. I really had a new mom and dad.

The next morning, I found a Facebook message from my brother Ben. I smiled as I read his friendly note.

I'm sure many other family members have already mentioned this to you… I find it fascinating that you are an artist. All of us are artistically inclined. Both my older sister and I graduated from Cal Arts, and my dad taught there forever. How cool that you have the same passion for artistic expression we do. Your sketches on Facebook are full of a depth of nostalgia that is both comforting and warm.

I shook my head in wonder. Every new family member I had encountered so far was artistically inclined. The fact I was part of two creative families resonated with me, but somehow did not surprise me. Deep down I felt that, at least for me, nature trumped nurture.

No matter how often my pragmatic parents had told me to get my head out of the clouds, my inner artist had always come through. But this insistent urge, this thing that made me different, was part of a lineage. I fit right in with my people, and I could be proud of my ancestry and my identity.

Later that day, my sister Nina also messaged. She said she had wondered about me for decades, and that she'd love to get to know me. Then, another delightful surprise:

> *I saw that you have a son in Seattle? I guess that makes me his aunt. So weird. I have lived in Bothell, thirty miles from there, for the last fifteen years.*

I had heard about adoptive families finding biological relatives living close to them, but how strange and wonderful that it was happening to me. I imagined my birth sister and Matt passing on the street as strangers, and I itched to tell him. To give him the gift of new family that was transforming my life.

And then it struck me: I could tell Matt in person. Mike, our middle son, and I were flying out to visit him in three weeks, after all. We could all meet Nina together.

My heart beat fast as my fingers flew over the keys, explaining my planned trip and asking if she might be able to get together. Her reply was quick. She'd definitely make time for us.

How was it possible I had such wonderful relatives, open to my presence in their lives? Many reunions turn out well, but mine was proceeding like a fairy tale.

Karen and I texted nearly every day for the first couple weeks. She might visit after she shot a new movie, *Ooga Booga*, a tongue-in-cheek horror film based on the Zuni doll from *Trilogy of Terror*. She was busy but, "So happy to have you with me, as tho' you never left." I held my phone to my heart after reading that one.

My new sister Nina and I sent long messages on Facebook, getting to know each other. She loved the idea of meeting us all when I would be in town. She had moved up to Seattle with her two preschool boys in the '90s. That took such strength of character. And she had made it work, completing her schooling, and pursuing a career as a teacher at a nearby college. I couldn't wait to meet her.

I kept working on my family tree on Ancestry and emailed Beny for information on his lineage. His families on both sides were Tuscan from way back, from a few small towns nestled close together not far from Florence. He provided lots of facts and then posted images from a trip to Italy so I could put faces with names. On Facebook, I was thrilled to friend two cousins who lived in the village where Beny's grandparents grew up.

Each Thursday our Art Guild pals were eager to hear the latest; each Sunday at church we chatted with friends who shared our astonishment. Denise, on the other hand, was quieter than usual and seemed to feel left out, so Rich and I tried to give her extra attention. And late in the evenings, after she went to bed, the two of us cuddled on the couch, reveling in the newness that had entered both our lives.

Those joyful weeks were a gift, a time for my heart to fill with love, for my mind to embrace my role as a daughter again, for my severed roots to mend and take hold.

I would need all my new strength to face what was coming next.

CHAPTER 8

September 2012

I HUMMED AS I DROVE THE OLD CORSICA we'd inherited from my adoptive dad along a country road. My cell rang; it was Karen. We chatted about her new movie. Her role had been easy to shoot so she was back from filming already. Then she paused.

"Darling, there's something I need to tell you. I wasn't sure if I should, but I discussed it with Stephen. We feel you should know." I frowned; her voice carried a tense note that made me uneasy.

I pulled over into a parking lot, put the car in park, and listened as she continued.

"This will be hard to hear, and there's no easy way to express it. I'm battling cancer again." She took a breath. Time halted. She went on. "I had it before, did you know? And I beat it. Stephen's brother has learned...."

The throbbing of my heart drowned out her voice. Dread seized my chest. She might die. People who get cancer a second time die. I just found her! Oh my God, I can't lose her. How can this be happening?!

In my next breath a plan to meet her sprang to life. I climbed out of the car and paced on the gravel, my heart racing, the ground shifting under my feet.

Karen continued, "So Stephen and I might not visit..."

"Mom," I interrupted, "I can come to you! I purchased tickets for Seattle for two weeks from now. Since I fly Southwest, I can add a flight to LA!"

After a silent second Karen asked, "When would you arrive?"

"It would be the 17th or 18th."

Her speech quickened with decisiveness. "Perfect! You can stay with us for a week, in our extra room. Stephen can pick you up at the airport."

She surprised me by her immediate engagement with my idea and by inviting me into her home. My arms felt suddenly empty. I needed to hold her. Now.

"But can you afford it?" She asked. "I'd help, but Stephen is swamped with bills between my health and Celine's schooling."

"We'll work it out somehow, Mom," I assured her.

When Rich got home from guiding on the pontoon, we talked at the kitchen table. In a quavering voice, I told him about Karen's condition. He reached for my hand. "I guess we didn't think about the fact that finding new parents would mean losing them, too."

I nodded. "At least not so soon."

I explained my idea to add a flight after Seattle and asked his opinion on the added time and expense. He hesitated but considered the plan. "I can stay here with Denise for another week so you can meet Karen. But I don't know where the money is going to come from. We're already stretching ourselves to get you and Mike to Seattle."

His response did not deflate me; our reunion had to become a reality. "There has to be a way. My Art Guild friends might help. I'll ask them tomorrow."

The next morning, Denise and I joined the ladies in a room at the local library. These dear women had opened their arms and hearts to us soon after we moved here. Most of them were a generation older, and they embraced us like mothers, encouraging our art and teaching me the ropes of country life. It thrilled them that I had found Karen.

Doreen, our unappointed leader, was born in England. She had a sunny disposition, lyrical accent, and wavy blonde hair. Every week she related amusing anecdotes or burst into spontaneous song. She was particularly riveted when I shared the news of my birth mother: she was a true Karen Black fan. She had been watching Karen's movies and online interviews nonstop during the month since my amazing discovery.

Doreen's friend Mary was there each week, too. She had short gray hair and an easy smile above her denim painting shirt. She was an intuitive Christian, and she sensed something wrong as soon as I walked in the room that day.

"What is it?" She asked as we hugged hello.

"Let's talk about it later," I said, a little embarrassed that the concern on my face was so obvious.

"When you're ready."

Doreen was extra bubbly that morning. "I found *Capricorn One* online last night, Diane. How I love your mother in it! Does she smoke? She looks so good with a cigarette!"

"No, Doreen, she did years ago, but quit." My voice sounded curt, so I added, "Jack Nicholson told her, 'Blackie, everyone will want to smoke when they watch you light up.' But she's against it now."

This got a few smiles, but then the silence grew awkward. I had trouble making small talk, and after a few minutes, I gave up trying. "I have something to say, you guys," I began. "Karen shared bad news yesterday. She… she has cancer." My words hung in the air as paintbrushes and pencils clinked onto tables.

Doreen was the first to speak. "Oh, dear God, no! Did she say what kind?"

"It's called Ampullary cancer, very rare. It's in the digestive tract where the stomach meets the intestines." Seeing the horror on everyone's faces, I hastened to add, "She had it two years ago and got rid of it. And she was upbeat when she explained a hopeful treatment."

"Well she would be positive with you," said Doreen, "But telling you must have been so difficult for her. Right when you just reconnected."

Nancy, a petite, bighearted lady, was sitting next to me. Her worried eyes met mine. "Did they discover it before you found her, Diane?"

"I'm not sure..." How long had Karen known?

Mary looked up from her lap. "How wonderful that you met her now. I mean, it would be better if she wasn't sick, of course, but if something happens—God forbid—at least you've connected with her."

"Thanks, Mary, you're right. And guess what? In a couple weeks I'm going out to spend time with Matt and Becca and the grandboys in Seattle. I told Karen I could fly to Los Angeles afterward, and she suggested I stay with her for a whole week!"

"That's lovely!" Doreen responded. The ladies voiced their agreement and excitement for me.

Now was the time to appeal for help, but I hesitated. The right words eluded me, and I worried about poisoning this sweet, loving space with such a forward request. I remained silent as the conversation moved on.

On the way home, I got a call from Mary. "Diane, it may not be my place to ask, but I know the extra airfare to LA can't be cheap. Can you manage it, or do you need help?"

Relief flooded me. "Oh, Mary, I couldn't bring myself to ask, but..."

"Well, don't you worry. I have two hundred dollars put away. I planned a trip to see a friend and it never happened. I prayed about what to do with the money, and today I felt I should offer it to you."

"Wow, unbelievable, Mary. The ticket is $190!"

"You see? The Lord's hands are holding you, Diane."

"How can I ever thank you? You're helping me achieve a lifelong dream. I can't express how much it means."

"Please, you know how much we all love you. And you're always there for us. Consider us even. I'll send a check tomorrow." She hung up before I could protest.

Back at home, my excitement overflowed as I recounted Mary's kind offer to Rich. He was not happy to accept the money, but he was relieved everything would work out. So, it was set; I'd meet my birth mother in three weeks.

Trees cast long sunrise shadows over our road as Rich and I walked to the driveway on Monday, September 10, with my luggage. Today my trip began: first stop, a week in Seattle with Mike. Then when Mike flew home, I'd fly to LA alone to meet Karen.

Our son was busy arranging our suitcases in the Corsica's trunk while we said our goodbyes. My two-week trip would be the longest we'd ever been apart in over thirty years of marriage.

We held hands for a long moment. "I know I keep saying this, Rich, but I'm so thankful you're staying with Denise so I can go."

"You've wanted this all your life, Di. Just pray for me, and I'll be praying for you." He hugged me. "Love you."

"I will. Love you, too."

I climbed into the passenger seat. Mike said goodbye to his dad and settled behind the wheel for the two-hour trip to Nashville International, the closest major airport. As he drove, I kept glancing at his silhouette. He looked so Italian with his brown eyes and dark hair. How had I not noticed before? His twenty-seven-year-old features matched young photos of my half brother Ben. It was intoxicating to see him in the new light of my birth father's lineage.

I'm on my way to meet my mother and brothers and sisters, I mused, with the Tennessee hills rolling by. Ben Benedetti and his wife, who lived north of LA, seemed thrilled at the chance to take me to lunch. I would get to meet my adopted sister, Celine, who lived with Stephen and Karen. And to my amazement, Hunter would be flying into town as well. So, like puzzle pieces falling together from on high, I was meeting my birth mother and four of five siblings within two weeks. It was surreal and happening so quickly. I needed something to keep me grounded.

I reached into the back seat, pulled out my journal, and settled in to make a chart of my new family members, trying to memorize everyone. I put a star beside the ones I was flying to meet:

Mom's Side	_Dad's Side_
*Karen	Beny
*Her husband Stephen	His wife Joan
*Half brother Hunter	*Half sister Nina
*Adopted sister Celine	*Half brother Ben
	Stepsister Kirsten

Plus, there were everyone's partners and spouses; a niece and four nephews; and Karen's siblings. Beny was an only child. And cousins, so many cousins. As children, Denise and I didn't have any cousins around; our few relatives lived far away and after my mother's breakdown we rarely saw them. So I was giddy with the prospect of having so many relations to get to know.

Mike and I had seats together on the plane, with a window to share. He read Crichton's Next while I spent time on my computer organizing photos. My carry-on included a small album of pre-digital pictures—glimpses of my childhood and our children's. The laptop held images of teenage boys and onward to our grandkids, Matt's sons Gibson and Porter. I wanted my mom to see my life and my children. I hoped she would get to know her grandkids. If only there was time. If only she got better.

After several hours, Mike was having a turn at the window. "Hey, Ma, do you think that could be Mount Rainier already?" He pointed into the distance.

I leaned over him and glimpsed a tiny triangle on the horizon. "Aren't we still too far away?"

It turned out the sky was so clear we were able to see Rainier's summit approaching for more than a half hour. I tipped my head back in my chair and closed my eyes, daydreaming of the future, the years coming toward me like that mountain. If Karen beats this cancer, we could have plenty of time. Her mom lived to be ninety-seven. Even with the disease looming, there was hope for decades together. I resolved to make every moment count, whatever was waiting for me on the other side of that peak.

———•••———

Our eldest son came to pick us up at SeaTac airport with three-year-old Gibson in tow. Their family's new Mazda SUV was large enough to accommodate Matt's six-foot-seven frame. He folded me into a huge bear hug, and I hefted the little blondie Gibson up for a kiss. I spent the ride in the back seat with my grandson, admiring his blue eyes and listening to his chatter with rapt interest while my own boys chatted up front.

Matt's curly brown hair swept against the roof of the car as he turned to talk. "So, Ma," he said, "how overwhelmed are you?"

"Damn overwhelmed, going from having one sister to a giant family!"

"It must be weird. What's the relative count so far?"

"Thirty I know of, including cousins on Karen's side."

"Becca and I have been watching Karen's interviews on YouTube, and I understand where you get your craziness! You seem to be a tame version of her. It was uncanny seeing her in the Vice interview, sitting curled on the couch like you do. And she talked to her cat and kept getting distracted. She walked away for a second in the middle of a question, too. I so see you in her!"

I laughed at the truthful comparison. "Dad and I watched that video too and noticed her gestures are like mine. Uncanny is a good word for it."

We took a bridge over the shipyards and emerged in wooded

West Seattle. Their apartment was on the second floor of a house. The guys dragged our luggage up the outdoor stairway to their deck where Matt's blonde wife Becca, and their toddler Porter, greeted us with more hugs. The closeness of kinship made me light and cheery.

Our days together overflowed with small adventures. One day we walked through Pike Place Market where I took photos and bought Denise a shirt with a fish design. Another time we spent an hour in a music store equipped for young customers' fun, filled with handheld noisemakers little Porter loved. Mike and Gibson discovered a unique old-school typewriter rigged to make cool sounds when they tapped the keys. I enjoyed photographing the action.

Then Matt asked to see a violin so Gibson could try it. "Since my great grandpa played the violin for the Chicago Symphony, maybe the talent will be inherited," he said, alluding to Karen's grandfather, Arthur Ziegler. Matt had accepted his genetic roots, I noted with satisfaction.

During the first few days of our time in Seattle, my new sister Nina and I texted plans. She invited us over for dinner on Thursday night. So, that afternoon, we piled into the SUV and took the thirty-minute drive up to suburban Bothell.

I stood hesitating on the sidewalk, waiting for Matt to walk with me up to the house. On the cement stoop, I squeezed his hand, rang the bell, and peered into the beveled glass window. Jeaned legs appeared and started down a half-flight of stairs. I straightened and held my breath. The door opened.

Nina greeted us with a big smile, wearing a rust-colored T-shirt that featured a Volkswagen bus on a desert road. She didn't resemble me, even face-to-face; she was blonde and must have inherited her features from her mother Joan. But her open good-natured expression and her informal choice of clothing drew me to her right away.

Nina spoke first. "Well hello, long-lost relatives!" We hugged, and I handed her my gift, a sketchpad. She and I were both artists.

"Thanks! Wow, so cool to meet you at last!"

I found my voice. "Hi, Nina! It's amazing to be here. This is Matt and Becca, I guess you recognize them from Facebook."

"Yes, and this must be Gibson! Hello, young man." She shook his little hand, then stooped. "Hi, Porter!" She said to the toddler who gave her a big smile. "Come on in. I'll give you the grand tour." She carried my gift and Becca's dessert and led us up the stairs into a sunlit great room. She introduced us to her burly boyfriend Jonathan. They stood eye-to-eye, and I realized Nina must be close to six-feet tall.

"Jonathan was adopted too," Nina mentioned, hinting at a topic for conversation. "And this is my son Tyler," she said as we moved into a sitting area. Tyler stood and nodded, shaking hands with Matt and Mike. He held a small white dog in the crook of his arm. The kids settled in together to talk while Jonathan headed to the kitchen to check on dinner.

Nina showed me around their eclectic home, pointing out her large abstract paintings, a contrast to my realistic drawings. I liked her bold colors and textures. We strolled out onto their raised deck, past a row of festive, colored wine bottle lights hanging from a wood trellis, then downstairs into the backyard.

"There used to be more of those giant arborvitaes," she said, pointing near the back of her large yard which overlooked a wild stretch of land. "We have a nice view now, but it's because of a fire. One night we woke up to a blaze and the sound of a firetruck a minute later. A couple trees and a good chunk of our yard burned."

"Wow, how scary!" I stuck out my lower lip in a pout.

"Hey! You have a Benedetti lip!" Nina laughed, rolling her lip the same way to prove it. It felt quietly spectacular to see this physical similarity with my new sister. This was another step toward seeing myself more clearly.

The conversation turned to lighter things. Matt came into the yard with my camera and snapped a picture of us together. We walked back to the deck, and as we climbed the stairs, Nina noticed our sandaled feet.

"And look at those Benedetti toes!" She said. We placed our sandaled feet side by side for a photo. "You have the fat big toe and longer middle one, like all of us." My big feet floated above the ground, here with my real biological sister.

Nina went into the kitchen to set the table, and as dinner finished cooking, I chatted with her boyfriend on the deck.

"Hey, Jonathan, Nina said you're adopted too?" I asked, as I eased into a patio chair across from him.

"Yep," he answered, a quick frown on his heavy brow. "So how did you find your birth mom?"

"When Illinois opened their records, I ordered my birth certificate. Karen's name was on it. All I did was Google her, and since she was famous, she had a Wikipedia page. Her fame made it easy."

"But how did you contact her?" He asked.

"Oh, on Facebook. I sent her a private message and she replied! She's been so wonderful," I answered, glowing. "You want to find your mother too?"

"Yeah. I think I'm ready to, but I'm nervous about it. We've been looking for her, but so far, no success. We talked 20 years ago, but I wasn't prepared for a relationship, so I lost track of her. I hope we can find her again... but I'm not sure how I'd take it if she rejects me."

His transparency impressed me. "No matter what, both of you will know you tried, and that'll be meaningful. I've gotten a lot of satisfaction just by knowing my roots. Even if I hadn't met any of you, I would've been glad I took the leap. Although, I'm blessed beyond belief with two whole new families! You'll never be certain unless you try."

Jonathan gave a pensive nod. Nina came out to get us, and we joined the family filing into the kitchen. Her son Aiden bounced in the front door as we were gathering. His cropped blond hair stuck up in a cowlick.

"Hello, surprise cousins!" He exclaimed, getting a laugh from us. His boisterous nature contrasted with his brother Tyler's quiet reticence. Aiden reminded me of our Ricky.

Over Jonathan's delicious chicken, we got to know each other. We chatted about our lives, the troubles and perks of birth order, and the contrast between being a sibling and being a parent. My heart swelled to see this group of strangers becoming a family.

During a lull, I asked the question that had been on my mind. "Nina, when did your dad tell you and Ben about me?"

"Our dad," she corrected, smiling. "We were 14 and 15, I think. At Christmas one year, he told us we had another sibling. Our parents were always transparent with us. I even tried looking for you when the Internet got better websites about 10 years ago. But I didn't have enough information, so I stopped. My half sister, Kirsten, my mom's daughter, is your age. He and mom married when she was eight. She was born in 1958."

I gasped. My birth father had raised a girl while I was a child. "I was born in 59! Do you know they named me Nina?"

"My mom told me. It's interesting. I might be your namesake."

"It says a lot about Beny—our dad—that he told you about me when you were young." I shook my head, trying to take it in, thankful my birth father hadn't forgotten me.

Before we left, we rounded up our four young men out on the deck and took pictures of them goofing around like cousins. Then Nina strolled out front with us. We walked together, trailing behind as Becca packed the kids into the SUV.

"It was so remarkable meeting you and your beautiful family!" She said. "I was nervous, but I didn't need to be. You're so comfortable."

"I couldn't tell you were nervous at all! I was anxious, too, but as soon as you answered the door you put me at ease."

"Thanks!" Nina smiled. "Well, you better go," she said, nodding toward my waiting kids. We hugged for a long time.

On the way home to Matt's house, I sat in the back next to little Porter's car seat. His drowsy eyes gazed out the window as I floated in the wonder of the day, watching the waning sunlight glint off the passing city. Memories of this bright day flickered past, shining out toward the future.

During the following days, Karen and I texted to prepare for our upcoming visit. Each text I received made me smile because her happiness shone in her words:

I am feeling SO WELL today! So glad I am improving in time for family wonder and fun!!! I feel I've known you for years.

As I reread each text late at night, a mixture of peace, excitement, apprehension, and love swirled inside me. Sometimes my chest hurt, my heart was so full of deep connection to her. I had the basic human bond now. For fifty-three years I'd lived with an emptiness at my core; it was why I didn't know myself, and why I always felt apart instead of a part. As if I was a plant expected to grow with no roots, a cut flower propped up in water.

CHAPTER 9

Tuesday, September 18

On a cool, damp morning, Matt drove me to SeaTac airport very early; no minutes to shower, only time to choose clothing. I hastily picked a cocoa and white blouse with tan capris, brushed my teeth and hair, and sleepwalked out to Matt's truck. I hadn't slept well. Dawn blushed the sky as I said goodbye to my son at the departure terminal.

In a window seat on the jet, I propped my jacket against the wall, peeked under the shade a few times, and dozed. When the flight attendant came by, I sat up and ordered coffee. Sipping the warmth, I considered the day ahead. I'll meet Karen for real today. My stomach churned. For the first time since we'd made plans to meet, I had second thoughts. What was I doing, staying for a week in the Hollywood home of people I had never met? What if I was awkward? What if I didn't connect with them? I prayed for courage and took deep breaths, letting myself relax. By the time I entered the airport, I was ready for my adventure.

Karen's husband, Stephen, had my flight itinerary, and on the way to my luggage, I texted him as I walked out into a hot LA morning and found a spot to sit. The sun warmed my shoulders as I took deep breaths, trying to calm my pounding heart again. A black BMW pulled up to the curb. Out stepped a tanned man who smiled at me, waving.

"Hey, Diane!" He walked over, bending to embrace me. "So good to meet you!"

"Hi, Stephen, thanks for picking me up." His eyes held me with affection like a loved one returning from a trip. I smiled at his pleasant nature, but my jitters wouldn't be quashed.

As he navigated city streets, we described our ongoing creative projects. Stephen was a video editor working on a movie trailer; I had a book design to complete. We spoke about Karen. They had been married twenty-eight years, and she had told him about my birth long ago.

We wove through Bel-Air, an opulent district stretching up an expansive slope. I'd never seen such wealth firsthand. Giant stone walls or close-set cedars allowed glimpses of estates from the winding road.

"I'm out of my element," I told him, holding my hands together on my lap to avoid biting my nails.

"People are just people here," he assured me, as the car crested a hill into a manicured middle-class neighborhood. Bright pink bougainvillea flowed over a low wall and waist-high red geraniums grew like bushes along a picket fence. We pulled into a driveway of a blonde brick ranch home. A tree laden with white blossoms framed the front door.

"You nervous?" He asked, as we stepped up.

"Oh, I am so nervous."

"I'm sure she is too."

He held the door for me and we walked in, through a day-lit space to a living room where their adopted daughter, Celine, met me with a quick hug. She was in her mid-twenties, stunning and slender, with waist-length hair. But I barely noticed this, because over her shoulder, my birth mother stood a few feet from me. Her tearful eyes fixed on mine as time slowed. I moved toward her.

Karen was more beautiful and fragile than I had imagined. Her face shone with wonder, mirroring mine I was sure. One more step and she was in my arms, small and delicate and floral scented. Right away I became protective. We held each other a long while.

I spoke first, in a whisper. "All I want to do is hug you!"

"Last time I saw you, you were this big," she said, pulling back and holding her hands apart just-so. "And you were not happy. You were scratching your little face with your fingernails."

She fastened my gaze. "Love those brown eyes. Beny's right, you do look like both of us!"

What a healing statement that was for me. I burst with relief to hold my birth mother and hear her voice. Relief mixed with wonder and amazement. Love overflowed, inside and out, as I fulfilled this lifelong dream. We were right in the middle of a miracle. From the moment she came into my life with her message of acceptance, our kinship completed me. Yet grief tinged my joy, because our time might be brief.

Karen led me to a deep-seated yellow couch under a window. We sank into it and faced each other. I memorized her face, her stunning blue eyes. She wore a lavender polo shirt and pale slacks; her brown hair was all frizzy curls. I took in the surrounding homey comfort: soft seating, vintage furnishings, warm stucco walls. A high sloping ceiling created an airy space above us. Skylights lit the room.

"Thank you so much for making this possible," she said, with tears in her eyes.

"I've always wanted to find you, and Stephen said you searched, as well," I said.

"We did! My brother Peter's so good at discovering everybody. He would go to state records, but no matter where we tried... I mean, who would we search for? Nina, that's the only name we had, and the date you were born.

"So, my friend Lee would say, 'Oh it's March 4th, she's thinking of you.' Lee's coming over Friday night. She's Celine's godmother." Karen nodded toward her daughter sitting on a green chaise near us. "And she's Hunter's godmother, but Hunter and I were apart for eleven years. It broke me to pieces."

"I didn't know that happened," I said, surprised. I looked down and saw that we still held hands, so I squeezed hers.

She gave me a slow once-over. "You're awfully pretty. I love your face. So here you are, your whole figure… I like your hands, they're Beny's hands. Isn't that funny, you come, and I look at your body!"

We laughed as her soft gaze held me. "Well, sure, curiosity is normal! I wondered about you, too. And it's weird, but I always wondered what I looked like. Growing up without my own people made it hard for me to see myself, somehow. Knowing who you are would've helped me."

"Celine didn't have that problem, did you?" Karen turned to her.

"No, but I totally understand that," Celine answered. Her adoption had been an open one while mine was closed.

"You do look like a blend of these two," I said, pointing to our mom and Stephen.

Karen said, "Yes, especially as a youngster. She's part Irish and so is Stephen. Let me show you something." She got up and walked into the dining room.

"I have a similar heritage, so it works," said Celine.

Would I have understood myself better if Italian or Czech parents had raised me? Could I have been more self-possessed? Recognizing my own Bohemian features had helped me, so it was possible.

Karen came back with a photo of little Celine and Daddy Stephen and plopped down next to me. "See how much alike they are?" The resemblance was striking.

She paused, regarding me again. "I can't believe you're here! You're a wonderful weight, couldn't be better."

"I'm at a hundred forty-two right now."

"I'm a hundred fifteen," she said, looking worried, "I lost forty pounds."

"That's perfect for your height," I said, wanting to encourage her. Celine nodded, but her eyes hinted that illness had caused the weight loss.

We changed subjects while Celine disappeared into the kitchen. I curled up toward Karen. She reached for my hands and our eyes linked.

"Anticipation kept hitting me day by day. Earlier I was terrified," I admitted.

"Yes, entrance is nerve-racking. But it's interesting that it's always been cozy between us, never at all strained."

"I sensed that connection to you right away."

She gazed out the window, her eyes glazed as if seeing memories. "You know I had you in a county hospital."

"Yes, Cook County," I said. "And I remember the Foundlings Home, that's where we went to adopt my sister. I imagine you stayed there while you were pregnant?"

"Yes, that's right. I lived in that maternity home four months. We all had jobs, mine was dusting. I wanted to work in the kitchen. I love to cook, but the housemothers wouldn't let me. When my labor started, they took me to the county hospital a few blocks away to deliver in a stark room with lots of lights. They gave me an epidural, so I didn't feel a thing. There was a big boulder," her hands shaped a mound on her belly, "and I watched it moving down my stomach. I don't remember pushing. It moved by itself, and then the baby–you–came out, and the doctor hurried you away. I looked at the clock on the wall behind me like this," she tipped her head back, "because I wanted to know what time you were born. It was 3:30 in the afternoon.

"And they gave me a bed in a huge room, and all the mothers...." her voice broke, but she continued, "the mothers were next to me. There must have been twenty, in a long row. And what happened was, the nurses brought the babies to them for nursing, and they didn't bring you. So, I felt desperate."

I covered my mouth with my hand. How awful that must have been for her. "All your hormones at that point are screaming, 'I want my baby—I'd imagine.'"

She was quiet and crumpled as if still experiencing the pain. She sounded short of breath. "It's more the soul, the spirit. It's an abrogation of the way life should be."

"Abrogation?" I asked. I didn't know the word.

"It means something is wrong, there's a breaking off. It was terrible, oh my god, the loss I felt watching other people with their babies. Because I've always been an earth mother anyway, as I'm sure you are. You want to nurse, and they don't bring your baby."

I had nursed all my boys. "Oh, that must have been so tough," was all I could say. I reached for her hand.

She relaxed back into the couch, breathing hard as if glad she had gotten through the story. Her face softened, and she smiled. "Oh, you're funny to say it's tough! That's ironic!" She looked up at Stephen, who sat on the arm of the chair next to her, and spoke gibberish to him.

He turned to me with a droll expression. "So. Karen has a baby talk… and you just heard it," he explained. I laughed, surprised and amused.

"Have you always done that, Karen?" Asked Stephen.

She thought a moment. "When I had Hunter, I started. Celine used to hate it, but now she uses it sometimes too. So does Karyn Rachtman, who is like my other child. She's the daughter of a guy I went with before I met Stephen."

Celine brought us plates of steamy chicken casserole. It tasted fantastic; all I'd eaten was a Kind bar and airplane peanuts. While we munched, Celine talked about her birth mother, and a half brother she'd met a few times. "It's nice to know your families," she said.

I told them about meeting Nina. "Does she look like you?" Karen asked.

"No, not much at all. Our feet are alike though! I have Benedetti toes." I laughed and wiggled them.

Chapter 9: Tuesday, September 18

After our meal, Stephen gathered our empty plates. Karen and I slouched on the couch with our feet on the coffee table. I was a little a girl again, hanging out with new friends.

"You're giving me a weird experience," my mother began, focusing on me, her voice soft. "Let me try to explain. I have three children, and they'll all be here soon, which I never thought would happen." She stopped, taking that in, blinking, playing with her hair.

"When Celine was four," she went on, "we went to see Hunter, and his father and stepmother took him out of the house. We stayed, waiting in the backyard all afternoon, and they never came home. There are other stories I could tell, too.

"So, I knew Hunter's father, what he was capable of. When I looked at Hunter, I saw the father in him, like a rock, a hard place. And I don't know Celine's father—I can somewhat see Stephen in her, but not in the same way.

"But I can see Beny in you, Diane. And it makes me wish Beny were here. It makes me understand the triangle of family—in a way that has not been mine. It's a real lesson." Her eyes pierced me. "You're formidable, darling. You really are."

No response came to mind. The compliment hit me as profound, even as I puzzled over her meaning.

"You are. You have your purpose, and…" Here she moved her hand forward, fingers pointing ahead. She spoke with her whole body.

"My mommy and me," she continued, "we both have a very… um… she decides she's gonna publish a book. She sits down and writes the book and gets it published and wins awards. And even when she was eighty, she was still writing books. At ninety, she wrote her autobiography."

"Wow," I said, enthralled by Karen's presence and impressed by her mother's determination. And I was bowled over by the possibility of reading my grandmother's life story.

Karen continued, "And she refused to die, she was ninety-seven when she died. She was like that. She created a future and delivered

that future unto herself and others. And that's a part of me, isn't it?"
She looked up at Stephen, who nodded.

"And you're like that, too," Karen said to me.

So that's what she meant by formidable. Did I have this quality?
The fact I took the step to find her and the chance to meet her proved
this point.

"It's kind of stubbornness," Stephen interjected.

"No, I'm not, I'm so easy, my god…" countered Karen.

"No, but when you have an intention," Stephen explained, "you
go after it."

"Yeah," agreed Karen.

I sat up. "The brick wall might be this way," I suggested, putting
an arm straight out from myself and walking along it with my other
hand. "And you're gonna follow it."

"I like it! The wall's a pretty color too. Purple and yellow." My
mother smiled, her eyes sparkling. I pulled in a long breath and felt a
deep sense of belonging.

"Let me tell you a story," I said. She nodded, and I clasped my
hands around my knees. "My husband worked as a fireman for 22
years. Before we moved, he was president of his local union, too. The
intense job and strained politics were too much for him. I worried he'd
drop dead of a heart attack from the stress."

"So. In the fire service, fifty-and-out means when you are fifty
with twenty years on the job, you can retire. And I said, you're gonna
do that, that's what we're gonna do. And he said, 'I can't.' I don't
know. It was tough for him, but I insisted."

"Good." My mother sounded proud of me.

"We put the house on the market, and we sold it and moved. We
closed on the new place in Kentucky on September 8, 2008. And
September 16th-ish, the big crash hit.…"

"Oh wow," said Karen, her eyes widening, a smile playing on
her lips.

"And we wouldn't have been able to do it, all our stocks, you know. He would still be a fireman and likely on his second heart attack."

Karen nodded in appreciation. "Good for you! That's so great. He helps people learn how to fish, right?"

"Yep. He's a fishing guide. He's living his dream."

The conversation rambled after that and lingered on Karen's plans for a party.

"You'll meet my pal, Lee Purcell. Let me show you a picture," Karen said. She retrieved a photo from the hallway. "Friday night's going to be a big deal," she said, scooting in next to me, picture now in hand. She held a tiny photo of herself and Lee, looking like teenagers. "This was 1970."

As Karen, Stephen, and Celine bounced stories back and forth, I enjoyed their camaraderie, a lightheartedness I had never experienced in my adoptive family. Even Rich and I, while raising our kids, never developed the bantering ease that these folks had together. Their creative natures shone as they played off each other like best friends.

"So anyway, Lee's an actress. She's done a lot of television and film," Karen continued. "She was nominated for two Emmys, and she had her own series once."

"And what's her last name?" I asked.

"Purcell. Lee Purcell."

"The IMDb website is my new friend," I said, making a mental note to look her up.

"We want to ask you something," Mom began and glanced at Stephen. "We think it's important to keep our reunion between us for now. What I mean is, we'd like you not to be too public about it."

I looked from her to Stephen, puzzled by what she meant. There was silence.

"Don't post it on Facebook," her husband said. "Don't go to the press."

"They'd eat her alive," Mom said, and patted my knee. "I don't want you to get hurt."

"Okay, I don't mind," I said, tucking my chin. Their constraint stung, and I doubted it was all for my benefit.

"It'll be our secret for now," said Mom. I nodded and smiled like a conspirator, but I hated to hide our joyful story. Some of the easiness, the belonging, drained out of me. But I kept my mouth shut tight because I dared not threaten our new relationship, which suddenly felt tenuous.

"Come on, let's go outside," she invited, taking my hand.

I shook off the disappointment, for the time being, and we walked under a tattered gazebo into a sunlit sitting area. A round bistro table, a tablecloth of lilac hydrangeas, and spring blossom scents in the gentle breeze surrounded us as we sat side by side on a white wicker love seat. Stephen stood before us taking photos and then retreated into the house, leaving us to chat.

"Tell me about your time with those handsome little boys!" My mother said.

I told her of our visit: Gibson trying the violin like my great-grandfather Arthur Ziegler, meeting Nina Benedetti. "I'll meet my brother Ben tomorrow; he and his wife are taking me out to breakfast. Did you ever meet Beny's kids?" I asked.

"Yes, several times. I used to go to parties at their house when they lived in Newhall."

As she spoke, I marveled at how Karen's gestures, her high cheekbones, the side of her face, were all so much like mine. Our eyes were very different, though, mine small and darkest brown, hers large and blue with lovely marbled starbursts.

"Your eyes are beautiful," I told her, entranced. "So striking, and much larger than mine."

"Thank you, but I'll tell you a secret, they really are small. I'm remembered by my eyes, but they're watercolor paintings. Their size is an illusion I create. I'll show you how I do it while you're here," she offered, a smile spreading across her face.

The contrast between her easy smile and my adoptive mother's endless scowl hit me hard, robbing the moment, temporarily, of joy. Why couldn't Karen have raised me? How different my life would have been in the warmth of her glow. I steered my thoughts back to the beautiful present moment and the cadence of her voice. I could sit here forever.

Too soon we walked back into the house where Stephen met us. "Let me show you to your room." He reached for one of my suitcases. I towed the other and accompanied him down the hall, passing more family photos than I could count. Unlike in the photo albums in my adoptive home, I was related to these people. These pictures were more tangible evidence of my humanity; knowing the people in these photos could have bolstered my identity when I'd been a child searching strangers' faces for some sign of belonging. I hoped to peruse the photos soon.

Stephen led me to a small guest-room-office. He nodded to the empty glass desk next to a twin bed. "I moved my electronics to the dining room. So, this will be your place. Make yourself at home." He left and shut the door behind him.

I plunked down on the bed and peeked out the window at the tree above the patio wall. I'm here, I'm really here! I phoned Rich and shared the joy, then busied myself unpacking.

That night we all hung out around the coffee table, relaxing on the floor and on the big couch. Celine's boyfriend, Josh, brought in Chinese. When the load of food covered the glass table, I asked if I could say grace. Stephen said sure, and they reached for each other's hands, and we prayed in that tiny circle of found family. This simple gesture conveyed their acceptance of my faith and filled me with gratitude.

After dinner I remembered to give Karen my gift, a pencil portrait of her. She raved over it and placed it on their credenza outside the kitchen.

Later in my darkened room, I relived my shining day. The movie Sleepless in Seattle came to my mind. Tom Hanks' character, Sam, had a little boy who wanted him to meet Annie, played by Meg Ryan. The film was a series of almost-meetings. They finally found each other in the last scene, just when you'd decided they never would. In that sweet moment, Sam took Annie's hand, and they walked to the elevator together with his delighted son.

Today I had that kind of homecoming experience. It felt cozy, as Karen would say, with an air of magic. Peace infused me, and the movie scene reverberated in my mind as I lay on the edge of sleep.

"Sam," Annie said as they held hands in the elevator. "It's nice to meet you."

Yes, just like that.

CHAPTER 10

Early Wednesday, September 19

THE SILENCE IN THE LIVING ROOM let me know I was the only one awake as I padded to the front door. My dad's son, Ben Benedetti, lived forty minutes from Karen, up the 405 freeway in Santa Clarita. I expected him and his wife, Valisa, to arrive at 8:00 a.m. to treat me to breakfast.

Outside, the clarity of the sunlight took my breath away. This was my first experience of the brightness and color of an LA summer morning. The delicate citrus scent of the lemon tree next to their house added to the entrancing atmosphere. But I only had a moment to breathe it all in before a black sedan rolled into the driveway.

A tall Italian-looking man stepped from the driver's seat with a big smile on his face. I immediately recognized him from his pictures on Facebook.

"Hello there!" Ben said heartily, greeting me with a great bear hug. "It's nice to finally meet you."

"Absolutely!" I said, from inside his hug. I scooted back and peered up at him to find he had my eyes. It was odd and thrilling, seeing my own eyes blinking at me from another face. Then I took in his other features: his nose, mouth, chin, and thick brown hair made him an older copy of my son Mike, as I'd expected.

"Hi, Diane!" A woman's voice broke my spell. Valisa ambled around the car to welcome me.

"Hi, Valisa!" I said, hugging her. We had been messaging on Facebook, so this was a comfortable meeting. Her hair was long and blonde; she had an ample figure and a fair complexion. She and Ben exchanged a glance of agreement, sparking my curiosity, as we piled into the car for a short drive to Jerry's Famous Deli on Ventura Boulevard.

Inside the glass door of Jerry's, we followed a hostess into an airy dining space filled with 1950s decor and the muted hum of conversation. She seated us in one of the red booths, and I scooted in next to my brother.

As we exchanged small talk, Ben kept nodding at Valisa, who had tears in her eyes. Finally he said, "She's so like her, it's spooky!"

Ben turned toward me. "You are reminding us of my grandma Lola," he explained. Lola had passed away more than a decade earlier.

"Oh!" Their faces were earnest and I suppressed a smile, wanting to laugh for joy but unsure how much sadness their tears held.

"It's like we're sitting here talking with someone who died," said Valisa, shaking her head in disbelief.

Ben nodded and chuckled, so I smiled. "How do I remind you of your grandma?" I asked.

"Your bone structure matches hers. Plus, your gestures and manner of speaking." Chills ran up my spine as he continued. "It's uncanny. Grandma was one the most wonderful, cherished people in my life. I only wish you could have met her." I nodded and swallowed hard. I wished that so much.

With that, our conversation turned to our histories. Ben and Valisa had been together since their teenage years, same as Rich and me. When I told them I grew up in the western suburbs of Chicago, their faces brightened.

"Was it close to Brookfield?" Ben asked. "That's where Grandpa and Grandma moved to when Dad was twelve."

"Cool, that's less than five miles from Westchester, where I lived! And I know he was a youngster in Little Tuscany in Chicago, because he sent me his book to read."

"Oh, what a great idea! Glad to hear you have it," said Ben.

"It meant so much to read about his childhood. And it was funny, but even though he grew up twenty years before me, his memories are similar to mine. In his book, there were the green carts of knife sharpeners with their singsong bells. And in my neighborhood, a bent old man pushed one of those carts down the middle of our street each week. My mother shooed me out the door with nickels and kitchen shears when we heard his bell. So, I feel a connection to our dad because the world of the forties hadn't completely faded away by the sixties."

We continued talking warmly. After a bit I asked, "Valisa, can you take a picture of my brother and me?" She nodded and I passed her my Nikon camera. I slid over near Ben and put my hand on his arm. He covered it with his other hand and leaned toward me. It was a sweet moment.

We took more photos in the parking lot. On the way back to Karen's, I sat in the front seat with my brother, who kept the conversation going. "Like I've expressed before, you come from a very artistic family. With dad being an actor, then a director and producer, he's been a creative all his life. The arts were a big part of our life." Too soon we pulled into the drive.

"It's been truly special meeting you. You feel like family already," Ben said.

"So do you," I agreed, hugging him goodbye. Knowing I was so like my Grandma Lola made them cry. I shook my head in wonderment as I climbed the front steps.

— ••• —

The house was quiet, so I inched the door closed behind me. Stephen worked in the dining room on his large monitor amid a swarm of electronics. We said a brief hello; he told me my mom was resting, so I tiptoed back into my bedroom and phoned Rich even though he was on the boat. I left a message, eager to relate what a great time I'd had with Ben and Valisa.

Afterward I wandered to the living room. The coffee table books had intrigued me, so I settled into the couch and perused them. One volume was The Stewardess is Flying the Plane! American Films of the '70s. My mom Karen was on the cover as Nancy Pryor, wearing headphones with her brow furrowed. Both my birth parents had spent their lives in the performing arts. Karen's path had led from New York's Broadway to Hollywood's cinema. Beny had become a professor and then Dean of Theater at Cal Arts. He'd gone on to win awards for film producing. I had a lineage to be proud of; I was part of two accomplished families.

A large, colorful book caught my eye: an illustrated edition of John Singer Sargent's work. I turned the full-color pages, admiring the astonishing paintings. The perfect way he had captured natural light made me want to study oil painting. This new aspiration became an instant commitment: I would make it a reality. I would learn to paint. Karen's compliment came to mind; maybe I had this formidable quality she had seen in me. Perhaps I did create my future like my mother and grandmother.

Just then, my mom's bedroom door creaked open, and she appeared in a white button-down shirt and loose pants. In the afternoon light, she was an angelic vision, her backlit curls framing the expression of wonder on her face. How meaningful it must have been to her—not knowing what had happened to me for decades—to discover I was whole and happy, an individual interested in the arts. We gazed at each other with half smiles.

Then I witnessed Karen's unique, attentive presence. She seemed to perceive my thoughts and respond to them.

"John Singer Sargent, one of my favorite artists," she said, walking over to join me on the couch. "I love the way he painted light! He and Sisley created scenes you could step right into because the light is perfect."

"It makes me want to try oil painting," I said, thrilled that she, too, noticed the light in the landscapes.

"Oh, you would love it! You have a gift, Diane. Your drawings have such a soul." And her eyes shone with earnest meaning. She reached up and touched my shoulder. "You want to have tea?"

"Sure, sounds good," I said.

"Come and talk with me while I set up a tray." I followed my mom to the kitchen island. She brought out a red flowered tray and opened a cabinet stacked with delicate china teacups.

"How was your visit with Beny's son?" She asked as she worked.

I leaned on the counter and described my morning. "Ben has my eyes."

She raised one eyebrow. "That must have been interesting."

"They said my gestures reminded them of their Grandma Lola. But I think I inherited your way of moving."

"You remind me of my Grandma Emma, too, Diane. I'll find a photo to show you. Why don't you go gather albums from the hallway, and we'll look at them out on the patio?"

"Okay, and I'll grab the one I brought, too—of when our kids were young." I couldn't wait to share our pictures.

I retrieved the albums while mom finished the tea. When I got back, arms loaded, Stephen stepped into the kitchen from the dining room where he worked.

"Can I help you carry that?" He asked Karen. He leaned over and gave her a gentle kiss. Their love for each other permeated the room. Stephen led us out, and I followed Karen into the shadow of the house. Her right leg gave once and she stumbled. This sign of weakness shook me back down to earth. Was this frailness because of her cancer? I had put her illness out of my mind, and now the possible brevity of our time together punctured my dreamlike state. I took a deep breath and sobered myself.

Stephen placed the tea tray on a table in the gazebo shade, smiled, and left us. While birds and breeze sang in the trees, Mom poured. "This is my favorite tea, Ahmad Darjeeling. Are you a tea drinker?"

"I like tea, but I need my coffee every morning," I answered. I again settled in the now, leaving the later to fend for itself, and as we chatted about health and her new herbal treatment, her confidence and vitality floated me back to the clouds.

Soon we flipped the black paper pages of her vintage photo albums. She described the people and places. She stopped at a picture of her family in old-fashioned beachwear, posing in front of a dune. "This is Moonlight Beach where we have reunions," she said, her words sparkling with recollection. "How I love the ocean, Diane!" The photo sang with hope, kindling a new dream: to play in the surf with my mother.

"This is your Aunt Gail and Uncle Peter—he's older than my sister and me—and your Grandma Elsie and Grandpa Norman!" She pointed and smiled.

I had seen a younger photo of my grandparents on Ancestry.com. In this image, Elsie was a glamorous redhead instead of a brunette. Norman was handsome and svelte, but he looked full of himself. Of course, I didn't voice this observation.

"Oh, here's a picture of my Grandma Emma." Karen touched a small sepia portrait.

"Is she your mom's or your dad's mother?" I asked.

"My mom's," she said. "Your two have similar features. And she was gentle and soft-spoken like you."

I peered at this window into my past, this lady who was my great grandma. Her dark hair was pulled back, and she wore a high-necked Victorian blouse. Her eyelids drooped over small dark eyes, just like mine did. She had my slender nose and thin lips, my ears with no lobes. I touched the smooth place my ear met my face. I looked like my great grandma! I asked Karen to tell me about these folks.

"Your Grandpa Norman was a salesman when we kids were

growing up," she said, "and your grandma was a brilliant writer."

"Yes! I ordered three of her books on Amazon. Your Wikipedia page noted she was an author."

"How wonderful of you!" She said, looking surprised.

"I intend to learn all I can about my roots, because I never had them before," I explained. "Knowing my ancestors connects me to humanity. It gives me a grounding, a foundation. I'm not an island anymore."

"Well, you should talk to my brother Peter! He's interested in genealogy too. He did a ton of research in the eighties and found out oodles about our family history. I remember some of it. On my mom's side, the Reifs and the Shimons came over from Germany and Bohemia in the 1850s. Emma's father, John Shimon, was a country doctor, a very learned man. Both families settled around Manitowoc, Wisconsin."

I brightened at the mention of that town. "Mom, my adoptive parents used to bring us to Wisconsin every summer. On the way, we drove through Manitowoc. I loved it! I looked forward to it and gazed out the window to watch the houses go by on the rolling hills. There was something magical about the place. I asked my dad to stop there each year, but he never did."

She looked astonished. "What did you want to do there?"

"I don't know... just be there, I guess."

"Diane, that's amazing. You have hundreds of relatives in Manitowoc."

Now I was the astonished one. Chills ran along my spine as I remembered my deep longing and the disappointment each year when we didn't stop. Of all the towns in Wisconsin, my adoptive parents drove through this one on vacations, this village that inextricably drew me in. And I was never allowed to stay. "Spooky! Like my genes knew I belonged there."

"I believe it's more than genetic. We are more than cells and chemicals; we are spiritual beings. I think you felt that connection with your spirit."

"I believe we all have a spirit, or soul, too. That's something we have in common." This simple belief was the shared foundation of many faiths, I realized.

We settled back into browsing our albums. I soaked in more of our family history, and she reveled in the photos of her grandsons.

"Our oldest, Matt, has his own business in Seattle now. Mike lived out there a while, but we brought him home to Kentucky after he had a pulmonary embolism."

"Oh, how awful!" She said.

"Yeah, he almost died! At first, the hospital released him with painkillers, but another doctor looked at the chest x-ray and called him back in, saving his life. It scared us."

We chatted about parenting and laughed in disbelief that my youngest son, Ricky, and Celine, were born six months apart. So we paralleled each other while we raised them. I remembered many times watching my children at play, wondering what my birth mother might be doing. I never dreamed she'd be sitting on another park bench somewhere, enjoying her own child's antics. Another amazing synchronicity.

After a while, she suggested making a mural on her patio wall together. My heart jumped at the chance to be creative with my birth mother. She knew I loved to draw, and she wanted to do it with me. My adoptive mother had not thought like this, she had not tried to enter my world, to get down on the floor and play, to let me show her how to sketch, to dig in the garden with me. And she had never celebrated who I was, as Karen had already done by telling me I was formidable. I looked with wonder at this woman who was making an effort to get to know me. She smiled back. We agreed on flowers as a theme for our mural, decided to work on the concrete surface with permanent markers, and planned to start the next day.

Stephen came out with his cell phone in his hand. "Hunter's in town," he announced, and Karen beamed. "He's borrowing his friend

Pete's car and will be here soon."

As Stephen walked back inside, Karen sat back in her wicker chair, her gaze far away. "Your brother was a child actor, Diane. He was brilliant in Paris, Texas when he was nine. Hunter means more to me than anyone, Diane…." Her voice drifted off, then she added in a whisper, "I lost him, you know."

CHAPTER 11

Late Wednesday, September 19

THE GREEN GAZEBO COVER fended off the midday sun. Our teacups had been empty a while, but our conversation absorbed me so much I hadn't noticed.

"Hunter's father took him away when he was eleven. Took him out of my life and away from his acting career, too." Mom continued. "I only had my family for a few weeks. It was the Christmas after Celine's birth, and Hunter begged me not to send him to his father's. But I was busy with the baby, and I had a movie, and I sent him anyway.

"When he came back, he announced he wanted to live with his father. We tried to keep him, of course, but in court, he said his dad offered him more stability! That man was anything but stable. I still don't know how he manipulated Hunter against us, but within two years, my son was gone for good. That boy was everything to me..." she trailed off, her eyes distant as though reliving the painful memory.

"But he's back. He called me from college and said he wanted to be in my life again. We've been close ever since, close in a way like that time never happened." She paused, then added, "And yet, the man Hunter is disconnected with the child I had. I feel the connective moments' absence. Do you understand?"

I searched for a way to express what I'd heard her say. "You weren't there to see the change over the years. You missed his whole teenage experience." I frowned, realizing she must have mourned his loss. I added, "I bet it hurt a lot."

"Yes, that's it exactly. You listen well!" Then her disquiet evaporated as her eyes sparkled and danced. "All my children, together for the first time! The dinner party on Friday night is to celebrate. Hunter can cook—he's a fabulous cook. And Stephen will help get the house ready."

We chatted more, and then she told me she was hungry. "I had a Whipple procedure a few years ago," she said, "to get rid of the stupid cancer the first time. It worked. You know I was cancer-free for a whole year. But they take out part of your intestines, so it's hard to digest at all. I eat and eat and still lose weight. I'm always ravenous." She wrinkled her nose. "And I can't enjoy all the stuff I used to love, like Chicago hot dogs. And eating makes me so tired."

Inside, she headed for the kitchen, and I retired to my room, since I'd had a big breakfast. Instead of eating, I opened my journal and noted our magical Manitowoc conversation.

As I wrote, it occurred to me I should recount our whole story. I stopped and looked out the window at the white patio wall. Writing in my journal seemed a waste—my grandsons might not even learn cursive. So I'd need to type it. I opened my computer and a Word document, and beginning with my flight to LA, I typed brief notes and impressions. I didn't get far along when there was a soft knock on my door. It was Stephen.

"Hunter's here."

"Be right out!" I named the document "Karen's House," saved it, and straightened my purple T-shirt and jean shorts. I looked in the mirrored closet door at my reflection bouncing on my toes. I stopped and took a deep breath. "You have two brothers! You are meeting them both in one day!" My brown eyes¬ twinkled back at me, and I headed out into the hallway toward the living room, where the afternoon sun cast a warm yellow hue.

And there he was, talking to Stephen. Hunter's masculine, angular face resembled Matt's. He had chin-length brown hair swept back by the sunglasses on top of his head. A short-cropped beard and layered clothing completed his stylish look.

He turned to me, locking his eyes with mine and giving me a natural half smile.

"Hi, Hunter," I said, tucking my chin, suddenly shy.

"Hello, Diane," he said, stepping forward and gathering me into a gentle hug. Stephen went back to work on his computer in the dining room, telling us Karen was napping after her lunch. We kept our voices low.

Hunter looked at me. "You look so much like Mom it's crazy!"

"Thanks," I said. "You look like my son Matt."

"Cool. How are you doing, sis? All this must overwhelm you!" His eyes expressed sincerity and caring, and his voice carried a measured cadence. I liked him right away and loved that he had called me his sister.

"Yes," I said, and smiled, "but in a good way!"

"I can't imagine having so many new people in your life. And finding Mom, what a trip!"

"It's fun to relate my story and see people who remember her react with astonishment."

He smiled. "Tell me about your time so far." We walked over to sit in the living room, he on the chaise and I on the couch. I described meeting Mom and having breakfast with Ben.

"So, you have a brother on your dad's side!"

"And two sisters."

"That's amazing."

"What about you? Stephen said you live in Dallas? And you're married, right?

"Yes, to Elyse, and we have a nine-month-old baby girl, Jane."

This surprised me. "Mom was already a grandma! Do you carry pictures?"

He pulled out his wallet and presented a cute blondie in a yellow romper.

"So adorable! I'm an aunt again!"

Hunter smiled, studying me in silence. "Hey, I have people to meet about directing, and I'm staying with a buddy of mine, Pete, borrowing his car. So, I won't be here all the time, but I want you to call me if you need anything, okay? If you just wanna chat, or whatever. I'm an early riser, so mornings are good."

"I've been getting up early here, too, with the time difference."

"Maybe we could have coffee one day." He moved over and sat next to me, and we exchanged cell numbers. "I gotta talk to Stephen a minute," he said as he rose and stepped into the dining room. "Hey, Stephen, how long does mom sleep after lunch?"

They spoke in hushed tones, and I leaned back and considered our low-key meeting. Hunter had a gracious, deliberate, winsome nature. He was a fuzzy blanket around my insecurities, a big brother to his big sister.

"Okay, sis, I gotta run, I'll be back for dinner. Love you." He spoke as if those words were an everyday thing.

"Love you, too!" I said and meant it. After the door closed behind him, I considered pinching myself, but decided to let the dream continue.

After meeting Hunter, I hiked to Whole Foods to get myself a few things, a four-block walk through their charming neighborhood. The shaded road curved downhill between rows of elegant homes. I walked along the sidewalk, comfortable in my shorts and sandals, and enjoyed the colorful yards filled with flowers and trees that my Midwestern eyes didn't recognize. One yard had a small fountain built into a walled entryway, bubbling into black rocks, misting my feet.

The profusion of blooms matched my surreal tumble into wonderland. When I was a little girl daydreaming of my birth mother in my crabapple tree, I never suspected what a marvelous journey awaited me.

That evening when Hunter returned, we ordered dinner from Chili's online menu, and Stephen brought our food home. As we spread supper on the coffee table, a slim blonde woman in a stylish black jean jacket came through the door. Celine smiled, jumped up and hugged her.

Our visitor parked next to Karen on the couch, and they embraced a long while.

"Diane, this is my brilliant friend Ondi Timoner, who just had to meet you!" Mom said. "We worked together on the episode of 'Switched' that featured Celine."

Ondi extended her hand to me as I sat on the floor near them. She glanced back and forth between Karen and me. "I see similarities," she said to Mom, who nodded.

Then Celine broke in, "You wanna stay for dinner?"

"I only have half an hour until I pick up Ian, but I'll have a bite with you," Ondi said, as we settled on the floor around the table.

During the meal the conversation was lighthearted. Mom told an anecdote about a detective and a photo of a 'one-eyed' man. Stephen recounted a riddle. They spoke with accents that were as humorous as the jokes. How comfortable they were with each other. Hunter and I exchanged amused glances.

I was so engrossed in the conversation, surrounded by family, that my food went largely untouched. Mom told me, "Ondi makes documentaries, outstanding ones. She won the Grand Jury Prize at Sundance twice."

Stephen leaned toward me and explained, "That's a prestigious juried film festival."

"And Ondi might get Deep Purple made into a movie," added Mom, her expression a poignant question.

"Did you tell her about it?" Ondi asked.

"She's already read it!" Mom said with a smile.

"Diane, your mother is a fantastic writer, and this screenplay you read, well, she wrote that about you."

I nodded. "Yes. It amazed me." My feelings about it went so deep I had few words. I often, especially in those first few weeks around my birth family, could not verbalize my emotions.

"You can never know how much it means to your mom, Diane, that you found her. And she's a treasure for you, so cherish her." She clasped Karen's hands. Their expressions exchanged sadness as they said goodbye. The unspoken word, cancer, darkened the room.

After Ondi left us, the creative talk continued. Artistic projects were the hub of most conversations between Karen and her friends and family. This was an entirely new experience for me. A fresh wind caught my sails as the notion that people could spend whole evenings discussing original ideas enthralled and enlivened me. Again, I snagged on the memory of my childhood feeling of isolation, of the somberness of our home. This lively interaction was what I had been missing. I never learned this form of expression because my parents doused my spontaneity, and I didn't have the confidence to let it shine in spite of them. And then, I married a non-creative and threw myself into raising our kids. So I never surrounded myself with artistic people. I felt no regret; I had no idea what I missed out on. Until now.

Later, while we still lounged in the living room, I asked when Mom had told my siblings about me.

"I think it was in April," said Celine, turning to Hunter.

"I was thinking March, but April could be right," he answered.

"This year?" I asked in amazement. "Only six months ago?"

They had learned of me at the same time I had sent in the forms for my birth certificate. Somehow this news fit with the idea that she didn't want to be public with our reunion. Had she felt shame about giving me up? I dared not ask.

"Yes, it was this spring," said Karen. "That's when I asked Peter to help find you. But we got nowhere… all we had to go on was the name I had given you, Nina, and a date. But then you found me!"

Teardrops glistened on her face. "I never thought this would happen," she said. "The universe has given me a great gift!" Hunter took her hand and their fingers intertwined. My birth mother and her children, shedding tears and appreciating this salient moment together.

CHAPTER 12

Thursday September 20

THURSDAY MORNING, I woke up humming. Today my mom and I planned to make a mural together. Mom—the word came easily now after just a few days together.

First, she needed her breakfast. Every day she woke up and drank fresh carrot and apple juice to help her pH balance, so her ozone and iodine treatments could be effective. I asked how I could help, and Stephen had recruited me to clean the juicer.

The house slept as I tiptoed to the kitchen. I started my coffee, enjoying the light breeze playing through the open window over the sink. My mom had draped vintage linen dishtowels over the curtains, with cute embroidered girls on them. I smiled at her nostalgia as I tackled the juicer. I tugged at the stainless-steel contraption, taking it apart to scrape out the stinky carrot mush left from yesterday's juice. Outside, I scraped the catch basin into their compost under the lemon tree in the backyard.

The tree needed pruning, and underneath it, weeds grew thick. I padded around the corner to the patio. Rips marred the faded green gazebo cover. Beyond it, the stark cement wall waiting for our artwork stood behind dying potted plants. Maybe the cancer was to blame for this dearth of care. Karen's care might consume this family more than it appeared to. I could revive the space with my gardening skills, but I was a guest. This week.

In my imagination I took my place as the eldest child, visiting often over the years to lend a hand, being a daughter to my mother, planting flowers in her wilderness. This optimism helped me soak up our scant time together while she was still whole. I'm convinced my naïve joy was sunlight for Karen's heart, a river in the desert of her cancer.

Later while I prepped a salad for lunch, Karen walked into the kitchen, looking disheveled but radiant. She showed me an easy, delicious dressing with olive oil, the juice of a lemon, and a sprinkle of soy sauce. Stephen worked in the next room while we chatted, and in the middle of our conversation, he called to us.

"You know what? I've been listening, and I can't tell who's talking! Your voices are identical!"

A smile started in my chest and burst out onto my face. All these years, I've sounded just like my mother!

My mom agreed with him. "Very similar, yes! Although decades of living in California has softened my Midwestern accent. My sister, your Aunt Gail, has the voice too. Our family would mistake us for each other on the phone." She smiled at the memory. We ate our salads at the coffee table and then headed outside to start the mural.

I found a place to plug in my Mac, and we plunked down in the white wicker loveseat to discuss our ideas. We faced the six-foot patio wall.

"I miss trees," my mother commented. "There are no good trees in Southern California."

I pointed above the wall to the massive tree with tear-drop leaves shading us from the midday sun. "That's a nice one."

"A gum tree's okay I guess." She shrugged. "But not like the ones back home."

I noted its thick, low branches. "When I was younger, I loved climbing trees."

Karen said, "Oh my god, me too! I spent my childhood in trees. I still climb them, at least I did before the cancer."

The brilliant blue green of her eyes engulfed me; the tired slump of her shoulders didn't register until much later. "I had a certain branch in an old crabapple tree," I told her. "I loved to hang out up there and eat the tiny red fruit."

She blinked back at me. "Mine was a pear tree, and I did the same thing."

My throat caught as a memory surfaced; being in my backyard branches, yearning for her. "I prayed for you all my life, Mom."

She drew in a breath of shocked gratitude. "You are teaching me so much about family," she whispered. I let her words wash over me, cleansing dark spaces. Despite our severed lives we had a bond all these years. Family ties live deep within us.

She opened up, then, about her first pregnancy. She had been a kid, just fifteen, and Charlie was her friend. It had been a childish exploration. But they'd been forced to marry, and Charlie was not kind to her. Her eyes darkened at the memory, and she seemed relieved when she spoke of the miscarriage, and leaving that difficult life behind her. I wasn't sure how to respond, except with nods and looks of understanding, although I'd never had a similar experience.

The conversation returned to our mural, and we chose the theme of colorful flowers. Karen sat cross-legged next to the gazebo, and I took a spot next to her with my laptop beside me. We quieted and started our flowers. Mine was an orange tiger lily, and hers was a blue daisy.

She broke the silence. "Tell me your favorite childhood memory."

"The day I learned to read! The first-grade teacher was standing in the front corner of our class with a big Dick and Jane book on an easel. She touched the words with a stick while she spoke them. When she read 'look,' the connection between the letters and the sounds clicked for me. I had a sudden awareness, like I woke up—like I unlocked a secret only grown-ups knew. I was so proud of myself that I ran all the way home to tell my dad."

"The same thing happened to me," she said, incredulous. "I read Little Women in first grade."

I sketched in awed silence beside her, struck anew with our similarity despite our separation. Then I asked, "What's your favorite memory?"

"The farm in Wisconsin," she answered in a flash. "That's where all my best memories happened. My sister and I would lie out on the screen porch at night talking for hours, listening to the wind in the trees, relishing the smell of the air. I miss the Midwest."

Vacations in Door County came to mind. "My dad took us up to Wisconsin every year, and we stayed in a cabin with a screen porch. That's where I learned that I loved nature."

Mom shook her head. "How is it possible we had such similar childhoods?"

"It's incredible," I answered.

In a soft and lilting voice, she began a song: "Blue skies, smiling at me…"

I recognized the old tune from my dad's jazz records. Even though my singing voice was hoarse, I joined in with this mother I had never known. We sang of blue skies, bluebirds, and blue days.

My heart soared along with her powerful voice. My dad would have loved to hear how his music helped us share this moment. I missed him.

"I'm amazed you know that song!" She said when the moment ended.

"My dad played jazz music in our home every day," I told her.

She took my hand. "I sang to you when you were in my womb."

Her love surrounded me, at once brand new and age old, gentle as waves on the sand and vast as breakers at sea. My breath and heartbeat filled my ears.

When she asked me to describe a watershed moment in my life, I told her the story of losing my adoptive dad. How the four months I helped him in the nursing home had matured me, how my father's silent faith had shone, helping me to lean into God's strength and peace.

"All of us who sustain a relationship with God have gone through hard times and found Him faithful," I said.

Then Karen shared wisdom from her beliefs. "In Scientology, there are three parts to every relationship: affinity, communication, and reality. When you share at least two of these, you can be friends. The ones closest to you share all three. And for me, affinity is the great binder in the universe. It bonds us to life and to one another."

That was a good insight, and so similar to the love and fellowship of Christianity. I could see Karen believed her faith with her heart and soul. We were alike in the depth of our thinking and feeling and believing. When she expressed herself, I could grasp and digest her meaning, as if she was more me than I was.

After we sketched a while, we were lying on the ground discussing the mural in front of us. Karen said, "Our styles are different, and I like yours better. Mine is a communication about a drawing, and yours is a communication about a flower. I like mine, but I love yours. I have an emotional reaction to it. And that is how all your artwork is. It affects people."

She validated me. She empowered me with her words and the realness with which she said them. I soaked her into my pores; such a refreshing contrast to the woman who had raised me. Karen was an encouraging mother, and we played together today.

Weeks later, as I shared the photos of that day, a friend noticed the tiredness in Karen's body, the gauntness of her frame. Her whole-hearted presence with me had masked her physical frailty. My birth mom had spent herself for our relationship. As I looked ahead and dreamed of more times together, the cancer hovered like a storm cloud on the horizon.

CHAPTER 13

Friday, September 21

A DESIGN PROJECT needed my attention Friday morning, so after cleaning the juicer, I ate breakfast in front of my computer. When I was done, I headed to the kitchen with my dishes and found Celine relaxing on the chaise. I was glad to have her to myself a minute, because she was always busy with beauty school, or somewhere with her boyfriend, Josh. I sat on the couch across from her. She pulled her long blond hair upward and deftly spun it into a top-knot bun as we chatted. Slim and lithe with delicate features, she exuded social confidence with her easy manner.

"I love that Mom came up with the mural idea! It was nice for you to work on it together yesterday," Celine said.

"Spending the day with her meant a lot to me," I confided, "since I missed out on her in my earlier life." I looked down at my lap, wondering if I should have expressed that.

"Yeah, but you had a good life on your own. You raised three kids, right?" She asked, as if encouraging me to think positively on the past.

"True, and I don't regret how my life has gone." I tried to sort out my feelings as I spoke. "But she has such a zest for living, I wish I'd known her." I shrugged. I didn't want to tell Celine how my adoptive mother squelched my zeal and constrained me to live in a flatter way, too insecure for a wholehearted dive into the arts. I steered our con-versation in another direction.

"So, you're in your mid-twenties, right?" I asked.

"Twenty-five," she answered.

"So is my youngest, Ricky. You're the same age as your nephew."

We laughed. She said, "I hope I get to meet him sometime. I want to meet all your kids."

"Well maybe next summer, if you guys have a family reunion again." I already looked forward to it.

"Well, it depends on my mom's health," Celine glanced down the hallway toward Karen's bedroom. "I mean, our mom. You know she beat cancer before, right?"

"Yeah, she told me. Cancer-free for a year, right?"

"Yep! She has a lot of determination." Celine brightened up. "She's fighting this in every way, including alternative therapy, that ozone and iodine regimen she's on. Plus, she eats super healthy and drinks that awful carrot juice every day, too. I know she can whoop cancer's butt again."

From what I'd seen so far, I easily believed our mother could win this battle. I leaned back, soaking up Celine's optimism. "I hope that with all my heart."

After washing my breakfast dishes, I decided to continue the mural, hoping to complete it so Karen had it to remember me by. A vase of dried hydrangea blooms was hiding behind boxes near the back door, perfect as a subject. The scent of the lemon tree surprised me again as I stepped outside. Our markers were on the table under the gazebo, so I set the flower vase near the patio wall and sat down to add these new blooms to our work in progress. Shaping the tuft of small blossoms on the wall absorbed my attention until the midday sun made the sweat drip from the tip of my nose. After pouring water on my head a few times, I had to stop. I hoped Karen would continue it when she felt better. It was only a smattering of flowers so far and needed to be tied together.

Back inside, I retreated to my room with a fresh glass of water, and after I cooled down, I called Rich. Sitting on my bed by the window, I highlighted our mural day and told him about the upcoming party.

"Some of my mom's friends will be here tonight. I'm looking forward to meeting Lee, who's been her friend since forever. Then there's Angela, who's a director, and Karyn Rachtman who my mom says is like another daughter to her. She does music for movies; she chose the songs for Pulp Fiction! And more people will be here, but I don't remember their names now." I leaned back against the headboard, "Mom told me, 'These are the friends who have to meet you or die!' I can't wait."

"Amazing stuff!" He commented. "I'm so glad we could do this for you. How are you holding up?"

"I'm tired, been helping a lot, but I'm so grateful to be here. How are you guys doing?"

"We're fine. Denise just asked again when you'd be coming back and showed me today's masterpiece," he said. He was dependable as the sunrise, and I loved him for that. We talked a little more, and then I told him I'd call tomorrow.

As I was hanging up, I heard muted yelling coming from the direction of my mom's room. I got up and opened my door. Hunter had arrived from his friend's house. He was in the shadowed hallway, shifting his weight back and forth, his phone glowing up at his face. He glanced at me. "Welcome to the family," he said in a wry tone.

More fiery language emanated from behind mom's double doors. It was Mom's voice, screaming that Celine was not helping. I couldn't hear clearly, but both their voices were intense and angry. My first reaction was, I wanted to march in there and tell them to stop it. I worked my fists, realizing I had no place to interfere. I was the eldest child, but I couldn't step into that role. I had no history with these people. As I stood near my quiet brother, Celine stepped into the hall and closed the doors behind her. She stopped next to Hunter, and a look of understanding passed between them. We moved away from the room.

I asked, "Has she always been volatile, or is it new with her illness?" This was a side of my new mother I hadn't yet seen, and I wondered if it would have been part of my life, too, if she'd kept me.

Celine said, "It's worse now, but yeah, it's not new." She was frowning but seemed calm already, taking the outburst in stride. She went into her bedroom.

Hunter and I walked out of the dark hallway into late afternoon light, and pausing in the living room, he told me something. "You know I didn't live with mom and Stephen when I was a teenager."

'Yeah, Mom told me."

"Well, I went to live with my dad and stepmom when I was eleven, because I wanted stability." He said in a hushed tone, raising an eyebrow.

I wouldn't have understood this ten minutes ago, but now I had an inkling what he meant. I nodded, glancing toward the bedroom.

"Mom said your father basically took you from them," I told him. "That he made you quit acting."

"I wanted to quit. After Invaders, I knew it wasn't what I wanted. There was a lot of family ugliness over custody, too." He shook his head.

Their views on the matter certainly were in contrast. "I'm sorry you had to go through all that."

"It's in the past." He smiled. "I reached out to her again when I was in college. I decided I wanted to heal our relationship."

"I'm glad you did." I wouldn't have met him otherwise, and his calm nature was providing stability for me right now. I was a bit unhinged, knowing Karen could lose it like that. I was glad I hadn't argued about her restriction against posting our story. How deep was our bond, really? Maybe I could still lose her affection. I hugged myself as I followed Hunter into the kitchen.

We turned to the dinner prep. He had volunteered as chef for the evening, and we stuck to the tasks at hand, keeping conversation light.

A half hour later, Hunter had dinner under his control, and he graciously let me bow out. Now in my small room, I stood between the glass desk and the twin bed. Posters of Karen's movies surrounded me. A Hitchcock Family Plot poster featured her behind sunglasses and blonde bangs, surrounded by a black hat and tall-collared trench coat. Near it there was a smaller poster for a Cannes film, Can She Bake a Cherry Pie? My mom looked like a younger me in that one, a profile shot of her with tousled '80s hair. Our silhouettes were identical back then.

Then there was a poster of her standing in a desert, blazing sun obscuring her eyes, highlights on her high cheekbones. I glanced at myself in the mirrored closet door. If I stood just-so, directly under the ceiling fixture, my forehead shadowing my eyes, my facial structure looked just like hers. I stared at my reflection. I need to grow my hair, and start getting my eyebrows waxed, I decided. And get some makeup. I'd never been much for primping, but now I wanted to be more feminine, more like my mother. How different my life would have been if I could have accessed my birth certificate when I turned eighteen. She was an A-list celebrity....

I walked forward, ruining the visual illusion and turning my mind away from the past to the present. Tonight was for celebrating that we were together now. I reached for my black dress and started getting ready. My nerves jangled in anticipation.

The aroma of the roasting chicken wafted through the house as I walked out of the hallway. The light of the setting sun angled on the wall ahead of me, and I paused to look at my mom's pretty home. The open space I entered was arranged in a horseshoe around the kitchen. Above me, the ceiling slanted up toward the middle. To my left, at the front of the house, a bay window shone sunset rose between the front door and dining room. Two flowered love seats faced each other under the window. To my right, the living room skylight glowed twilight above the large couch. Open vertical blinds revealed the evening, the patio, and our mural.

The decor featured family: a large painting by Stephen's mother, almost abstract, of him as a young child. Two colorful pastels were Celine's childhood artwork. A dozen family photos, old and new, guided my eyes around the rooms where our party would take place. An antique wooden ice chest stood next to me; on top sat a palm-sized metal rectangle. I reached for it and felt its weight and cool smoothness in my hand. There was a message carved: Dwell in Possibility. I read hope into it, then sighed and set it down.

Rounding the corner of the kitchen, I paused to watch Hunter cook, with his western shirtsleeves rolled up. His back was to me as he shifted his weight, swayed and stirred, leaned to check a pot on the stove, side to side like a slow-motion dance. He was music for my eyes, a real live brother, a piece of my mother. He seemed to have gotten her love for cooking, something that had definitely skipped me. The counter was covered in spices and bowls and utensils. There were three pans on the range, and two chickens in the oven. Hunter looked right at home.

"Hey, bro, how's it going?" I said as I walked around the island.

He turned. "You look nice!"

"Thanks! Can I help?"

"Nah, I'm good. Why don't you ask Mom?"

Mom and Stephen were in the dining room discussing the furniture. "I don't see how that'll work," Mom said.

"It'll work, you'll see," assured Stephen.

I poked my head in. "Is there anything I can do?" The long antique table was not yet set.

Mom's eyes met mine. "Let me see you! Lovely. You look great in black!"

"You look amazing!" I said. It was the first time I'd seen her dressed up. She wore a silky white blouse, a pair of gray slacks, and a silver fresh-water pearl necklace. Her hair was full of curls falling down to her shoulders. Her blue eyes were full of anticipation. After watching her manage her illness all week, I was thrilled to see her so happy. I suddenly understood her earlier outburst. Of course, she was highly stressed this afternoon, juggling so much. Now she was nearly done and ready to have fun.

Just then the front door opened, and in stepped a woman with long, full, curly red hair. After greeting her, Karen turned to me. "Diane, I want you to meet my good friend Angela Garcia Combs," my mom said, beaming.

Angela embraced me. She was an inch or two taller than my five-eight frame and solidly slender in a deep green dress. Her smile was contagious.

"You've done a great thing reaching out to your mom. It means more to her than you can know." Angela's eyes sparkled as she took my mother's hand.

"How did you two meet?" I asked.

"It was Henry," said Mom.

Stephen had been standing back with his arms crossed, taking it all in with an amicable smile. At the mention of Henry, he rolled his eyes.

Angela saw the question in my eyes, "Henry Jaglom is–"

"Insane!" Said Mom, grinning.

"—a nut," continued Angela. "He's a quirky independent film-maker and *all* the great actors know him. He invited me to a small party about ten years ago, and I sat next to your mom—"

"And we were instantly pals!" Mom finished the sentence. "I could tell right away Angela was uniquely brilliant. She's a superb director."

Stephen cleared his throat. "People will get here soon," he nudged.

"Right," said Mom. "Angela's here early to help make things beautiful. She has a good eye for decorating."

"I just want to help you implement your vision for the evening," Angela said.

Mom asked me, "Can you clear off the coffee table, darling?" And they turned their attention to the dining area, setting out candles and discussing seating.

I walked around to the coffee table and found a place against a wall for the collection of large art books. After I wiped the glass tabletop, I retreated to my room, glad for a minute to be alone. I sat on the side of the bed, elbows on knees with my face in my hands. This felt so surreal, being here in Hollywood with this family I'd never met before, being accepted and loved. And now a dinner party where I was to be the guest of honor. If they only knew I'd never even been to a formal dinner party before.

Nowhere in my experience was there anything to compare this with. Rich and I were raised middle class; his family was blue collar and celebrated with barbecue and beer. Since the white-collar parents who raised me didn't socialize much, I had no experience with formal etiquette and had adopted the Bay's customs. I was truly out of my element tonight. I was scared. I worried I'd do or say something stupid, so I sat quietly for a few minutes to silence my nerves and send up a quick prayer. Then I got up, smoothed my dress and headed back out.

Hunter was standing near the front door with a slim, well-dressed woman who looked about my age. Their hands were clasped between them. She was saying how good it was to see him. Her forest-green cardigan complemented her auburn hair. She turned to me, and her eyes were a stunning caramel shade.

"Diane, this is our friend, Lee Purcell," said Hunter.

Lee looked at me like she was seeing a vision, then walked up and took my hands. "Your mom has wished for this all her life," she said, and then gave me a tender hug. "You are beautiful! You look like her, but not like her. I gotta see a picture of Beny. Karen, does she look like Beny?"

Mom was walking into the front room when she answered, "Yes, she's a blend of both of us, and very beautiful. Hello, darling! Thank you for coming." They hugged and kissed. "I want you to see what my talented daughter made for me!" Mom gestured for me to follow her into the living room. She reached for the pencil portrait I'd made for her that she'd placed on the credenza.

"It looks just like you!" Lee said. "Really nice work, Diane. Has Karen told you she sketches people too? She made a funny one of me when I was staying at her house years ago. I still have it somewhere."

"Why don't you two talk while I finish up in the dining room," said Mom, and Lee and I sat on the couch. I clasped my hands hard to still myself, keeping them in my lap so I wouldn't fidget.

"Lee, Mom told me a lot about you," I said, "but I have to say, there's no way you're anywhere near her age! It's hard to believe you've been friends since she first came out to California."

"Thanks! You have to remember your mom was nearly thirty when she got to Hollywood. I was much younger. But yes, we've been friends since back then. We first met on a talk show around 1970, while promoting our respective movies. Hers was *Five Easy Pieces* and mine was my first film, *Adam at 6 am*."

"Tell me a story about living with my mom," I said spontaneously.

Lee looked far away with misty eyes. "What fun we had, Diane." Then she laughed. "Okay, here's the one about the sketch. I stayed with your mom for a while in her big house here in LA. One of the bathrooms had two sinks, a long countertop, and a huge mirror. This is where we'd get ready in the morning, sitting on the edge of each sink with our feet on the countertop, naked, putting on our makeup in the mirror. And one day she drew me like that, naked with a shower cap on my head! That's Karen."

I imagined the scene and smiled at the thought of my mom young and free. How cool to have a friendship like that.

Lee leaned over to me. "Your mom is priceless, Diane. Treasure her. She's wanted to find you for all the years I've known her. You are a miracle in her life right now."

More people had come in while we were talking, so we turned our attention to the group, but I had gained a friend in those few minutes. Lee would be there for me often in the months to come.

My mom and the rest of the guests joined us in the living room seating area—the big couch, matching chair, coffee table, and chaise. Karyn Rachtman was there, a beautiful dark-haired young woman. Karyn looked at my Karen with a lot of love. Everyone seemed to want to sit near my mom on the couch, so I sat on the carpet next to her. The energy of her friends' love filled the room.

Once we were all seated, they right away wanted to know how I'd found Karen. I relayed the whole story of finding her, and Karen told her part also. Then she told the story of my birth: watching the big boulder moving down her stomach, the angst of watching the doctor take me away, and seeing me once in the nursery through the glass.

Her friends asked if I was beautiful. Karen said, "No, she was disturbed! She had scratched her little cheek with her nails."

And someone commented, "Of course she was disturbed; she'd been taken away from her mother." Then they asked me how old I was when I was adopted. When I said nine weeks they gasped.

"There's so much research now about how important those weeks are for bonding," Celine said.

My mom looked pensive. "We were right there when Celine was born. I caught her and carried her to a tub of warm water."

Hearing this, I wondered if that was why I'd had such a big hole in my heart all those years. Maybe that was why I had never bonded with my adoptive mother, too. I spoke that last thought out loud. I was unsure about if I should have voice to the thought—Karen seemed pretty upset about it—but it was part of my story. "And now I don't feel that void anymore," I assured them. "Ever since Karen first answered me on Facebook, there's been a quiet, still place in my heart that is new, where the void used to be."

Hunter entered then and announced that dinner was ready. The group heaved a collective sigh, as if glad for the reprieve from this heavy conversation. We trooped into the dining room. There were two candelabra centerpieces on the dark mahogany table, a white lace tablecloth, dainty mix-and-match china and good silver. It was a tight squeeze, and a card table extended the dining surface, but all twelve of us fit. Hunter's cooking was delicious. Dinner went by quickly, and I was so absorbed in the small talk, I didn't remember to be self-conscious.

After the meal, we sat in the living room again. People had brought finger-food desserts which Angela spread out on the coffee table. We played a creative game while we nibbled. Stephen announced I was first, and everyone had to think of the most fabulous, far-out vacation possible for me. I had to pick my favorite of their ideas.

There were some amazing choices. Angela told of a place in France where there were wild white horses. Stephen's idea was an island off the coast of Italy with a private beach just for family. Both of these places were real; they had been there. Hunter's friend Josh had me visiting all the great museums of Europe. Josh's partner, Mark, came up with a cool one—to spend a week being whoever or whatever you wanted to be, person or animal. I picked Karen's idea: a South Seas paradise, thatched huts on stilts in the water surrounded by family, snorkeling and hanging out.

Then she was next and told us we had to come up with a new career for her. Angela's notion won; it was to be an English teacher for at-risk teens. Karen said she had always loved English and would enjoy validating kids who needed it. She really did have a gift for making people feel special.

The evening wound down with Lee the last remaining guest. The three of us, Mom, me, and Lee, sat chatting on the couch. They told stories together the way longtime friends can, laughing and finishing each other's thoughts. Lee told about meeting on the talk show. She remembered Karen floating toward her, like an apparition, wearing something outrageous with lots of scarves. They became friends right away, and later were roommates. Their stories painted such a nice picture of my mom's early life for me.

Even now, looking back through time's haze, I still see Karen and Lee holding hands on the soft golden couch, reminiscing, and the same wonder fills me as when I was with them in that tender moment.

CHAPTER 14

Saturday, September 22

EARLY SATURDAY AFTERNOON, less than twenty-four hours before I would board my plane back to Nashville Airport, I had already checked in online and printed my boarding pass. My bags were packed, and now I was sitting in the living room with my mom and Celine. Stephen was on the chaise, and Hunter was in the kitchen cleaning up from lunch.

"What should we do with Diane today?" Asked Mom, "It's her last day, you guys should take her somewhere fun."

I hope they take me to the ocean. It had been years since I stood in the waves, feeling the power of the sea, on a vacation when our kids were young. I couldn't believe I was only a few miles from the coast and I might not get to see it. But ideas were already flying around.

"We could go for a ride on Sunset Strip," suggested Celine.

"I could take her down to Culver City," said Stephen. "Maybe she'd like to see a movie studio?" He asked, with a question in his eyes. I should want that since my mom's a movie star. But it wasn't high on my list. I shook my head.

Hunter walked in, wiping his hands on a dishtowel. He sat on the arm of an overstuffed chair. "How about Mulholland Drive?" He said.

I listened impatiently, hoping someone would suggest what I really wanted to do. After several more comments, I spoke up with a smile. "How about we ask Diane what she wants to do?"

Everyone stopped talking. Mom chuckled. "Well, that would be the smart thing. Good for you!" She put her hand on my arm. "What does Diane want to do?"

"Diane wants to go to the ocean," I said firmly and looked around, seeing nods of approval. My new family seemed to think this was a fine idea.

Hunter and Celine looked at each other. "Venice Beach?" Celine asked, raising her eyebrows.

Hunter's gray eyes brightened with his half smile. "Yeah." He nodded. "Perfect."

Celine lent me a swimsuit to wear under my clothes, and an hour later Hunter, Celine, Josh, and I piled into a compact car. Celine drove, negotiating the 405, merging into the carpool lane. Traffic was surprisingly light, and we soon arrived at the beach.

As the car doors clunked shut, I caught a whiff of sea air and admired my surroundings. The breeze carried a mixture of faint music and crowd murmur from the boardwalk where we headed. Soon we were engulfed in a blur of vivid T-shirts and wild costumes of people walking, skating, and skateboarding all around us. A muscular man wrapped in a fat live snake skated past, leaving me in his wake. Venice Beach was a colorful carnival with painted buildings and art vendors selling bright murals, metal monster sculptures, and other creations. But I kept turning toward the ocean, wanting to get out there.

After we strolled a few blocks, we came across a walkway leading out onto the sand. I tugged Hunter's sleeve. "Come on, let's go!" I said.

The beach was expansive, several hundred yards wide, with a rise that hid the water. Right away, the noise from the boardwalk faded into a surreal quiet, only the swish of our steps on the sand. A distant drumming floated on the wind. We were approaching a group of people playing percussion instruments.

"That's the drum circle. I used to hang out there," explained Celine.

We walked up and listened a few minutes. Musicians were standing with hand drums and cowbells or sitting on blankets with bongos and snares. Their sound moved me, at once mysterious and playful, full of wistful, rhythmic essence. A fitting soundtrack to this wonder-filled week.

When they took a break, we continued our hike. The sound of breakers filled the air as we crested the rise. Finally, the ocean, a gold and silver glow spreading to the horizon. My brother stopped and gazed out. I rolled up my jeans and trotted into the cold water—brisk but not freezing—until I was knee deep. A wave pushed me, and my feet slid on the sand, the water dragging the grains away from my toes. How I had missed these sensations. The next wave sprayed my chest, so I decided to swim. I ran back where Celine, Josh, and Hunter stood chatting, dropped my jeans, and asked them to snap a couple of pictures of me swimming.

They seemed amused watching me. I waded to my waist and followed the waves, waiting for one to crest. I crouched, squinting into the late afternoon sun until a whitecap was about to swallow me. Then I launched toward shore and the ocean lifted and sailed me until the grit of sand on my belly slowed me. Sitting up, I wiped hair from my face as more foam tousled me, and another wave tossed me in farther. It was heaven, to enjoy the power of the ocean without fear, letting it play with me, resting in its embrace. I pulled myself up and ran out to body surf again.

When I had my fill, I toweled off, feeling the aliveness that only time in the ocean can bring. Josh took a photo of us three siblings, capturing the joy.

On the way back to the car, Hunter pointed out a four-story building. "That's the Cadillac Hotel," he said. "I used to stay there when I was in town to work. This beach holds a lot of memories for me." He paused. "I wouldn't have come here if you hadn't suggested it, and I'm glad we did; it felt good to be here again."

We walked stride for stride. "I like you," I said. "You have a measured, calm manner about you that feels nice."

"It's a reaction to being raised by actors," he confided. "I had to find my own sense of stability."

"I thought I had a chance to find Mom when you were only two," I told him. "When I turned eighteen, I wrote her a letter, planning to send it when I got my birth certificate. But the law had changed. My records were sealed." A few steps later, I added, "If I'd found her, I might have helped raise you."

"But you would have missed out on your experiences without us," Hunter said.

"Maybe," I considered. "But maybe my life wouldn't have changed much. Either way, knowing my baby brother would have been amazing."

He shook his head, smiled and frowned at the same time. I'm not sure how he took it, but I was brave enough to speak what was on my mind now, to say things I would have kept to myself before I met my mother. Why did she make me brave? She made me feel seen: she validated who I innately was. I hoped to encourage people like she did.

Celine and Josh caught up with us. And we found the car and started home. Venice Beach disappeared around a curve, becoming a memory like my week with my new family. In my life, I was gliding on the crest of a wave, floating toward the beach, learning to trust myself to the power of the sea. I hoped I had time to keep playing and avoid the rocky shore.

That evening, while my mom and I were hanging out on the big couch, she asked if any of our kids were artists.

"Yes and no. Mike used to make intricate origami as a child. And Ricky writes songs. Want to hear one?"

When she said yes, I found a sound file he had posted on Facebook and played it. She listened intently to his rapid-fire rap. "Play it again," she insisted, and leaned in with a spellbound expression.

"Stephen, come and hear this. My grandson is a genius."

Then she stood up and beckoned to us. "Here's what you do. Have a friend make a video of him walking by all different Chicago landmarks, dubbing the song. Move the camera in front of him." She stood me in front of her and then walked toward me, pretending to sing and look around the city as I backed up ahead of her enjoying her vivacity.

She went on, "He would have to practice getting the timing perfect. Then edit the clips together creatively and put it on YouTube and see what happens."

"Wow, Mom, what a great idea!" I wished Ricky could have seen her reaction.

"You know, I have a great friend, Harriet Schock, who's a brilliant songwriter and wrote a book about the craft."

"I'll look her up," I said.

When Sunday morning arrived, I was ready to leave, but Karen was still in bed. I knocked and entered quietly. In the silent darkness, she patted the sheet next to her, so I crawled in and put my head on her shoulder. It was a somber moment, and dread descended on me. This might be our last moment ever. What if I never saw her again? I expressed my worry. She took my hand and assured me: affinity lasts forever.

I thanked her for talking about it and don't remember all her words, only the love I felt for her and from her, my birth mother. Then I kissed her goodbye.

I comforted myself with the idea that we might have years to share. Women on both sides of Karen's family lived a long time, so it was not a stretch to hope for twenty years.

Stephen took me to the airport in the early morning sun, and Rich picked me up midday in Nashville and greeted me with a big hug. He put my luggage in the truck bed, and on the passenger seat I found a live plant—bright pink mums. I sent Karen a photo of them, and we texted back and forth. I told her she was more wonderful than I ever imagined my birth mother to be.

Rich listened while I talked the whole two hours home. I flew in the clouds, relating highlights of each day as he drove the scenic route home. Late afternoon sunlight seemed to vibrate through the trees above the road, its golden glow matching the electricity energizing me.

Photos

From Our Life Apart

Karen Ziegler, 1948

Diane Koehnemann, 1968

Above: Denise and Diane, soon after Denise came home from the Foundlings Home in 1963.

Below: The Koehnemann family in 1963: Don, Jodie, Denise and Diane

Above: Denise, Dad, and Diane in Door County, WI, 1968

Below Left: Diane in 1969. Below Right: The sisters in 1972 when Denise came home from Childrens Memorial Hospital.

Above left: Diane and Rich, 1977. Above right: Diane, Rich and baby Matthew, 1983

Below: Rich, Ricky, Mike, and Matt, Mingo Falls, NC, 1995

Above: Rich and Diane, 2020

Below: Diane and Denise, 2020

Above: Karen on the set of "A Gunfight," 1971

Below: Lee Purcell and Karen, early eighties

KAREN

Above: Karen, husband Kit Carson and son Hunter, 1975

Below: Karen and Hunter, 1977

Above Left: Karen as Rayette in Five Easy Pieces, 1970
Above Right: Karen and Hunter in Invaders from Mars, 1986

Below: Classic Karen Black, 1975

Above: Karen and husband Stephen Eckelberry about 1986

Below: Karen and adopted daughter Celine, about 1992

Above: brother Peter, mother Elsie, Karen and sister Gail,
Mission Beach, CA, about 1990

Below: Karen and Hunter, 1999

Photos

From Our Time Together

Diane and Karen on their first day together, September 2012

Photo compared when I first received my birth certificate.

Above: Diane, 1981, and Karen, 1966

Below: Diane 1986, and Karen, 1954

Photos from the Seattle trip on the way to meeting Karen in LA.

Above: Sons Matt and Mike, Grandson Gibson, Daughter-in-law Becca, Diane

Below: Diane and sister Nina Benedetti

Above: Karen and Diane's reunion in Karen's home

Below: Sharing family photos

Above: Working on a mural together on Karen's patio wall

Below: Karen with all her children: Diane, Hunter Carson, and Celine Eckelberry

Above: Reunion with birth father Robert "Beny" Benedetti

Below: Beny and his wife Joan with Diane

Above: Brother Ben Benedetti with Diane

Below left: Uncle Peter Ziegler and Diane;

Below right: Photo of Beny and Karen, 1958, from Peter's photo album

Above: Diane and Karen at my birthday party

Below: Hunter and Diane at Venice Beach

Loved ones surround Karen at the party in her home:

Above, Daughter Celine and Karyn Rachtman

Left, Angela Garcia Combs; Right, Lee Purcell

Above: Hunter Carson, wife Elyse and daughter Jane

Below: Diane and Karen's sister Gail Brown Duggan

Loved ones surround Karen in her hospital room:

Above: Lee Purcell and Harriet Schock

Below: Hunter, Karen, Harriet, Jane (with Elyse), Gail

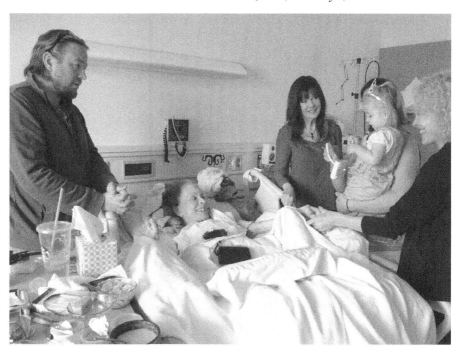

CHAPTER 15

October 2012

THE LADIES AT THE ART GUILD couldn't wait to see my photos. They were proud of the miracle that had happened in my life, almost as pleased as if I was their daughter. Enthusiasm filled the room as I told of our time together.

Denise, on the other hand, felt left out. I had to tone down my exuberance around her. She tried saying that Karen was her mother, too, but I told her that wasn't true; she had her own birth mother.

"My birth mom might be famous, too," she guessed.

"I'll tell you what, Neecy, I'll send for your birth records, and we'll see if we can find her." I sent for her forms later that week.

It was hard for me not to post about my time on Facebook. I had told Karen I didn't mind keeping us out of the public eye, but it annoyed me now. This was the most unbelievable thing that had ever happened in my life, and I couldn't share it? But I kept my word and didn't post her name. I could not risk being rejected by going against her wishes.

A couple weeks went by. I wrote more about my time at Karen's home, I messaged with my new siblings, and lunched with friends who were excited to hear my story. One day my email inbox surprised me with an oil painting opportunity. A Kentucky artist would be holding a workshop in Paducah in a few weeks. I called Karen with the news, and she caught my excitement right away. A few of my drawings had sold that month at the local gallery, so I had just enough art money to attend.

The two-day workshop was in a historic brick building in Paducah's quaint downtown. Large windows lined the north side of the artists' space, bringing in clean, indirect light. I was jittery with excitement as I walked in the first morning. There were six students, all of us women, most of us mature. The instructor was a man around my age, a well-known regional artist, and a good teacher.

He dove right into a hands-on lesson. We crowded around his easel as he squeezed paint onto his wooden palette, explaining how to mix colors from the limited number of tubes he required: a certain yellow, red, a blue, white and gray. The hues of nature appeared like magic while he mashed blobs of paint together with his palette knife.

When it was our turn, we tried to mimic what he had done. Not as easy as he made it look, but over the next hours I learned to predict what tone would result as I mixed. It was fascinating, visceral, and satisfying. I was hooked.

On the drive home that afternoon, the world became a painting; my ability to see had been transformed. The shapes of colors overlaid trees, buildings, and the road I traveled. These colors depended on the light hitting the surfaces. In the sun, red bricks looked orange, gray road glowed golden, green trees chartreuse. Shaded brick was violet, shadowed trees were blue. Why had I never noticed this before? Why did learning to mix a limited palette open my eyes to this truth? I didn't know, but somehow, I could capture light with paint now. It was a salient moment.

I phoned my mother again and left a message expressing my amazement and discovery. It would be the first of many messages I would leave for her. Karen didn't answer her phone often. She texted me the next day, though, saying how contagious my enthusiasm had been, and how much it reminded her of her own exhilaration for life.

After that, I didn't hear from her for a while. I worried, first about her health, then that she had moved on, that I had only been an event, and she might not keep me in her life.

A month after I returned from LA, autumn rains came to Kentucky. The air was still warm enough to leave the doors open, bringing in the patter of raindrops and rumble of thunder, and the scent of the wetted world.

"If there's anything good about my birth mom being so far away," I told Rich, as I stood at the doorway, "it's southern California weather. I bet there's not a flu and pneumonia season there."

That evening, Hunter called. Our mom was home from the hospital, but no one had told me she'd been there in the first place.

"I can't believe Stephen didn't tell me!" I said, pacing on our porch, pulling my jacket around me. "She's doing all right now, though?"

"Yeah, it was pretty scary for a day or too. The pneumonia was filling up her lungs. But she's tough. She'll be okay."

"Well, that explains why she hasn't called me in a while. But why wouldn't Stephen tell me?"

"It's not you. They're scattered. Sometimes I don't know stuff either. They assume the other told me. Don't sweat it. I'm gonna make sure you stay in the loop from now on." Hunter's unruffled manner comforted me again. He treated me like I always imagined a big brother would, even though I was sixteen when he was born, and he didn't know I existed until a few months ago.

But his reassurance didn't take away the heaviness I felt. I had lived half a century without my birth mother, and the thought of losing her so soon was unbearable. I was having trouble standing straight, like gravity had doubled my weight. I finally internalized that she was fighting for her life. Her frailty, the sag in her shoulders and unsteady gait, all came back to me. How she pushed herself to spend that time with me. A deep thankfulness blended with my new dread.

I started calling her once a week, but her phone went straight to a voice mail message: "You've reached Karen Black's cell. You can leave a message here, but for a quicker response, send her an email…" I left upbeat voicemails and emails, because I wanted to be a positive part of her life.

She often didn't respond to either form of communication. I struggled with sadness as these silent days went by. I tried to see her point of view: after all, I reasoned, she was waging war with cancer. But I worried that I didn't mean as much to her as she did to me. Texting garnered a reply most often, and though I missed the sound of her voice, at least I found out what was going on. She amazed me with encouraging words, expressing her care for me even though she was going through so much. This was the opposite of my adoptive mother, who let negative words flood out, never seeming to care how they hurt me. Maybe because of that, I coveted communications from Karen and cherished each one I received even more.

During this time, while my heart was heavy, something unexpected happened.

One early night, Rich called me over to his computer desk in the kitchen. He was on Facebook, and he wanted to show me something Stephen had posted.

"It's your mom singing," Rich said. I stood behind him to watch the video.

Karen was dressed up in a plum sweater, sitting at a piano in a festive living room, next to a woman I hadn't met. The ambient sound of a party surrounded them. My first thoughts were, she looks so well! When was this? Later, I found out it was a 2012 Academy Award party. The woman next to her at the piano was her friend, Azalia Snail.

They were smiling, heartily belting out a rendition of the Gershwin song, "Summertime." My heart seemed to forget how to beat as I heard her exuberant voice singing the lyrics, addressed to a child:

One of these mornings you're gonna rise up singing
And you'll spread your wings and you'll take to the sky
But till that morning, there ain't nothin' can harm you
With daddy and mammy standin' by…"[4]

I stood stunned. Sudden, powerful emotions filled my chest and tears poured from my eyes. Was she thinking of me as she sang, remembering the baby she'd named Nina?

Rich wasn't sure how to react. "You okay, Di?"

"Yeah... I don't know... maybe not. I need a minute," I said and retreated into our bedroom when the video was over. Switching on the nightstand lamp, I sat heavily on the bed and sobbed. When the tears subsided, I wiped my eyes and wrote in my journal to try and make sense of my perplexing reaction:

Today I heard my birth mother sing, really sing. Her voice did something to my heart I want to understand. A dark, locked place inside me broke open. Out poured feelings of sorrow, of abandonment—I've never felt abandoned since the earliest time I can remember. The trauma was hidden deep inside. And the reason it came out is because here was my mother, so alive and on fire in her soul, and I did not grow up with this light in my life. I was an ember kept burning only from within, when I could have nestled close to her and become a flame. We are so much alike! I have never had anyone at all who truly understood me, and here she is, myself mirrored, and she denied me this most precious relationship.

Maybe it's even a stirring of memory from when Karen was carrying me—she told me she sang to me back then. I could be reliving the internal struggle of a newborn being torn from my mother. This makes sense with the depth of emotion I feel, and with abandonment coming to the surface.

Some of the emotion is positive, too, more like a fire burning in my soul, like something has been rekindled. I hope and pray for more time with my birth mom!!

The next day, I texted Karen about hearing the song. I told her that listening to her sing did something deep in my heart I didn't understand yet, as if a long-buried place was awakened.

She replied, Oh my. It's like the freedom in your soul can be likened to mine!

Her response touched me so deeply, I didn't mention the rest. She didn't need to read it in a text, anyway. Instead, I expressed myself in a poem, and thoughts began to pour into my journal. What might I have gone through as a lonely infant? If I had felt abandoned, how did I make it through nine weeks living in the sterile adoption agency? Did I have a kind nurse? Maybe she was the same woman who let Karen see me in the nursery. How did I adjust to a brand-new life afterward? As I wrestled with these questions, emotions roiled. One day while I wrote, a truth surfaced about something that had puzzled me since childhood.

In my mind, I was back in my crabapple tree in the backyard, enjoying the tiny pink blossoms in spring and sour red fruit in summer. I again felt the peace and sadness I had called my melancholy. A unique, dual emotion that didn't have a true name, a mingling of emptiness, wholeness, and serenity. There was something inexpressibly wonderful about it. Through the years, at quiet times alone, I would sit still and let it draw me inward to a cozy space in my heart.

My pen paused above the page as realization dawned. Tears came. I knew what the melancholy was, why I cherished this place inside me that felt safe but sad: it was all I had left of my birth mother. It was a warm natal recollection of Karen, from within her womb, wrapped in the trauma of abandonment.

I had found her in my own heart. She'd been with me all my life.

Ember

How could you
deny me you

all these years
the vast empty places
echo
where you belonged

your song
rips through my heart
unstops a hardened place
not known before

there it is:
you abandoned me

I should have joined your song
the song that completes me
that touches me like fire
in my bones.

but you did not know
your fire followed me
I have been an ember
when I could have been a flame

God give me time
please please sweet time
help me to forgive her
I have just found my life

CHAPTER 16

November & December 2012

CRISP FALL LEAVES SWIRLED in a harsh wind, skittered over the road, and disappeared into the woods. I huddled on the porch swing in the pale morning light, watching nature mirror my mood as gust tore leaf from branch. Inwardly, I shared their forced journey through empty space. Buffeted by intense emotions since hearing Karen sing, buried abandonment, grief, and pain had knocked me headlong.

As the wind whistled, my mind drifted again to my life's beginning. The memory of Karen's womb was so sweet, so powerful an impression, I had still tasted it as an infant. But that sweetness had come wrapped in a hollow blanket, a howling void.

Her song unearthed anger I never knew existed. She had hurt me by leaving me as an infant; I was mad at her. I had to forgive her. I needed to heal and get past this. Examining what I knew, I sought to understand her point of view.

During the week we were together, she had told me about her pregnancy at fifteen. It had happened the first time she'd had sex, with her friend Charlie Black. He was eighteen; she was only fifteen. Her father had been furious. Their parents met and decided the kids must marry. The adults spoke of her in the third person, and from then on she grew accustomed to powerlessness.

So, Karen and Charlie found themselves in the back of a car, driving south to Alabama where they could legally marry. Then they shared an apartment in Muncie, Indiana, where he attended college. Karen became a housewife, cooking and cleaning while going to high school pregnant, where she faced derision from her peers. Charlie ridiculed her in front of his friends, too. She was miserable.

It happened that she miscarried. Relieved, she headed home to Barrington, hoping to find forgiveness. But her father barred her from returning, so she drove back to Muncie.

When Charlie transferred to Purdue University, Karen took control of her life and applied for early college entry. She was accepted and went to Purdue, breaking it off with Charlie but keeping his last name. Later she entered Northwestern School of Drama, where she met Beny.

When she found herself pregnant again, she did not tell her parents. Society in general, in the late fifties, disdained unwed pregnancy. In that climate, she firmly believed she could not have both a baby and a career. She chose her art over me, and over Beny, too, because she told me he had offered to marry her.

Karen suffered for this choice. Her heart ached without her child to hold. She lived with the emptiness as I did, but instead of burying it, she turned it into fuel for acting and writing. Her screenplay, Deep Purple, told the story of Minerva Sassoon, an abused woman searching for the daughter she gave up for adoption. She found a neglected, impoverished girl and cared for her, convinced she had found the baby she had given up. Minerva's attention helped the girl, Frances, feel seen, feel loved for the first time. In the end they knew they were not mother and daughter, but they saved each other and left their abusers together. Karen told me writing this film was her way of dealing with the guilt of surrendering me.

Her consuming passion was to communicate her vision to the eyes and ears of others. Her art drove her. As a fellow artist, I understood this nonnegotiable urge to create. Karen had said, "If I had kept you,

I'd be a secretary." She'd have been imprisoned in the work-a-day world with unexpressed art tearing her apart.

Instead, she sailed on to pursue dreams and star in films while I lived a secure childhood in obscure suburbia playing with friends until the streetlights shone. Our family vacationed each year at a place where I forged great memories. My adoptive parents were not abusive nor poor. Though we had our share of difficult times, I was safe. I was loved.

As winter weeks went by, seeing and understanding these things helped me make peace with Karen's decision, forgive her, and once again become glad for the expansive life she enjoyed. But gladness mingled with sorrow. More tumors grew, more chemo ravaged her. My heart wrapped tendrils around her; my mind always turned to her.

Later that month, Rich's father, Larry, fell and broke a hip. We traveled up north to stay with his mother, Dorothy, at Thanksgiving. Larry was in the hospital. Tests had also shown lesions on his lungs. Matt brought his sons to Chicago, and they visited their Great Grandpa Larry, whose failing health kept declining. Rich hated to see his strong father losing the will to live. This man, who had worked two jobs most of his life to provide for his family, lingered for several more months and passed away that spring. My husband and I endured a season of heart-rending times.

On Thanksgiving, Karen sent me a text saying, hope your day is full of cozy joy! Love! Nothing about the round of chemo she faced. My adoptive mom used to tell me about every little trouble in her life, so Karen's silence about her health unnerved me. Didn't she think of me as her daughter? When she sent a voice mail birthday song to our grandson Gibson that week, I focused on the loss of their opportunity for relationship, instead of celebrating this small connection. Grief haunted me with visions of a past that never was and a future that wouldn't be. My heart was tumbling downhill in the rain, picking up mud as it rolled.

I yearned to be with Karen and hold her hand. At the same time, I took comfort in knowing she had good friends, and she would have hands to hold.

To buoy my mood, I wrote her an old-fashioned letter on stationery. I spoke about our family time with Dorothy, my mother-in-law. We were making a genealogy tree of the Bay and Guthrie clans. I described Rich, our sons and our grandsons. And I told her: Nobody in my life communicates the way you do. I have been an island, without creative people to emulate, never knowing what made me different. I am like you!

A few weeks later, when I asked if she'd gotten it, I treasured her answer. She said she had taken my "beautiful handwritten letter" to the hospital with her so she could read and reread it.

Back in Kentucky, my need to hear Karen's voice grew stronger. Relief flooded me each time she texted, about once a week. One day in December, I expressed how much I wanted to talk to her.

She called the next morning. Her first question was, as usual, "Where are you?" This afternoon, I relaxed on our bed, enjoying the natural light filtering through our bamboo blinds.

"Do you think about me every day?" She asked, her voice tight.

"Yes," I answered honestly.

"Diane, being my daughter is more of an idea than a reality. I birthed you fifty years ago, but I wasn't there for you. We weren't in each other's life."

"But you are my mother. And we're a lot alike," I countered.

"We have lots of similarities, but plenty of ways we're different. You're making me feel crowded."

My stomach sank as I realized I was pushing her away. I could not lose her this way. She continued, "Please be present where you are. And don't worry about me. I'm well cared for."

"I know. And thank you for telling me. I don't want to make you uncomfortable." I was short of breath, hoping she would continue to love me.

"So, you're all right with this? I wasn't sure how you'd feel about this kind of communication."

"I'm glad for it, because what you're saying is real, and I like that." I breathed easier.

She said, "We're alike in that way."

"Part of why I'm thinking of you so much," I explained, "is because I'm looking at my past in a new light, now that I know you and know myself better because of you." I again did not express the feelings of abandonment and grief I'd been working through.

"Oh!" She said. "I like that." Her voice lost its edge, then, and she opened up and told me how she feared an ablation she would undergo to remove a tumor pressing on her spine. "Such a large thing they'll take out of me. How will I walk, how will I eat, who will take care of me?"

This made me yearn to jump in my car, drive to the airport and take the next flight out to California. That was impossible, and I just said, "I wish I could be there for you."

I took some time with the lights off in my room, thinking through what she'd said, clearing the fog in my head. I decided to take her advice to heart.

The next day when I took our dogs outside, I stepped into a literal fog. It engulfed me, fading into glowing whiteness amid the forest trees. While I played ball with our black lab, enjoying the rhythm of throw and retrieve, my mother's words resonated: "Be present where you are." I remembered the day she walked into her living room while I perused the John Singer Sergeant art book. She had effortlessly entered my moment to discuss the light in the paintings, exactly what I was admiring. Now, ethereal light surrounded me. Could I learn to notice details of the here-and-now by choice?

A deep breath, an exhalation, and I stilled my mind. Water drops pattered on the wet earth from dripping oak branches above. Birdcall echoed into the distance. The lichen on the trunk beside me, the etched bark, the muted tone of the trees in the middle distance, and the bright gray-white ghosts of trunks further down. Cool denim against my legs. The dog panting next to me, waiting on my throw.

This mindfulness already happened naturally while I painted outdoors and when I composed poetry. Now I had willed it, chosen to make it occur. If I mastered this ability, it could help me, not only in times of solitude, but also in social settings. It would enable me to listen well and be there for others. The first word I ever read was look, and now my birth mother had helped me see how to integrate this concept as a guiding principle in my life.

Slowly my heart loosened its too-tight grip on Karen, and I relaxed into my new daughterhood, respecting Karen's need for space, texting her weekly and replying to her texts, but not making any phone calls. Stephen video-called at Christmas. What a treasure to see Karen smiling on my computer screen, standing wobbly beside their beautiful tree. How thin she looked in her purple pajamas, but still bright and cheery, gushing about presents and plans. We exchanged gifts by mail. I sent her what she asked me for: a canvas print of me as a baby. She sent me a cozy sweater in the color she said was my best, a red violet.

Wearing the soft ribbed knit, I looked at myself in the mirror. My face reflected Karen and Beny, and both of their mothers, Elsie and Lola. A comfortable sense of belonging filled me. From my unique vantage point of relational freshness and forgiveness, I had nothing but love and joy whenever I thought of my new family. I worked to extend this simplicity of affection to other relationships and make it a permanent part of my character.

Finding my blood relatives had rearranged my view of myself. Ancestry.com had uncovered the hidden history of me, and Karen's acceptance and communication had revealed aspects I had seen only as a sketch, a shadow. Now they were vivid: the natural world was my inspiration; I lacked any veneer and spoke from my heart; my passion was my art. My joyful exuberance now had a source—Karen. And seeing so much of her in me, I planted myself squarely in my native soil.

And in this new state of self-awareness and groundedness, my view of God expanded. Wrestling with my traditional faith since Karen told me she had cancer, I came to realize that any one set of doctrines could not fully explain the divine. In the same way, the picket fence around our yard could never contain a wild forest: roots would grow under it; seeds would blow over it. God's love burgeoned beyond any boundaries we set.

And I wrote another poem, this one about the identity I was now wearing, or more precisely, being: my real self that had reemerged since finding Karen. My roots had given me wings.

Flame

I am new
like a small child
like leaves in spring
like first-heard song
scattering through the air

Freshly born
I ride the waves
of newday hours
open eyes and
widened heart

seeing me by knowing you
Who was i before?

Empty places hold
new fullness here,
re-defining
life within my soul

Finding Karen Black

Time
I pray for time
We are we for once
or can it be for more?

Ever forward we are we
In unity my soul is free
Hidden hurt is seen and freed
so newness rains within
Breathing hurts in this rare air
we won't be here again.

CHAPTER 17

January & February 2013

ONE MORNING MY EYES OPENED in sudden inspiration. I could not believe I hadn't remembered it before: The letter I'd written to my birth mother in 1977 when I was eighteen. I could send it to her now.

Springing out of bed, I swung open my closet door, turned on the light, and unburied a red bin at the back. I dragged it out and scrounged inside. Under my Saturn V rocket model, my high school diary and poem book, and a box of Rich's love letters, I spotted the envelope. I pulled it out and opened it. There were two photos of me and Rich and the yellowed notebook paper of my letter. I held it up gingerly like the treasure it was: five pages of my teenage heart.

With everything in a new envelope, I slipped it into our country mailbox, flag up.

Another day, wrapped in a throw blanket on the couch, my computer in my lap, I searched for Alfred Sisley. I snapped a picture of an intriguing painting and texted it to Karen. She surprised me with a phone call.

We exchanged ideas on capturing natural light with paint. I told her what I had learned; that the surface reflection influences the color of any object: direct sun added a golden tone, shade took on the blues of the sky. She suggested it took a season for an artist to develop an intuitive ability to mix the colors one's eyes perceived.

She said, "It's the passion to get the color spot-on that makes a painter great. If you succeed, you can walk into the painting. It is Truth."

This was like something that had impressed me while watching two of her recent films, Nothing Special and Maria My Love. So, I said, "That's what you do, you create Truth in your acting. How do you make your characters so real?"

"It comes from a passion for people, for watching behavior, gestures and their meanings." She paused. "I work from need: the hoarding lady in Maria, she needed her things to stay put. Don't think while you act: plan well, then react on the stage or in the film. Memorize everything, yes, but don't rely on that. Make a big imagination for yourself, then relive the event you imagined as you say your line."

Her call was twenty-five minutes of the most energizing conversation I've ever had.

Some time later, I decided to audition for a play at the Paducah Market House Theatre. In an email to my birth father, Beny, I mentioned my plan. He sent me one of his books on acting, The Actor in You, and I read over its eye-opening advice. He and Karen had both contributed to help aspiring actors hone their craft.

Curiosity fueled my courage, and I stood on stage, reading lines and interacting with people who knew what they were doing. It was stimulating fun, providing me a brief glimpse into what both my parents had spent their lives doing.

Later in January, an envelope from the state of Illinois arrived, addressed to Denise. She and I sat at the kitchen table and unfolded her original birth certificate. I showed her where her mother's name was, and she read it: "Janice Marie Huff." No father cited, and my sister didn't ask.

My voice choked as I read their ages. "Neecy, your birth mom was only fourteen." Her dad had been sixteen.

"Oh," she paused, her face blank. Then, a spark: "She was in high school."

"Yes," I agreed. "She was just a kid."

I searched the web for two weeks and found no leads. Then, the high school idea came back to me, and I discovered a yearbook search site. Digging in, I unearthed three photos of a Janice Huff, the right age, in an outlying Chicago suburb. She was in yearbooks as a freshman, junior, and senior. The sophomore book didn't include her—1963, the year of my sister's birth.

I met a dead end when I tried to find out more. But I framed the photo that looked most like Denise, and she set it on her table with other family photos. This satisfied her, and she didn't ask for anything more.

One evening in early February, while Rich, Denise, and I were watching television, my cell rang. "It's Stephen," I said. "I'm gonna take it in the bedroom." I closed the door behind me, to block the TV noise, and answered.

Stephen seemed hesitant, and I held my breath, but he said, "Karen is fine. Well, not fine but not in danger. She has a procedure coming up, an ablation to burn out one tumor developing in her back. Last time it was excruciating, and she needed a lot of help. This time, I have a deadline looming, so I'm very busy..."

He's going to ask me to care for Karen. My heart skipped a beat.

"... Celine has a heavy class load and a job, and we can't afford home health right now. If I paid for your plane ticket, would you be willing to fly out? I realize this is asking a lot. You wouldn't be a guest, it would be hard work..."

"Yes, Stephen, yes! I would love to lend a hand. I feel helpless here so far away! Of course, I will." I didn't have to ask Rich. He knew how fearful I was of losing Karen. "So, when is this?" I asked.

He told me the details: a couple weeks ago she had a liter of liquid removed from the space between her organs. The tumors were causing this. "But she's still working. On the 9th and 10th she's recording lessons on acting with Russell Brown, and then she has a reading on the 16th with rehearsals. The ablation surgery is scheduled for the 20th…"

Rich entered the room. I covered the phone and showed him my notes. He nodded and whispered, "Whatever you need to do, we'll be okay."

Meanwhile on the phone, Stephen was rambling. I could tell he was stressed. "… I'll pick you up and get you settled. You can stay in my study again. There's a new stray kitten to share the room with… you'll help Karen with pillows for her legs. I'll teach you how to make her breakfast…. She'll be bed-bound. Angela Garcia Combs is a marvelous cook and will bring meals, you'll just heat them up. By the way, Angela wants you to call her."

I hung up, dazed but thankful I would soon see my mother again. Then I had a pang of guilt for thinking of myself. Was I being shallow? No, because of her illness I was getting another chance to be with her, to be a daughter in her need, to show her love. My heart should be free to rejoice at this opportunity without feeling guilty.

The next day I called Angela, Karen's red-haired friend I'd met at the dinner party. I pictured her long curls and keen glance as she spoke.

"You're a great light in her life," she assured me. "Sometimes she feels engulfed in a prism of darkness. You're here at the right moment. She needs to be loved, and we all saw your genuine love for her."

I was glad my affection was so evident.

"I want to tell you about her cancer," Angela went on. "It was a robust strain, but they caught it early, so there's hope. She went to a doctor for stomach pains, and they found a carcinoma on the place the gall bladder and pancreas connect. She and Stephen flew to the Mayo Clinic in Minneapolis. This was in 2009."

"She told me she'd had it before," I said, fretful.

"Well, they did the Whipple, a radical procedure, but she was cancer-free. After a year they discovered two tiny spots, in the same region as the original site. It hadn't metastasized—it still hasn't—so far radiation and chemo have kept it from getting into her lymph nodes." I didn't know what to say. At my hesitation she added, "This cancer is not genetic."

It caught me off guard to realize I now had a medical history. No more writing adopted on the forms. And even though it wasn't hereditary, my answer would now be yes to the question, *is there cancer in your family?*

CHAPTER 18

Wednesday & Thursday, February 20–21

MY EYELIDS WERE HEAVY as I shuffled in line, waiting to board my six a.m. flight. Peace cocooned me, because each step brought me closer to holding and helping my mother. Swirling emotions threatened the calm surface, however. Fear kept fighting through, and concern for her health created a dark counterpoint. I was stranded in emotional paradox in the claustrophobic corridor, like a bad dream. Finally, I found a window seat and took out my pillow, hoping to fall asleep as the plane rose above Nashville. The Cumberland River glinted in the morning sun.

Stephen had asked me to stay at least three weeks. While I took care of my mom's daily needs, I would get to know her better and tell her more about my life, too, sharing photos and videos. In my carry-on was a small art bag I'd brought along in the hopes I'd have time to paint a neighborhood scene, as well.

Then a sudden realization—I'd be there on my birthday! We'd be together on that day for only the second time in our lives. I lifted the shade and followed cloud shadows drifting over patchwork farmlands, thankfulness swelling with every breath.

Stephen picked me up from Los Angeles Airport once again, looking bedraggled. Karen's procedure had gone well, he told me, and she was recovering at the hospital. He'd pick her up after dropping me at their home.

We stopped for breakfast at a retro diner where Stephen knew the waiters. He seemed to perk up in familiar surroundings. The coffee helped, too. We had a hearty American breakfast and good conversation. Born in Belgium, he grew up in Paris with five brothers. The family moved around often; he had a cosmopolitan upbringing. His mother was an artist, but Stephen took after his businessman father. He had been in love with Karen even before he met her at a Scientology conference years ago.

When we arrived at their house, he helped bring in my luggage and then left right away for the hospital. Celine was at school. I was alone in the warm glow of sunlit windows. I wandered among the antique furnishings and found a photo of my grandma Elsie as a teen with a 1920s flapper hairdo. She was a young girl, trying on coyness and sensuality, yet retaining freshness and innocence. I brought the photo over to the chaise, unpacked my sketchbook, and drew a likeness that captured her naïveté.

As I worked, it occurred to me that creating visual art had something in common with acting: intention. I aimed to show innocence, and this idea came through to my hand as it moved over the paper, the same as an actor's body brings to life the character she creates.

Before long, Stephen opened the front door with Karen leaning her weight on his arm. They walked slowly to her bedroom, Stephen shushing me with a finger as they passed. Her eyes flickered toward me, but pain prevented her from speaking. I waited in the hall as he eased her into bed and made her comfortable. Then he motioned me in, and I tucked my head to my chest and lifted my suddenly heavy feet through the doorway. In the darkened room I approached their big four-poster bed, where my mom lay on her back, knees propped on pillows. She patted the covers next to her, and I sat down, leaning in for a gentle hug. Gaunt and frail, she gave me a small smile. Her hair was wispy, and she ran her fingers through it as she spoke.

"You look thinner than the last time I saw you," she said, her voice a whisper.

"I've lost weight, you're right," I said. Fifteen pounds had disappeared from the stress and worry over her, in spite of the healing I'd also been doing. I wrestled daily with conflicting emotions that kept me restless and entangled: joy twisting with grief and new life grappling with impending death. But I didn't tell her any of this.

Instead I asked, "How did the ablation go?"

"Great, they got all the tumor, but now my right kidney is swollen like a rock." She lifted her shirt and pressed on the side of her abdomen, showing me the outline of a three-inch lump. I doused a gasp and struggled to keep my face calm. "I think maybe another tumor is pressing on the ureter."

"I'm glad I'm here," I managed, keeping my voice even. "I felt helpless so far away."

We didn't talk long because she needed sleep. I stood up, shaky from seeing her fragility, sorry I had let her lack of communication bother me.

I stepped across the hallway and unpacked. The kitten I shared the study with, a thin black scrap of a cat, stretched on the twin bed. Cat urea tinged the air. Celine had posted a sign: Please close the window at night when Kitten is inside. I was allergic to some cats, and my eyes burned right away with this one.

I fled into the fresh air of the front room and sat in the sun. I was here! Relieved and thankful but apprehensive and grieving, I prayed for strength to balance the emotional strain.

On Thursday morning, I woke early, my head throbbing from the cat and my heart pounding with anxiety. The window opened with a tug and the kitten jumped out. A fresh California breeze tousled the curtains. As I breathed in the sweet air, there was a knock on the door: Stephen wanted to teach me how to make Karen's breakfast, so I dressed and joined him in the kitchen. He explained my responsibilities while he put together the stainless-steel juicer.

"Since Karen had the Whipple, her body doesn't use food well. She has to eat all the time to get enough nutrition, so we feed her nutrient-rich foods. Every morning she gets a full glass of carrot juice and a plate of fresh pineapple."

While he made the juice, I sliced and chunked the pineapple. He pointed out the plastic packets of liquid herbs and dolloped his home-made yogurt into a cup. We put all the food on a tray with a cup of tea.

"Okay," said Stephen, "She's awake and you can take it in to her. I have to run to the office this morning, and Celine is at school, so you're on your own."

I stood outside her double bedroom doors, hesitant to knock. This moment seemed pivotal. It was the first time I'd assisted her: I'd gone from guest to caregiver. How would she receive me? Once inside, however, I shook off these dismal thoughts as she greeted me in her soft, husky voice, sounding truly happy to see me.

"Good morning, darling. Come and put the tray over here." With difficulty, she scooted herself upright against the headboard to eat. "Put the tea on my table, okay? And can you help me open the herbs? They're specially prepared for me, to help fight the cancer along with my pH diet to combat the tumors." She ate some of what I'd brought her, but she didn't seem to get much down before pushing the tray away.

"I need to go back to sleep. I get exhausted after I eat because of the horrible Whipple procedure I had to remove the original cancer. It made it hard to digest food. Can you help put the pillows back under my legs?" She explained how she wanted them stacked, and I memorized her instructions.

Back in the quiet kitchen, I cleaned the juicer and carried the scrapings to the compost pile outside the back door. Then I went around to the patio. The tattered gazebo cover looked even more worn than I remembered. Leaves and cobwebs littered the concrete floor under withering plants and dusty furniture. "This place needs work!"

I said out loud, shaking my head. I had noticed this last time, and now I had a chance to help. The exercise would help me release my tension and agitation, and a spring cleaning would make a nice surprise for Karen. I'd have to ask Stephen to be sure it was all right.

As I stepped in the back door, the front door opened, and I heard a female voice call, "Hello?"

"Oh, Angela, come on in!" I hurried through the kitchen to help with the many boxes and bags she balanced.

Angela Combs brought her energetic presence in with the meals. She bustled into the kitchen telling me all about her menu choices. Before opening the fridge, she smiled. "I wonder where we'll put it all, because I've seen this crazy fridge before!"

She was right; behind the refrigerator door a bomb seemed to have exploded. What a jumbled mountain of foods! It looked ready to tumble out at any moment. There were restaurant packages, produce, half-eaten carry-out and mounds of plastic herb packages. Laughing, we organized it to fit in the bounty she had brought.

Angela's energy was the pick-me-up I needed. She told me about the wonderful surprise party she'd given Karen two years before, with a fantastic spread of all kinds of my mom's favorite foods. Tears rimmed her eyes as she told the story.

Mom shuffled out of her bedroom, then, and sat on the couch to chat with us. She seemed almost whole, engaging and laughing, even though she weighed next to nothing. Her good color and high spirits encouraged me.

That afternoon, Stephen spread out a futon on the living room floor. Karen and I lounged in front of the TV, chatting.

"Do you like my new reading glasses?" I asked.

"No, they look parochial," she replied. "Let me see them."

She put them on and pinched up her face like a strict teacher. She was right! I'd never been good at fashion. Now I had a new way to make style decisions—check myself in the mirror and ask what type of person my attire announced.

"Sunday will be fun," Mom said. "We'll be here on the futon with Karyn, Lee, and Celine, to watch the Oscars. They're special to me, Diane, you should have seen the dresses I used to wear to the Awards. There was this pale blue gown I adored, with a long train."

"Yes, I saw pictures of it," I said.

"You did? When?"

"When I first found you on Wikipedia, before you messaged me. I searched the internet for images of you because I'd wondered for so long. And you are famous, you know," I smirked.

She gave me a sidelong glance and rolled her eyes.

After a while we settled into viewing a vintage movie. While my mom enjoyed the film, I studied her profile to imprint it on my memory. I breathed in these small moments with her as if I were a little girl. She was being my mommy without realizing it. Should I tell her? Would it make her stop being herself? I kept my mouth shut. Then I remembered my big news.

"Hey, Mom, guess what?" I said, "I'll be here for my birthday!"

Her eyebrows raised. "Stephen, are you hearing this?" She called into the dining room, where he was working.

"No, what's up?" He said, pushing back his chair and starting into the room.

"We'll have Diane's birthday here!" Her smile shone in her words.

"Oh, that's poetry!" Stephen exclaimed.

"This puts me in a celebratory mood," Mom said. "Let's have a party!"

"Oh, Mom, I just want to spend the day with you," I said. And although I was thinking of her health, I also meant it. I wanted to savor the time with her and not have to share her with lots of other people. "I'd like a quiet evening with our family on my birthday."

They nodded to my request. But Mom said, "This still calls for a celebration." Her eyebrow raised, and the planning had begun.

It was nine o'clock that night when we sat down to dinner together on their four-poster bed: Karen, Stephen, and me. It was fun, not at all awkward. They both leaned against the headboard, and I sat cross-legged at the other end of the big king mattress, food spread between us. The conversation leaped through thoughtful perspectives and humorous commentary. Their banter was invigorating.

Peppered through it, we talked about big-picture things. At one point I said, "I love to sit and observe the room I'm in, noticing everything around me made by people I don't know, from all around the globe."

They nodded and said they'd thought of that plenty.

Mom added, "We like to talk about ways we're connected to the rest of humanity."

Stephen commented about how instrumental the industrial revolution was in that interdependence, and we discussed exploration. "Sailors took beer because it doesn't go bad; it goes flat," he said, "but the yeast eats any microbes. So, beer was one reason the new world was discovered! Also, tomatoes originated in the new world, not Italy."

Here he transformed into an Italian guy, saying, "We put these tomatoes on our pizza. They are so good, we say we discovered them in Italy!"

On and on, random topics and laughter filled our evening until Stephen cleaned up our dishes from the bed, and we said goodnight.

Back across the hall in my room, I jotted notes of the day and texted my brother Hunter; he had said I could contact him if I needed anything. I asked what he thought about an idea I'd had that evening: to meet my birth father Beny during my stay here. He and his wife, Joan, were at their winter condo in San Diego, not far south. Did my brother think it would be okay to leave our mom for a couple days? Hunter was so sweet to call back even though—I hadn't realized—it was eleven p.m. in Dallas. He said I definitely should meet my dad. There was an Amtrak along the coast, so I wouldn't have to borrow or rent a car.

The Amtrak website listed the train, aptly named the Coaster, and displayed a map of the route that hugged the coastline for most of the four-hour trip to San Diego. As I began to imagine the trip, it became easier to take the next step toward making it a reality. I would bring it up the next day.

CHAPTER 19

Friday–Sunday, February 22–24

My mom was having her breakfast in bed again on Friday morning. I walked up to her double door and knocked, holding her second glass of carrot juice.

"Come on in," she called.

I entered the spacious room, its pink walls and rose-patterned curtains glowing in morning light. Karen leaned against the mahogany headboard, a notebook open on her lap, her phone in one hand and a pen in the other. Breakfast was half-eaten on a tray. She exuded renewed energy.

"Thanks, darling, put it here." She nodded toward a small side table strewn with books, medicine and half empty cups. I cleared a spot and placed the juice glass next to her brass lamp. "Come here, let me look at you."

She set aside her notebook. I sat on the edge of the bed, hardly breathing as she touched my face, overwhelmed to be in such intimacy with her.

"What a wonderful thing you've done, Diane, coming all this way to help me," she said, putting her hand on mine.

"It means the world to me, Mom," I assured her.

Her eyes twinkled, and she flipped my hand over. She raised an eyebrow and asked, "Ever had your palm read?"

"No," I shook my head, intrigued into a grin. She leaned forward and studied my right hand for a moment, then grabbed the other one and looked back and forth between them.

"Palm reading is a Czech, Bohemian, or gypsy thing," my mom said, holding both my palms. She explained, "My great-aunt Mary taught me when I was a child. She was Grandma Emma's sister, up in Manitowoc. Now since you're right-handed, your left hand is potential, the right is reality."

"Interesting," I said, enjoying this unexpected moment.

"You have a clean hand." She put her fingertip in the center of my right palm and ran it vertically. "This is your professional line. It's double, and you have a big star at the top of it, all the way up at the base of your finger. That is a great talent."

She looked up at me with a piercing gaze. "You have to keep painting; you could be in museums."

I smiled at her earnest prediction of my glowing professional future.

"Also, another line crosses it; that is a second talent, like painting and also drawing." Then she followed a groove across my palm, under my fingers. "Your love line starts super early, like you were a loving infant." She paused. Then she went on without comment, "It's spotless, with only one long-term relationship." She touched one small crease just under my pinkie, which was the same on both hands. Just Rich, I mused.

"Under your love line is your head line. The left is longer than the right, which means you're not as intellectual as you could've been."

My birth father spent fifty years as a professor of theater at universities across the continent. With my passion for academics and my artistic bent, if Beny and Karen had raised me, who knows where I'd be now.

"Look under your forefinger on your left hand." She pointed out a curved crease. "Your head line is all tangled up with your life line. But on your right side it's separate. That means you and your family would have been like-minded, but you ended up more of an independent thinker."

"That's true. I'm not pragmatic like the parents who raised me," I said.

She looked up at me and smiled, letting go of my palms. "I don't necessarily believe in this, but once Czech always Czech."

"Well, thanks. That was fun! And I hope you're right about the museums."

I gathered up the used cups on her table and stood. She would sleep again soon, saving her limited strength. "The juicer needs cleaning," I told her as I left.

"Okay, Darcy," she called after me. I laughed at her baby-talk language. Hearing her call me a playful name made me feel like her daughter. She had once again focused outward, on me, not on her condition. I shook my head in amazement at her remarkable spirit.

Later that day, midday sun poured through the skylight as Mom and I sat in the living room discussing dinner. She wanted chicken, made a favorite way. A list of ingredients came tumbling out of her mouth until I stopped her with a raised hand.

"Wait a minute, Mom, let me get a sheet of notebook paper. Can you give me the whole recipe? I'd love to have it." I wrote as she spoke:

Karen Black's Roasted Chicken

Whole chicken, clean and dry
stuff with onion, celery and lemon
sprinkle with sea salt, pepper, thyme and rosemary
Make a broth with Better Than Bouillon
Place chicken in a roasting pan and pour in one inch of broth
Rinse Idaho potatoes and cut in 1/4-inch medallions
Peel carrots and leave them whole
Stand the potato pieces like little soldiers around the meat
Fit carrots in the pan, salt and pepper vegetables

Do not cover. Bake at 395° for one and a half hours
If after an hour meat is too brown, float foil over it.

Whole Foods had the ingredients, and the walk helped clear my head. My mind turned to the work I wanted to do on their patio as I enjoyed the freshness and color along the sidewalks.

When I got back, Karen was in bed, and Stephen was at his computer. I put the groceries in the fridge and wandered to the dining room. "Can I see what you're doing?" I asked.

"Oh sure! Come on over," Stephen invited. "I'm working on a trailer."

On his screen a confusing array of digital sliders surrounded the video file he was editing. Briefly he talked me through his fascinating process. Then I remembered my idea. "I want to ask you something," I said. He turned and gave me his full attention. "Can I clean up the patio as a surprise for Karen?"

"Are you up for that? I worry I'm already asking so much of you."

"No, no, I'd love to do it. I have down time while she's sleeping. What do you think of taking down the gazebo cover? It's in sad shape."

He straightened up. "I've wanted a new canopy forever. Let's do it!" He was on board, and his enthusiasm energized me.

Outside again, I took stock of the needed work. There was trimming, sweeping, and cleaning for starters. I looked at our faded mural and wondered if I might repaint it.

That night, Stephen helped me make the chicken. He was an inventive cook, and he added white wine, red peppers, and a seasoning called Spike. The result was tasty, and we all enjoyed it. While we ate, I asked about taking a day or two to meet my birth father.

"I don't want to put you in a bind by leaving. I won't do it unless you can be here to help," I said to Stephen. I looked back and forth between them. They were both listening without judgment or reaction.

"I haven't asked Beny yet. I wanted to check with you, first. Maybe next week?"

"Yes, of course," said Stephen, his gentle tone putting me at ease. He and Karen had exchanged a nod and a smile. "It's a perfect idea. We can put you on the train, no problem. There's a break in my schedule coming up, so I'll have time to help."

Mom's eyes lit up with inspiration. "And you could meet my brother, Peter! He lives between here and San Diego." She talked to Stephen about towns and roads. I relished her enthusiasm. Soon she was dialing the phone and talking with her brother.

Before bed, I sent my Uncle Peter an email saying I wanted to talk genealogy while we were together. He and I had been in touch over the months as he answered family history questions. We had found a common interest.

In a message to my dad Beny, I explained our idea. Could he pick me up from the train and keep me overnight? The question was quite forward, but the opportunity was too perfect. He might be open to meeting me. As I pressed send, my sudden jitters showed me how invested I was in his answer.

The cat in my room meowed at the window to wake me up on Saturday. I let her out and noticed my dull headache, itchy eyes, and stuffy nose. I guessed I would have to tell someone about my allergy, although I didn't want to put them out. Celine might let her kitten sleep in their room if I explained my discomfort. So far, she'd been at school, at work, or with her fiancée, Josh. I never had a moment to converse with her. I hoped she wasn't avoiding me, but I was so busy, I really didn't mind; my introverted nature craved alone time, really.

Before getting coffee, I checked my email. There was a reply from Beny. My finger hovered a second before clicking. Even though we'd emailed a dozen times, it would be magical to meet my birth father for the first time. My legs bounced as I read his positive response. We'd love to have you. You can stay overnight; we have a good guest bedroom/ bath. The best day for us would be Tuesday the 26th. After I replied, I messaged Uncle Peter and asked if the following day, Wednesday the 27th, worked for him. My travel plans were taking shape.

I spent most of that morning cleaning up the patio. Stephen and I wrestled with the old gazebo cover; I climbed onto the cement wall, and Stephen worked from a stepladder to pry the stiff canvas off its metal frame.

When I went inside for lunch, he called me over to his computer and showed me a new tan canopy he had found. We checked the dimensions, and he ordered it. I was proud that I'd organized an update to their outdoor living space like an eldest daughter would.

That night, Karen and I ate dinner together, again in her bed. We had Indian takeout, and I devoured my fragrant saag paneer while she explained a new hopeful cancer treatment in Budapest.

"Stephen's genius brother Nicolas found out about it," she said. "The facility has heavy water baths that cure patients from around the world! A nurse is coming this week to tell us the details. Stephen thinks this will be the answer for me."

"I wonder how it works," I said, skeptical.

"Something to do with pumping the water full of oxygen," she said. "Anyway, we'll find out." Optimism infused me from the light in my mom's eyes.

Late Sunday afternoon, she emerged from her room with her makeup on, in a striped sweater with a beatific smile on her face. It was Oscar night. She shuffled out of the hall and over to the futon in front of the wide screen television. She beckoned to help her sit, and I took her hand. She had put on her favorite lilac nail polish, and she'd had the energy to dress up. Encouraged, I helped her onto the futon and propped pillows behind her.

"Karyn should be here soon," she said, winded. "Lee called and said she can't make it." I'd miss seeing Lee but looked forward to time with Karyn Rachtman.

Mom flipped on the TV as the red carpet started. I was bringing drinks from the kitchen when Karyn let herself in the front door. She and my mom hooted a greeting, and she knelt for a hug, taking stock of my mom with a smile.

"Hi, Diane! Come and join us," she invited, as she settled into the futon. Energy flowed from her like water from a spring.

I was an outsider, a spectator peering into the life of these two friends, with the years of love that surrounded them. But I was also the luckiest girl ever: thrilled to be here sharing this time with my Oscar-nominated mother. I scooted in next to them and listened to their insiders' comments as the Academy Awards proceeded. I didn't retain much of what I heard; I floated on air.

My mom raved about one movie called Amour. It was a French film nominated for the foreign film category. She turned toward me, using her hands for emphasis as she explained. "Amour is a watershed movie, Diane. It's the unadorned present moment caught by a still camera. The brilliance of the performers draws us into the scene as if we're right there." She applauded when the film won the Oscar.

Karyn and Karen commented about different actors, speaking from personal experience. They knew these people on the screen. These famous actors were the wider circle of my mother's sphere. They were her peers.

At one point, late in the show, I sat in a chair at one side of the room. Mom was still on the futon where she'd nested the whole time. Karyn had curled up in the far corner of the couch looking forlorn, and I didn't know why. Her forehead furrowed; her eyes rimmed with tears. I had an impulse to go sit next to her and take her hand but didn't do it because I didn't know her well enough. The moment passed. Months later, I pieced together the larger perspective I'd missed.

At the previous year's Academy Awards party, my mother had sung "Summertime" with her friend Azalia—the song Stephen had posted on Facebook in October, the one that pierced my heart. Karyn was grappling with the extent of her friend's disease. My mom had been vibrant and healthy just one year ago.

CHAPTER 20

Monday & Tuesday, February 25–26

MONDAY MORNING, while Karen ate her breakfast of fresh pineapple, carrot juice, and yogurt, I mentioned there was a nearby street scene that I wanted to paint. She encouraged me to do it. So, while she rested, I packed up and hiked in dappled shade to the spot, set up my easel on the curb, and painted. A family walked past; their little dark-haired girl skipped along, waving a tree branch. It was darling, and I included her in my small piece.

When I returned after two hours, Karen was in the living room reclining on the sofa with her notebook and phone. She called me over, asking about my time painting. The wet painting was tricky to pull from its carrier. I brought it over, holding it by the edges, and sat down next to her.

"Oh my god, that's lovely!" She raved, "It makes you want to walk right up the street. What warm light. I love the shadows too."

I smiled at her beaming face and sparkling eyes. "You are so good at that, Mom."

"At what?" She asked.

"At making people feel good about themselves."

"Yes," she nodded. "It's what I do. I enhance. Thank you, darling."

Then she put her hand on mine. "So, tomorrow you go to meet Beny." I nodded. "You will love him. He has a gentle nature like yours.

191

And don't worry about me, Stephen has taken the day off to be with me. I'll be fine. Just enjoy yourself. Give him my love."

"Thanks, Mom, I will!" I began to be excited for my trip.

After lunch, I did my laundry and packed my carry-on and computer case. I had photos on my Mac to share with Beny and Joan—glimpses of my childhood, our boys and grandkids.

As I folded my dryer-warm clothes, I reviewed what I knew about this man who was my father. My sister Nina had told me they used to take road trips in a VW bus. When she, Ben and Kirsten were kids, Beny had a hippie vibe with long hair, headband, and a suede jacket with fringe. I chuckled to myself thinking of my "square" adoptive dad with his pocket protector.

Nina was born in Toronto while Beny was Chairman of Theatre at York University. They moved to LA after that, where he was Dean of Theatre at Cal Arts for many years. Then he was president of Ted Danson's Anasazi Productions at Paramount Studios. He won three Emmys and a Peabody; he wrote books and screenplays. His work engaged questions of social justice in compelling and sensitive ways.

The book he had sent me, The Long Italian Goodbye, was on the desk. I flipped to the title page with its handwritten note, To Diane with love, Beny. It was a true but fictionalized account of his boyhood in the Chicago neighborhood of Little Tuscany. In its pages I journeyed with him through a year of his ten-year-old life in the Italian culture I never knew. I met my grandparents and great-grandparents through his eyes. He even included family recipes. The book was priceless to me.

And now I would meet him in person. I was intimidated by his achievements but wasn't as nervous as stepping through Karen's front door the first time. There was a calm expectancy and a hope for connection. Tomorrow I would find another big piece of myself.

Tuesday morning Stephen drove me to the Amtrak station. On the Coaster, I got a window seat on the west side and watched the breakers crash as we swept by the sea on the four-hour trip.

Surfers bobbed on boards and gulls swooped for fish from the cloudy sky. I dreamed of family reunions. There had been several Ziegler get-togethers, before I connected with Karen, at the beach near my Uncle Peter's home south of LA. Peter and I planned to meet in Oceanside on my way back tomorrow. He would bring his genealogy photos to share more about my roots.

My thoughts turned to the fast-approaching reunion with Beny. I wanted to stand up and announce to the train car, I'm going to meet my father for the first time! The clouds dissipated, and the sun shone through to match my mood.

The San Diego stop approached. I gathered my things and disembarked into balmy air under the shade of a long, covered platform. I followed the crowd, my bag clunking along behind me. In the sunlight near the end of the station, a tall man and dark-haired woman watched the train riders walk toward them. They were Beny and Joan; I was sure. Strolling at an even pace to keep my composure, I looked up to see tears glinting on Joan's cheeks. I exhaled; I hadn't realized I was holding my breath. I studied my birth father's face and noticed his brown eyes and droopy eyelids were like mine. But that was about all I observed; I was so thrilled to be with him I couldn't hold a straight thought.

"There she is!" Joan said, and they both smiled. I stepped up and said hi. My father gathered me into a hug, and his wife gave me a tender embrace.

"How was your trip?" She asked.

"Wonderful! I got to photograph the ocean." I held their hands and gazed at them, thankful to be there. My father was a substantial presence with thick hands and gentle brown eyes. His voice was soft, not booming as I had imagined it to be. Joan was about my height with fine features and a hint of wrinkles at the corners of her eyes.

"We enjoy riding the Coaster from time to time," Beny was saying. "Let me take your bag." He turned and led us down a ramp to the parking lot.

"We thought we'd show you Balboa Park first," said Joan, "and there's a good restaurant there. Want to grab lunch?"

"Sounds great," I replied, my belly rumbling in agreement.

We dined at the Spanish-themed Prado restaurant overlooking the park, a spacious area of gardens and turn-of-the-century buildings. Balboa Park was the site of the 1915-16 Panama-California Exposition, a World's Fair. While we waited for our food, our conversation was pleasant and natural. My tension unwound. I showed them my new Fuji camera, and Joan offered to take a photo of me and Beny. It still hangs on my wall, our expressions full of delight.

With the food in front of us, I asked if I could say grace. They nodded, and we grasped hands while I thanked God for our time together. When I opened my eyes, they smiled. During the meal we chatted, telling stories back and forth: of how I met Karen and of places they had lived; of their kids and grandkids and my boys and grandsons. Beny realized his new status as a great-grandpa.

Their keen interest in what I had to say was genuine. This was something I'd seen in all of my new family: each of them was inquisitive about me, so we conversed in an atmosphere of curiosity and celebration.

After lunch, I handed Joan the camera again. As she got ready to shoot, Beny reached over and put his arm around me, and I became possessive of him at that moment, like I was with Karen. From then on, I thought of him as my dad.

We drove to a downtown high-rise, parked under the building, and took an elevator to their condo. Beny introduced me to their two chestnut brown dogs as we walked in. Their wagging tails and the brisk ruffling he gave them showed how much he loved them. We stepped into a great room with a balcony overlooking the city. The decor was modern, and a stark contrast to photos I'd seen of their warm, southwestern adobe home in Santa Fe. Cool colors and contemporary furnishings were the theme here. Joan showed me to their guest room where I unpacked and typed a few notes. Beny is sweet, like Karen said, and I love Joan too, I felt relaxed right away!

We soon left again, driving to Point Loma, hoping the overcast sky would break in time for a sunset. We entered Cabrillo Park just before closing time and headed down to an ocean access lot. The clouds continued, the salt spray crashed, and gurgles of waves washed the rocky shore. Too soon a ranger drove up and said the park was closing.

Joan offered me the front passenger seat, so I could chat with Beny. I climbed in next to my father. Dinner was next on the agenda, and as we drove, they took turns describing our destination, one of their favorite spots, The Fish Market Restaurant on San Diego Bay. They chatted about the food and the view, and a Bob Hope Memorial they wanted to show me. I soaked it all in.

Then after a pause, I spoke. "Beny, may I ask you something?"

"By all means," he said, nodding, with an open expression on his face.

"I'd like to know a little about your relationship with Karen. How long were you together?"

"Well, I'd say about three years. We met right away when I started at Northwestern. I've forgotten what class we shared, but I was enamored of her from the beginning. We moved in together, with my buddies near campus. It was a comfortable arrangement. The third year she left for New York with a group of our classmates. It was over between us by then, anyway. They went to make it on stage; New York was the place to be in theatre. I stayed behind—although I thought about going with them and often wondered how different my life's trajectory would have been—but there's no use speculating. At the time, I wanted to pursue stage lighting. I took a job at the Court Theatre at the University of Chicago."

He paused, so I ventured another question. "Why did you two break up? Did you grow apart?"

"Her going to New York was a relief of sorts. I didn't have to break it off. She left. And I had known from the start her career came first.

She was my first great love, and I still love her as a friend, but some people just aren't meant to be together. Let's just say, she brought out the worst in me. She was…" he hesitated, "… She could be a bit volatile."

I thought about the day I overheard the fight between Karen and Celine, back in September. Celine had said they fought now and then. I'd also read a couple old articles that had painted Karen Black's character in a cloudy light. And I'd seen her vigor firsthand—she, already gaunt from disease, with more energy and drive than anyone I'd ever known. To imagine her as hard to live with was not a stretch.

"If Karen had raised me, I suppose my life would have been more turbulent," I reasoned. Beny raised his eyebrows and pursed his lips; I heard a murmur of assent from Joan in the back seat. I was dismayed at my thought: Karen might not have been much better a mom than the one I'd had. This felt disloyal, but there it was. And then a new notion: Beny might have raised me, too.

I considered this man who shared my DNA, who had answered my questions so candidly. He reminded me of my adoptive father. They both were even-keeled men, thoughtful and laid-back. Beny's understated expressions of emotion were very much like my other dad's, although Don had been a Silent Generation man a full twenty years his senior. I was glad I had been raised by a father with a calm demeanor like Beny's.

"Thanks for talking about it," I told him, unsure of how to explain everything I was feeling: the pull of being grateful for finding Karen while a part of me was grateful for not finding her sooner. And my wish that he had been in my life.

"I'm glad to," he said plainly.

"Do you have anything you want to ask me?" I ventured.

He paused. "What were your parents like?"

I told him about my dad, Don: his patience, his love for old-time radio and jazz music. That he was a speech therapist who worked with grade school kids and then stroke victims. He was very intelligent but couldn't change a light bulb. I chuckled. I told him about the time when Rich and I were still in high school, and Rich was at my house. He noticed that our basement door didn't have a doorknob, only a hook-and-eye latch. He asked me why, and I said it had always been that way. It turned out my dad had no idea how to fix it. Rich bought a knob assembly and installed it, impressing my father no end.

Joan asked about my mother then. I shrugged as I told them about her breakdown when I was five; that my dad raised me and Denise; that our mother, Jodie, was never the same after that. But I was glad for my formative years, I said, glad for my early memories of helping my mom in my sweet preschool life. I remembered good days baking chocolate chip cookies and playing in the backyard.

They listened to my stories until we pulled into a parking lot.

The sky had cleared, and dusk softened to a pale rose. We walked past smooth-barked coral trees toward the restaurant at the water's edge. We stopped at a statuary tribute to Bob Hope's USO tours during World War II. My other father would have loved it.

Inside, we took an elevator upstairs to quiet loft seating. At our table beneath a window, we looked out at the bay. The first stars winked in the twilight. We ordered wine with our dinner, and while we ate and drank, we talked frankly about family and life. As the conversation wandered along the years, I felt like their generational peer. We had so much in common, like raising three children to adulthood, surviving their teen years and learning to let them go. My stepsister, Kirsten, who was just a year my senior, was a child at their wedding and was off to college while they raised Ben and Nina.

We described our childhoods, and the world we grew up in—though twenty years apart—was very similar. Landline telephones, burgeoning suburbs with tree-lined streets, no internet, playing outside until the streetlights came on. We shared nostalgia for that simpler life, along with moments of angst—like the time our youngest son, Ricky, ran away when he was twelve. Beny and Joan revealed that Nina had also run away when she was fourteen. We talked like family.

At some point I paused, putting down my fork. "I feel almost like we've always been family."

"You make us feel comfortable with you, too," said Joan, thoughtfully.

Beny added, "This does feel like a homecoming."

The moment resonated with the same sense of bonding I had experienced with Karen.

Later, back at their condo, I brought my computer into the living room and sat down next to Beny to show him the photos I'd brought. I leaned toward him as I scrolled. He asked questions here and there. Joan sat in a chair nearby, taking it all in. I was calm and cozy, curled next to my birth father.

I woke early for the train on Wednesday, packed and walked out to the quiet living area, wondering if I should raid the fridge. But I was the last one up.

"You want pancakes?" Beny asked, with batter in a bowl.

"Sure!" I answered. Soon the griddle sizzled, and the room filled with a warm sweet aroma.

Joan and I sat at the table. "So, Karen's brother Peter will pick you up at the Solana Beach station?" She asked.

"Yep. We'll have lunch, and he'll show me family pictures. Did I tell you two, he's the one who put all the information on Karen's family into the genealogy databases? That's the reason I found enough information to build a whole family tree on Ancestry.com."

Beny said, "I think we have a chart somewhere at the Santa Fe house, of my mother's family lineage in Italy. When we get home in a couple weeks, I'll see if I can dig it up for you."

"Thanks, that'd be so great! You might well imagine my fascination."

He nodded. "My parents' families, way back on both sides, all lived in a few tiny villages—called communes—in the area around

Pescia, the city of flowers, in Tuscany. We went there in the late eighties—I can post photos for you to see, also. It is gorgeous country, and we still have loads of family over there."

"I have cousins in Italy?" I exclaimed. I would have to look them up on Facebook. We finished breakfast, and I got my belongings together.

Joan met me at the door. "I'll say goodbye here, dear. I have a meeting this morning." We hugged. "It's been wonderful getting to know you."

"Thanks for being willing to meet me, and for all your hospitality."

Beny and I and took the elevator to the parking garage. We pulled out into a sunny morning, and he surprised me with a stop at an art supply store, where he bought me a set of my favorite watercolor pencils as a birthday gift. We arrived at the train station a bit early and drove on past the tracks. At a breezy waterside market, we chatted and strolled, making small talk, keeping it light. I sensed that he was most comfortable avoiding emotionality. In that way, too, he was like the man who raised me. We rode back and unloaded my luggage as the train pulled into the station.

Beny walked with me down the platform, pulling my suitcase. It was time to say goodbye, and I choked up in spite of myself. I stepped on board and Beny lifted my bag to me. I turned to face him. Our eyes were wet as I hugged his neck. He hugged back.

"Bye, Daddy," I said, the whispered word out before I even thought it.

"Bye, honey," he said, and I let him go, backed up a step, and watched him walk away, in wonder at our special time together. *He's my daddy*, I repeated as I boarded, wiping my tears away.

CHAPTER 21

Wednesday–Sunday, February 27–March 3

THE TRAIN RIDE TO SOLANA BEACH was short, and the morning was still fresh. I waited in front of the station in the sun until my Uncle Peter drove up in a cream-colored sedan with round edges. He got out, gave me a timid hug, and put my bag in the trunk. His movements were stiff, his straight thin frame on the edge of elderly. Peter was the oldest of the three Ziegler siblings; Karen was his youngest sister. He seemed introverted like me, and I worried we might have an awkward time.

With sporadic chit-chat, we drove a few miles to a seaside restaurant. Once there, a hostess led us past stained glass windows to a patio rimmed with boulders fronting the shoreline breakers. Surfers strolled by with their boards. A seagull floated around the umbrella-shaded tables, eyeing us, waiting for scraps. In this relaxing atmosphere I began to feel comfortable, and he seemed to also. We clicked over a common passion: genealogy.

"You know we tried to find you last spring," Peter said. "But without your adopted name, it was impossible. And Karen refused to put her name on the indexes, for fear of shysters. They'd targeted her before."

"Yes, she told me. Twice people claimed she was their mother, except the dates were wrong. But it was easy for me to find her once I got my birth certificate."

After lunch he spoke to a host who found us a quiet room to occupy, and then we brought in Peter's three-inch binders from his trunk. It felt like Christmas.

We sat side by side scouring through pages of sepia images with their hand-typed captions. I was transported through time to my childhood; Peter's voice, with the tenor of age, his binders, and his keen interest in the family history, all reminded me of my adoptive dad. How Dad K—then and there I renamed my adoptive father— how he would have loved to hear all I'd discovered! With a pang of grief, I wished I could still call him and relate my adventures.

My new uncle spoke with enthusiasm about his genealogy search back in the 1980s. He handed me stapled family record sheets, and as I skimmed them, I asked how he'd found these mounds of facts before the internet age.

"Each data point required looking up the original records," he answered. "I worked a short walk from the National Archives in Washington DC, so I spent many lunch hours researching rolls of microfiche census forms. Also, I visited Manitowoc where my mother's family immigrated in the 1840s. I inspected the original entries in their vital record books, something no one can do today. And I ordered records from state agencies at my expense. Everything took over a decade to gather."

"I'm so impressed!" I told him. He loved this stuff, and I must have been his best audience in years. I floated through it all, sitting with my legs tucked under me on the wooden chair like a kid. Captivated. My own people were here on these pages, in faded black and white.

We continued our way through the binders. Then Peter paused, his fingers ready to turn a binder leaf. "I think you will like this next one."

He flipped the page. I gasped. It was a color photo of Karen and Beny. I had never imagined that one existed—a picture of my mother and father when they were dating. Yet there they stood, dressed for an event with Karen's siblings and their dates in front of vintage curtains. Both wore black—Beny, hair slicked back, in a suit and thin red tie, Karen in a low-cut evening dress, dark curls around her face. They leaned into each other, grinning with the comfort of a well-matched pair.

I put my hand on Peter's. "You can't know how much it means to see this." I pressed my lips together to refrain from sobbing. I snapped a photo of the image, and he promised to email a scan. A waitress took our picture. Peter might add us to another binder, for the next generation to see. Too soon I had to catch the train to LA. This journey through time with my uncle had made him dear to me.

The way home was a long sunset over glimpsed beaches, bobbing surfers, and calm seas. The tracks clacked a rhythm as the coast flew by as fast as the years captured in Uncle Peter's books. I mused over both days with a fullness in my chest, thankful for the connections I had made.

The bed creaked as I sat next to Karen to say goodnight. Dim light drifted in the open doorway. Her cool hand rested in mine. A pillow framed her face, her legs propped just-so as if she hadn't moved in the two days I'd been away. Her world, once encompassing continents, had shrunk within these walls. The darkness my trip had dispelled washed over me. My voice cracked, but I tried to speak with zest. "Our visit was wonderful and perfect, mom! I love Beny. You were right, he's cozy. And Joan accepted me with open arms. We connected like family."

"I knew you'd love them, darling! I want to hear all about it tomorrow."

I retreated to my bedroom, where my feelings finally found their way to the surface. The joy of my reunion with Beny and Joan and the delight of discovering the photo of my birth parents collided with the grief of seeing Karen nearly bedridden and the terror of the unknowable future. I hung my head in my hands, feeling like an expressionist painting brought to life.

The next day, I stepped quietly into Karen's room to clear her breakfast tray, computer tucked under my arm. The California sun shone through the rose-printed curtains, illuminating the wispy curls that haloed her gaunt face. When I slid her half-eaten meal over and settled next to her on the four-poster bed, she smiled up at me and asked about my trip. I recounted my two days away. Then I paused. My heart flipped. "I have something to show you, Mom," I said, turning the computer toward her. "Uncle Peter had this snapshot in his binder."

Karen scooted upright, wincing with the effort. She peered at the vintage image on the screen and her blue eyes sparkled. "Oh my God!" She whispered. "I remember that dress and that night. Beny and I were going to a dance."

She leaned back, her fingers brushing the screen as if she could touch the past. "We had such good times, Diane. One of my best memories of Beny happened on a Saturday when he picked me up from the maternity home. I was pregnant—with you…." She paused and tears welled in her eyes as she related the story of their warm, pink day on the rocky shore of Lake Michigan.

As she spoke, my mind saw them smiling and content. Beny leaped over the waves between boulders and beckoned to Karen, who laughed and jumped and caught his hand.

She continued, "The safety pin holding my slacks up had opened! The point stuck into my stomach. When I showed him, he said, 'See, you were so happy you didn't even feel it.'"

I was silent, imprinting her story into my memory before asking, "Why did you break up, Mom?" I needed to hear her point of view.

"We really loved each other, Diane. But he was more like a pal, a chum," she explained. "We grew apart, and then I moved to New York, and he didn't."

In contrast, I stayed with someone who had been a friend first, and who was still more companion than lover. Rich and I shared a quiet love; Karen had searched for passion. It seemed she'd found both in Stephen.

After cleaning up breakfast I headed to my room and emailed the photo to Beny. He forwarded it to me and my siblings, Ben, Nina, and Kirsten, with this comment that cracked me up:

Wow! I think this is 1958, a year before Diane. Isn't Karen beautiful! And I'm ready for Jersey Boys!

That photo cemented them as a couple in my mind: There was a time my birth parents were together, and there's proof. They loved each other, and they loved me. I was picking up pieces of my identity, getting them to fit in a puzzle that for fifty years I only dreamed existed. A wish formed. To have a day with both of them together— the three of us, as a family. A desperate hope, maybe, a doubtful dream for a fading future. But so many dreams had come true, this one might too.

The next day I phoned Rich, excited to relate my trek into self-hood. After listening to me, he expressed the strain he was under at home. Denise was agitated, and he was exhausted, caring for her on top of working the busy spring fishing season. I was conflicted, wanting to head home to help, but with hopes set on being where I was, too. Karen was giving me a birthday party on March 8, I explained sheepishly, and she had already invited people. He sighed his understanding. I pulled up Southwest Airlines on my computer and we found an affordable flight on March 10.

After my trip to meet Beny and Peter, the days began to blend together. Patio work took up my mornings while Karen slept. Cleaning and sprucing, digging and raking. I wanted to surprise my mom when she was well enough to venture outdoors. The exertion was a release from my nervous tension.

On one of these mornings, I found a baby palm tree growing above the retaining wall. I loosened the orphan's roots, gave it a new home in a large pot I'd found in their garage, and placed it on the patio with other plants. Another day I attacked a brittle, twisted jasmine vine hidden in a corner. After deciding it looked alive enough to save, I unwound the brown tendrils from the green ones, and then gave it a good watering. On summer evenings, the courtyard would fill with the heavenly aroma of its blossoms. I decided my work here was a metaphor for what I hoped I was doing in Karen's life—healing old wounds, letting the sun in.

I finished sweaty and tired, ready for a shower, but peaceful and calm, after investing myself in the work and forgetting my ongoing skydive through emotional storm clouds.

This became my routine. At midday I'd be back in the kitchen, blending the juice of fresh lemons with olive oil and tamari sauce, then pouring this dressing into a bowl of mixed greens. Her lunch tray in my arms, I entered her room, set it beside her and rolled up the broken shades to bring in the California sunshine. She sat with pen in hand, papers strewn over the sheets, sometimes reading a screenplay sent to her for advice, other times talking on her phone to a publicist or a friend, or making a list of ideas, or in the midst of any of a dozen other tasks. As Celine once told me, "She lives in her bed."

Afternoons included two or three hours with Karen in the living room. We watched TV most days, swaddled in the futon on the floor. Then she would disappear into her bedroom, napping once again. She used her phone to call me or Celine or Stephen to bring her things.

One evening, almost two weeks into my stay, she called me. "Are you okay?" She asked after I'd answered the phone. "You seemed over-tired or over-something. You know if I do anything that is perplexing or irritating, or some kind of dumb thing, you can actually tell me. I want you to be happy."

With my phone to my ear, I grinned. "I'm okay, just feeling worn out. It's not you," I assured her, and meant it.

"Well, make sure you get enough rest," she insisted. I loved her motherly concern.

Another day, I navigated LA traffic from behind the wheel of their BMW, heading to a urologist appointment. Mom whimpered in pain from her prone position on the back seat. Stephen reached over to squeeze her hand while he gave me driving directions. He had asked me to drive so he could be available for Karen. I was once again grateful to be a help in her need—even while terrified of the LA traffic.

Karen's voice, heavy with pain, became wistful. "I still can't believe you're here. Thank you for being so wonderful to me. It's so much for me to take in. Why would you do all this?"

I gave my honest answer. "I am here to love you, Mom!"

When we had parked in a garage next to a medical building, Stephen helped Karen walk, her anguish clear in her stooped posture and uneven gait. A nurse ushered us into a lush office.

We took seats against a wall. The doctor entered and sat behind a desk, seeming to tower over us. He explained a procedure to replace a stent, which would relieve Mom's pain-inducing pressure. I listened while keeping my eyes on Karen to make sure she followed his train of thought. When she tried to express a concern, he glossed over it. I interrupted and reworded her question and got a response, proud to have done something an adult child should do: advocate for her mother.

On our slow, careful walk back to the car, she said as much. Her keen eyes looked at me as she spoke. "You were a daughter to me in there."

"I was trying to be." I asserted.

Later that week, I was folding my laundry when I heard a lot of clunking and squeaking from the living room. I headed down the hall to find Stephen busy setting up lamps, a large umbrella for ambient light and a tripod for his camera. Equipment and cords had taken over the area by the front door. The love seat was facing it all, and Karen was just sitting down, wearing makeup and a cashmere sweater. She looked as good as when I'd first met her. I questioned Stephen, gesturing to the gear.

"We're filming her acceptance speech for an achievement award. Why don't you sit in the dining room and watch?" He was all business.

I curled up on the extra sofa in the dining room office, content to witness my mom in her element.

Her measured voice was gracious as she accepted the award, expressing her love for her fans, smiling and looking at the camera the entire time.

After Stephen turned out the bright lights, he brought the camera to his makeshift studio and uploaded the video. Karen slid down and rested prone in the love seat.

When Stephen showed me the video a few minutes later, I was riveted. I'd seen her do this a minute ago, but, wow, this was not the same. The Karen on the screen was looking into me, speaking to my soul, impacting me with her words.

"How is this what I just watched you record? It seems so different, so… personal!" I stammered in amazement. They chuckled.

"This is what Karen does. She creates connection."

"I'll say!" My eyes were wide in admiration as I gazed at my mother, who had made the effort to connect with me, also.

"There's no scrim between me and my audience," Karen explained, her hand swooshing to the side. "No barrier. My connection is open and clear as if they are right in front of me. I'm always aware of them and confronting the fact they are there with me. I learned this early, at about fifteen, practicing for a school play in front of my friend Charlie Black. My character looked directly into his eyes. The barrier just fell, and it has been gone ever since."

Days later, Stephen showed me a recording of the awards ceremony. When the audience applauded, tears of pride blurred my vision.

CHAPTER 22

Monday–Saturday, March 4–9

I OPENED MY EYES and my heart skipped a beat. It was March 4, my birthday, and I was with the one who'd birthed me.

My nervous energy spilled into physical activity all morning, as I cleaned patio furniture, cooked soup, and straightened the kitchen.

I drove Karen to the Angeles Clinic for her CT scan appointment after lunch. She introduced me with a great flourish to the staff. Then we entered a private room. While we waited, she wanted to talk about childhood books we both read.

We agreed that *Heidi* was our favorite. Young Heidi's yearning for the freedom of the outdoors, and her love of being with nature, resonated in both of our hearts. The story affected my mom so much she never let herself read it again—for fear of tainting that blissful memory!

And we both treasured the Oz series by L. Frank Baum.

"Do you remember the scene where Dorothy discovered the queen had many heads?" She asked.

"Sure, I do, I loved that."

"I thought that was the greatest idea! What a cool ability!"

"Hey, Mom," I said, sitting forward. "Guess what? It's 3:30; the exact time I was born."

She switched gears and got a faraway look in her eyes. I expected excitement, but she was pensive and spoke with sincerity. She took my hand. "Don't tell Celine, but I think I might be dying."

Hearing this from her lips made my muscles tighten. I nodded and promised not to tell, disheartened at her reaction to what I thought would be a meaningful moment. She'd been frank about her experience of my birth, so I doubted she was avoiding the topic. Later I reflected that she might have felt safe enough to share her fear with me, but that day I ached. I was quiet for the ride home, trying to shake off the disappointment. I phoned Rich from my room and asked him to pray for me. I was becoming emotionally exhausted. He encouraged me to rest and think on the good things.

Late that evening the mood was light once again. We ate Indian food and celebrated my birthday as a family, lounging around the coffee table while I opened my gifts. Celine gave me a beaded choker and a bracelet she had made for me; Mom handed me two boxes: a shirt she had worn in a movie and a photo album filled with pictures of my newfound relatives, past and present. Stephen chuckled as he told me how they'd worked on it in secret all week.

Her card filled me with warmth:

Thank you for making something so extraordinary and full of wonder happen to me. Your beauty of soul, your will, have brought us together and enhance our family and our lives beyond speech. Happy, Happiest of Birthdays!

Then, she offered me one last gift box. Inside was an exquisite pendant, a large amber stone set in silver filigree, tarnished with age.

"That was your Grandma Elsie's," she said. Speechless, I cradled my heirloom in my palm. My grandmother had held this treasure; it was a connection I could keep.

Seeing how I loved it, my mom's face lit up with an idea. "I have her autobiography in a binder, Diane. You can read it while you're here."

"May I get a copy made at Kinko's? Then I can take it home." And cherish it forever, my mind added. My mom said yes. I looked at each of them, smiling through thankful tears.

———••·———

It was Friday, March 8, the day of the birthday celebration Karen had planned. I wasn't as excited as before the party back in September. That seemed long ago, when I had been full of youthful wonder, still naïve about the seriousness of her condition.

In contrast, this day proceeded with sobriety. I helped Karen eat and pick out clothes, going into her closet to bring out what she wanted. While we did this, I asked a question I hoped she'd say yes to. "Mom, could you put your eye makeup on me?"

"Oh, not now, Diane, I'm getting ready for tonight," she answered.

A few minutes after I'd returned to my room disenchanted, Stephen called me back into Karen's room.

"The reason you asked me to do your makeup was for the party, wasn't it?" She asked.

"Yes, I was hoping so," I nodded, glad she understood now.

She smiled. "Come on over here. I've got my cake eyeliner ready. Can you kneel so I can reach you?"

She sat on the edge of her bed, and I knelt on the floor in front of her. It was nice to feel her hands on my face—like my own touch, so natural. Her breath was without odor, just soft puffs on my skin. She concentrated and focused on my eyes.

"I draw my eyes on in watercolor," she explained as she dabbed a black cream above my lids with a tiny brush. "I create the shadow, darker at the back of the eyelid where light can't go, and a paler hue as I go up toward the brow. This makes it seem that I actually have eyes.

"Another trick is to put my false lashes above the outside corners of my eyes, and then bring my actual lashes up and glue them to the ends of the false ones. You don't want to try that, do you?"

I shook my head. Then she instructed, "hold still…it's hard to paint the little folds of skins on the corner of your eyelids…there, that'll do." She sat back, appraising her work.

"Thank you so much!" I shone up at her. Stephen took our picture as she worked.

In my room, I took close-up photos, to assist my imitation of her trademark eyes. Later that evening, several wide-eyed guests said how much I looked like Karen.

After the makeup moment, Stephen and I brought my mom out to the big ochre sofa and made her comfortable. She was fragile and stunning, an angel dressed in her plum sweater and fresh-water pearl necklace, placed just-so on pillows.

The first two guests arrived. Our red-haired Angela introduced me to a dark-haired Dana, who had a playful sparkle in her eyes. The two of them helped bring Karen's vision for the evening to life. They toted in decorations and food, set up serving ware on pretty linens, and achieved a party atmosphere. A candelabra appeared on the glass coffee table. Wine bottles lined the counter. All the while chatting and taking cheerful directions from Karen, Angela and Dana worked a magical transformation. I helped where I could. As others arrived, the three of us sat down on puffy ottomans in a corner.

"Have I told you, Diane, I'm jealous of you? I often wished Karen was my mother," Angela confessed, smiling. "My mom was not the nurturing type."

"Thanks! And the woman who raised me wasn't nurturing either," I said.

Dana nodded agreement, and the three of us shared stories of small childhood un-niceties, like harsh hair brushing, until my mom beckoned me over to meet a guest.

"This is my great friend, Don Moss," she told me. A middle-aged man with graying hair held her hands in his. He greeted me with a smile. "He's been encouraging me to get the Budapest treatments," my mom said.

"Karen's told me all about you, Diane," Don said. Then he extended an arm to a slender woman standing nearby and introduced me to his graceful wife Alexa. She and I found two chairs and chatted while Don bent beside Karen, speaking in quiet tones.

We exchanged small talk, and then she asked how I found Karen. After I told my story in brief, she wondered how my adoptive parents felt about our reunion.

"They passed years ago, so I didn't have to face their reactions. Although, my dad would have celebrated with me, been interested in all I'm doing and the genealogy I've found."

"And your mother?" She asked.

I sighed. "My mom would have feared I meant to hurt her. She was emotionally unstable, so I'm glad she didn't have to deal with it."

Alexa nodded pensively. We continued to chat, but soon my mom waved me over again. I excused myself and stood up. With a flourish of her arm Karen loudly announced, "Everyone, this is my daughter, Diane!"

My ears rang with a rush of blood, and I'm sure I was bright red as I looked around at a sea of smiling faces. There was a smattering of applause and raised wine glasses.

I knelt on the floor near her as she talked me up, had a guest bring her my plein-air painting and praised it, and told the story of the letter I'd sent, the one I wrote at eighteen.

"It was a real communication," she said with pride. "She expressed her teenage heart." Her public approval did my grown-up heart good.

Stephen wandered through the party, chatting and recording all night. He had done this so often, the camera had become an extension of his arm, and I made a face at him as he walked by pointing the lens at me.

Russell Brown, a young friend of Karen's, told me how much she meant to him. He had directed her in a recent film and convinced her to give a lesson on acting. They'd recorded it just two weeks before my arrival. While we talked, Lee Purcell and Celine sat near the front door, away from the crowd, leaning close together. Lee seemed to be speaking words of encouragement; Karen's illness was a heavy burden on young Celine.

They hugged, and Lee stood up to look around. Finding my eyes, she came over and embraced me as well. Her leopard-print shirt matched her amber hair and light brown eyes. She pulled me into the hallway, away from the party. We stepped into my room and sat together, she on the twin bed, I in the rolling chair. Out of her sack she pulled a small present, also wrapped in animal print.

"Happy Birthday!" She said. It was a stunning pair of sterling drop earrings.

"Oh, Lee they're beautiful!" I leaned my head as I put them on.

She told me Karen had always remembered me on my birthday. "I encouraged her to sign up for the reunion registries, but that's not the way she works. That's too official."

I thought about the years I had waited, hoping for my birth mother to put her name on those lists.

Then Lee reached for my hands and took a deep breath. "Be brave. This cancer...she might not beat it." I grimaced. She continued, "Say everything you need to say. Nothing is too small or too big or too stupid. If you want to know what her favorite color was when she was five, ask. And call me, anytime, for anything." She squeezed my hands. Wiping tears, we rejoined the others.

Back in the living room, I did a double take at a bird perched on a man's shoulder. Curious, I went to investigate, joining two young people on the ottomans. They introduced themselves as Aleisha and Byron Gore. She wore vivacious colors, and he was in all black, including a fedora. Their bird, gray and bigger than a parakeet, was just now preening itself.

"May I hold him?" I ventured. I looked over at Karen, wondering if she'd seen this, wishing to show her. She was deep in a conversation, so I turned back.

"His name is Burden." Byron lifted him toward me. "I don't know if he'll let you," he said.

I knew how to place my hand under a bird and push up, so Burden stepped onto my finger. We eyed each other. The young couple eyed me. I put my forehead against Burden's head, covering his back with my free hand, smelling his wonderful wispy bird scent, feeling his feathery softness and his trembling fragileness. I took a few fragrant breaths, then thanked him and handed him back.

The couple looked at me with something akin to awe, or maybe it was shock. Byron said, "He's never let anyone do that before."

Aleisha asked how I had connected with Karen. I rocked back, hands laced around a knee, and related my story: finding her in ten seconds, waiting two weeks to hear from her, and reading her lovely Facebook reply that had changed my life. Their faces reflected awe again.

Soon there came a break in the buzz of the evening as Stephen's voice called for quiet. Karen was scooting up to a sitting position as he hooked up a small audio device on the coffee table. He motioned us all to crowd around for an announcement. This came as a surprise; they hadn't told me they'd do this.

Friends already surrounded Karen on the couch, but the wide backrest was free, so I reclined above her, reaching down to squeeze her hand. Russell saw where I was, smiled and climbed up at the other end. There was anticipation in the air.

"We have been learning a great deal about a hopeful treatment option for Karen," Stephen began, as soon as everyone settled. "The doctor in charge of the facility in Budapest traveled here to meet us. Here's what he had to say."

Stephen played the audio. The doctor had been to the house the day I was in San Diego with Beny and Joan. The recording explained how the heavy water treatment worked, the steps needed for Karen to take part, and what outcome they could expect. As it played, real hope for a cure filled me for the first time in months.

"So, what we'd like, to begin with, are frequent flier miles to get her over there," Stephen said, when the audio silenced. "And your ideas for making this happen."

A lively discussion developed as thoughts bounced around the crowd. The biggest takeaway was the unanimous vote for a Go-Fund-Me page. I had never heard of crowdfunding. It had taken hold on the internet a year earlier, in 2012, after a new law made it possible for people to publicize their efforts to raise money. Independent film-makers loved it, and it worked. Everyone was sure Karen's fan base would respond.

The next day, my last at the house, Stephen and I put up the new gazebo cover. Then all three of us worked on the GoFundMe page. On my computer, I cropped a photo Stephen had taken on our first day together and put the image of Karen on the page we developed. They wrote the copy that would encourage and reward people for taking part. Enthusiasm began to infuse me.

Evening came with its mellow light drifting through the living room skylight. While we talked about the fundraiser, Mom asked if I would come along to Budapest and care for her during the weeks of her treatment. Thrilled, I said yes, as long as we brought in enough money to pay for my tickets. We chatted and dreamed of her recovery—and, while we'd be in Europe, traveling to Prague together, to see our ancestral homeland. The view was rosy through the colored glasses of our imagination.

Outside under the twilight tinted sky, I rested in a wicker chair on the transformed patio. Stephen helped Karen out the back door. I couldn't wait to see her reaction to all my hard work. As they rounded the corner, she noticed the new gazebo cover first and liked it. But, instead of exclaiming joy, she focused on a piece of furniture that had broken earlier in the day, under Stephen's weight, as he put up the new canopy. She said, "Where is my wicker love seat? Why did you replace it with this old piece of junk?"

Injured, I responded, "This piece broke today, and Stephen can fix it. I was trying out a new arrangement, it's no big deal to put it back the way you had it." Then I retrieved the love seat from around a corner and let her direct me to put it outside the gazebo. She lowered herself to a comfortable half-prone position in it, and I pulled my chair next to her. Stephen left us.

We chatted together as the sun set behind the house and a deep purple settled on the sky. After a time, she said, "I wish you would tell me anything that's troubling you, anything different you wish I'd do."

I wished she'd have celebrated all my hard work. She had deflated me with her lack of gratitude, but I didn't voice the thought. "I'm just glad to be here, to help you, to be part of this family," I said instead. This was also true.

"You're avoiding the question."

"Caught me," I responded, smiling and looking at her sidelong. "Well, I wish you would have noticed my effort on this patio. I spent a good deal of time sprucing it up for you."

She looked over and noticed the vines tucked in the corner. "Oh, the jasmine looks lovely! It will smell heavenly this summer. Thank you. Thank you for all of it."

She was facing away from most of the newness I'd achieved: the new palm tree in its pot, the trailing vines cascading onto the patio wall. And she was in pain. I winced, feeling selfish for wanting kudos.

I hadn't been as honest as I could have been with her. There were a couple of things that irked me: she still did not let me post that she was my mother on Facebook, and she hadn't looked at the photos and videos I'd brought, although I'd asked several times. But, in that moment, the fear of losing her love trumped frankness. I relied on her like a boat at the mooring in a storm: too much honesty might untie the rope of acceptance holding us together. But the decision to withhold my negative comments may have kept a deeper relationship from blossoming. It was fear I listened to, even in the midst of the brave things I was doing.

The next morning, I packed to go. In the semi-darkness of their room, I crawled into the four-poster bed and kissed my birth mother. Her lips were as soft as rose petals. I touched her smooth face with my fingertips, held my tears, and tried to memorize the moment.

We did not say the word *goodbye*.

CHAPTER 23

April & May

RICH MET ME AT THE NASHVILLE AIRPORT and drove me home after my long three-week stay. Seeing him put me at ease like coming home after a long trip always does. This time, instead of my liveliness after my first week with Karen, I was sedate. As we rode, we exchanged stories. One of his guiding trips included a family with four kids who all caught their first fish. His grin showed his delight, and my mood lifted. Halfway home I explained the Budapest treatment that could save Karen.

"She wants me to go with her," I said, turning toward him, wondering how he'd react.

"To Hungary?" He asked, glancing at me with consternation. I knew his answer already.

"Yes, and if she gets better like we expect, we can go visit Prague where our ancestors lived," I said in a last-ditch effort.

His face grew grave. "Let me think about it."

I frowned and tried not to lose hope.

When we walked in our door, Denise cried as she rushed up for a hug. She needed sameness and routine, and these long trips away were "upsetting her apple cart," as our mom used to say. The first thing she did was show me a scrape on her arm. She was relieved to have me back at home. We hugged. It was calming to be here, to be back to normalcy.

After I unpacked my bags, I checked GoFundMe and gasped at the donations posted. As days went by, Rich and I watched in amazement as Karen's fans poured out their support and the total swooped toward the goal of $30,000, and then surpassed it. She wrote a heartfelt thank you note on the page. Our hope for her healing continued as she grew stronger during April to prepare for her long flight to Hungary.

Each day after taking care of my responsibilities, I read more of my Grandma Elsie's unpublished autobiography. I kept the binder of copied, typewritten pages on my nightstand and curled up against my headboard, reading the histories of our Reif and Shimon families. They came from Germany and Bohemia to my beloved Manitowoc where they bought rich farmland for five dollars an acre.

My great-great grandpa, John Shimon, came over on a steamship as a child. He became a farmer and country doctor, building his own homestead, putting himself through medical school, and making sure his children had good educations. His farm stood a mile from the town of Reifs Mills along the Branch River. Through a cedar woods by the stream, his daughter Emma Shimon walked to meet young Peter Anton Reif.

These two became my great-grandparents. After their marriage, they did a thing unprecedented in their families: they left their rural life. They moved to Chicago for employment, since Peter was tired of the lumber business he had worked at for many years. My Grandma Elsie was their fourth child, born in 1910 in the bustling big city.

She described their summer vacations to Manitowoc in wistful detail. I got to know my ancestors and their rustic world through her vivid word-pictures. Her story affected me the same as Beny's book had done, allowing me to borrow memories of my family's past, experience their lives and fill in missing pieces of myself.

I also discovered more about my mother. Elsie's recollection of her nine-year-old daughter fascinated me:

Mrs. Cogswell gave the role of Cinderella to Karen because she had a sweet singing voice. In a scene where Cinderella is sweeping the floor, Karen, looking like a wistful little waif, sings a sad song. I stood in the wings watching her sweep and sing. Then I noticed the audience. They were silent, captivated by her acting and her voice, enthralled. I said to myself, "That girl has something."

As a child, Karen was more introspective than [her siblings] Peter or Gail. Everything in nature—people, animals and the environment—fascinated her. She was Karen in Wonderland. She had a vivid imagination and perceived things from her own original point of view. And she has remained that way.

My mom still had the wonder and uniqueness her mother had recognized.

In a rare phone call a few weeks after my return, we discussed how things might have been if she'd kept me. Karen said, "I would have put you in ballet so fast…. You would have kept growing and growing, and told me, 'Mom, I am too tall, I will never be a ballerina.'"

I giggled my agreement. I'd been one of the tallest in my grade school.

Then she said, "I want to call you Nina Diane, because you're still Nina to me."

"I'd love that, Mom!" I replied. It showed her growing acceptance of me as both the baby she birthed and her adult daughter.

Mother's Day held profound significance. I picked out a delicate heart necklace for Karen, found a card with a misty photo of hydrangeas, and filled two journal pages with attempts at a sentiment, before writing this one in my best penmanship:

I cannot imagine a better mother! You are strong and confident, but gentle and teachable. You have a quiet strength and a joyful, life-full spirit. And best of all, you are my MOM!

On the Second Sunday in May, our local florist drove up with a live forever rose bush covered with deep red-pink petals. The card read: To my daughter Nina Diane, love and kisses, Mom. Rich helped me plant the bush in the sun near our deck.

During this reprieve from the fear of Karen's imminent death, the persistent knot of anxiety in my gut unwound. My thin frame gained back the pounds I'd lost over the winter. I started to balance, breathe, and hope beyond bleak possibilities.

Something miraculous happened when I connected with Karen, a mysterious alchemy brought together the aspects of my identity and distilled them into a whole. What helped me see myself clearly at last? The simple acceptance of the one who'd birthed me? I thought on this for quite a while during those first weeks at home.

Yes, both my birth parents' acceptance was key, but so was the confidence they instilled, helping me believe in my own strength by seeing theirs. I had needed to accept myself. I now cherished my artistic temperament, my love of nature, my uniqueness, because all these were ties to my lineage; they were family traits I could be proud of.

I'd relished my time with Karen as if I were a young girl. And now I needed to shake out my new self like a teenager spreading her wings and learn to fly on my own.

Two months after my birthday, we checked the GoFundMe page and found the total topped $60,000. Stephen expressed his amazement and relief, because Karen's medical bills had long ago exceeded his resources. Inspired by this unfathomable success, I created my own GoFundMe page, to help me afford another painting workshop and supplies. Friends and family contributed over $700: enough to pay for the class and a quality plein-air easel. The class extended the first one, with the same instructor. We used small town street scenes to explore the stages of oil painting, from sketches to shapes to details.

A new world of artistic expression opened to me like a flower. But as May wound to a close, and my orange day lilies bloomed, my heart began to wither with dread. No one had mentioned the Budapest treatment in weeks. Stephen never mentioned flight plans and never posted why Karen hadn't gone. I didn't ask. I was too scared to know the truth.

On a quiet Sunday evening when crickets had just started their song outside the screen door and Rich, Denise, and I were in the living room watching TV, my cell rang.

"Hey, sis," Hunter said, in a low tone that sounded urgent.

"Hey, bro," I answered, standing up, waiting for the worst.

"Mom's back in the hospital," he began, and I exhaled. She was alive.

"They're trying to get nutrients into her. Stephen says she can't keep anything down because of the chemo. She's malnourished and weak. Pneumonia took hold." He paused. "Her doctor told Stephen yesterday she had 24 hours to live, but this morning she was better. The doctors give her weeks now."

I sank into a kitchen chair and asked the question. "Why didn't she go to Budapest for the water treatment?"

Hunter explained, "They didn't go because the doctor flew here again and tested her. He found that her weak lungs would collapse— she wouldn't survive the long flights. And the tumor on her back is pressing into nerves. She can barely walk. So, Budapest is really out."

A pause, while I wiped my wet cheeks, breathing. He continued, "Stephen had the special heavy water flown over here, in bottles and suppositories, but don't get your hopes up. This small quantity's not a substitute for the weeks of total immersion she'd have had over there. Now they're deciding whether to go for even more chemo. The doctor forgot to do a CT scan before the last round, so he's not sure if the tumors are shrinking."

He sighed, then added, "I'm gonna call you whenever I know anything. Stephen doesn't communicate because he has so much on his plate."

"Thank you! I've been living in suspended animation over here, waiting and hearing nothing."

"Hey, Mom is tough, she's got a lot of spirit. Don't count her out yet."

"I so wish she could have gone to Budapest."

"It wasn't in the cards," he said. "Listen, I gotta make more phone calls."

"Okay, hug Janey for me."

"Will do. Love you."

"Love you, too."

I emailed Beny right away to tell him. I hadn't called him Dad since I said goodbye on the train in San Diego, but I did so in my message. He wrote back, thanking me for telling him, asking me to continue to pass on news. And for the first time he signed *Love, Dad.*

In the days that followed, darkness consumed me. Anxiety clung, sleep fled, and appetite faded. Grief gripped me as I fought the fact cancer was taking my birth mother away. I walked the dogs without seeing my surroundings; I curled on the bed with the lights off. Rich wasn't sure how to help me.

Time rolled on in slow motion waves. The fact of Karen's fragile mortality kept crashing in on me like an angry sea pulling me into its undertow. The chains on my porch swing were lifelines, swaying me to safety in the ocean swell. I rocked and read and prayed. I was desperate to keep Karen in my life, for my own sake.

One morning, I remembered a piece of Karen's advice. She said, "When creative people are stymied, the only way out is to create, create, create." The sun streamed in my window, and the green world reminded me I had planned a new flower bed. The exertion might do me good, like when I fixed up the patio in LA. So, I put on my denim shirt and walked outside, donning my gloves and grabbing my shovel, heading into the dew of the garden.

The earth was malleable from late spring rains. My spade dug in as I stepped on it and jumped, over and over, until I had a curved line of dirt clods. Then I knelt in the damp grass and pulled them apart, using a trowel to detail a smooth edge.

While I worked, I prayed. I pleaded, *please don't take my mother. I can't imagine living without her again.* Tears dripped off my chin. And a truth intruded, one that made me sit back on my heels: what happened to Karen was her story, not mine. My part was to love her, not to keep her. I was grasping for more time instead of honoring the moments we had left. Either later or sooner, I would have to let my birth mother go.

A week later, another call from Hunter. "Hey, sis." His subdued voice evinced quiet pain.

"Hey." My breath caught in my throat.

"It's time."

With a pounding heart, I stood and paced, glancing at Rich, who turned off the TV and shushed Denise.

Hunter continued, "Stephen says we need to come out to say goodbye. I've got a flight tomorrow."

"All right, I'll get on the Southwest website."

Rich nodded, meaning go ahead. I opened my computer. Denise looked confused and frightened. Mike was here, and he rounded the corner of the hallway with a questioning look.

"Karen's condition is grave," I sighed. "I'm gonna go out there."

"I can drive you to the airport, Ma," he offered.

But Rich said, "No, I'll do it. I don't have clients for a few days." That was a comfort. I wished he could fly out with me, but we had discussed it. He must stay with Denise again.

A morning flight was available, but pricey. I was too embarrassed to ask for help, especially on such short notice. Even though it strained our finances, Rich transferred money, we bought my ticket, and I printed a boarding pass for the last seat on the plane. After sending my itinerary to Stephen and Hunter, I packed a carry-on and a backpack. Even though I couldn't type Karen's name on Facebook, my friends knew our story, and I asked for prayers.

CHAPTER 24

Tuesday, June 11

WE WERE DRIVING THROUGH the steep tree-covered hills near Nashville when my cell phone rang. It was Stephen. My heart jumped into my throat as I fumbled to pick up, holding my breath.

"Hey, Diane. Are you at the airport?" He asked. He sounded upbeat, and I exhaled.

"We're almost there."

"Well, your mom's doing better! The doctor was just here and thinks she's out of danger. Maybe you could cancel your flight?"

"I don't think so." I frowned at Rich, who'd heard what Stephen said. "Let me call you back." I hung up.

"Let's not turn around," I told Rich. "I want to be there with her."

He took a deep breath and looked as frustrated as me. "This is your last trip, no matter what. I can't keep watching your sister. It's too stressful for me and for her. And we're draining our savings."

"I understand," I said. Mulling it over, I couldn't imagine going back home to wait more. "What if I got the call she died? I want to be with her while she's alive."

Rich nodded. "While she'll be cognizant you're there."

So we continued on our way, and I called to let Stephen know. I breathed deep to calm my fraying nerves and focused on my flight.

I hoped there would be a window seat left, so I could curl up and watch the sky.

But my chances of a window vanished as I was last in line at the gate. On board I found a center spot and settled in. After takeoff, I pulled out my dot-grid notebook and fine point pen.

The young man next to me by the window said, "Oh, you're journaling. I'm going to do that!" And he pulled out a big leather-bound volume. "I brought it along because I've wanted to start again." He wore a checked shirt on his lean frame, had a sandy complexion, and an open, friendly face. We exchanged small talk while we wrote. He told me, "I just finished an indexing project."

"What's indexing? I recognize the word from somewhere."

"It's genealogy. We make digital records of historical documents."

I perked up. "Oh! That's where I heard it. I've been making a family tree on Ancestry. When I first started, they had just added a census... 1940?"

"Yes, we released it last year," he said. "If you don't mind me asking, how did you become interested in your history?"

I straightened and launched into my reunion story, mentioning how great it was that my Uncle Peter had done all our family research in the eighties. I explained, "I found out a lot about my roots because he uploaded all the info he gathered to the Mormon databases."

He nodded. "That's us. That's what we do. I'm Mormon, and I volunteer to index."

Surprise and appreciation put a smile on my face. I hadn't thought about the people who made my search possible from the other end of cyberspace. People like Jamie and Uncle Peter make a difference in many peoples' lives.

"What you do is important," I said. "Genealogy connects us humans together with the threads of our past. It showed me who I am. At least that's my experience, because I'm so much more like my birth parents than my adoptive side. I have a strong connection to my new families."

We chatted for most of the trip. And, as I looked at him during our conversation, I had a clear view of the sky. I got my window seat after all.

On the ground at LAX, I shouldered my backpack and pulled my carry-on to the curb. Morning light brightened the cement outside the sliding doors. Traffic hum surrounded me. Stephen had told me to take a Super Shuttle to Mom's hospital, Providence St. John's in Santa Monica. A van pulled up, and the driver stowed my bags. I texted Stephen to tell him I was on my way.

At the hospital, I found my mom's room number, then took the elevator up to the fourth floor. When I stepped out, Stephen met me and apologized for not picking me up. "It's been a crazy morning, way too many people came to see her, and she had trouble falling back to sleep. She's just now dozing off."

We walked a curved corridor to a bank of large windows. Karen's room was the last one on the left, facing west. The sun would be shining in there, but her door was closed.

Stephen said. "We need to keep everyone who comes to see her out here in the hall while she rests. She's such a light sleeper, any noise wakes her. Can you be the gatekeeper? Don't let anyone in."

It took a moment to realize he was leaving me out here. Bewildered, I agreed. What else could I do? He went in, closing the heavy door behind him. I shrugged off my backpack and settled beside my luggage on the cool carpet, bunched my knees to my chest and buried my head. My stomach hurt. After almost ten hours of travel, I longed to just watch my mother sleep. His caution made sense considering her close call yesterday, but that didn't diffuse my frustration.

Inclined against the wall, I stared up through the window at the clear afternoon sky, chiding myself for letting this trouble me. My stomach rumbled its discontent again, and I reached in my pack for an energy bar. I chewed, relaxed, and sighed. I'm here, thank you that I'm here. My mind drifted through the day, the safe travel and good conversation. Soon enough I'd see Karen.

An hour ticked by. No one else showed up. I was scrolling through Facebook when the door opened, and Stephen poked his head out. "She's awake."

I inhaled, stood up and shook the stiffness from my legs. A lump formed in my throat as I walked in, stepped around a half-drawn curtain, and saw my mother. Her hospital bed was in the middle of the room, headboard against the right wall. Golden light slanted in from the window straight ahead, where a wide sill held flowers and cards. Karen reclined beneath a sheet, surrounded by pillows. We made eye contact. The joy in her smile and the love in her eyes melted the hours of waiting away.

I leaned in and gave her a gentle hug and kiss. Her hair was wispy, and she looked thinner, rail thin, but her grip on my arm was firm.

"How was your flight?" She asked.

"Amazing!" I said, explaining my conversation with the young man. "You know Uncle Peter loaded our family info into the Mormon database in the eighties? People like Jamie keep them updated. That's how I found so many relatives on Ancestry.com just by knowing your name and birth date."

She seemed caught up in my enthusiasm, but I couldn't get over how gaunt her face had become in the season I'd been absent from her.

"Tell me about your day," I said.

She did. Stephen left us, and I had a few minutes alone with her. We held hands while she spoke. A doctor had visited early, interrupting a lovely sleep. Friends had stopped by and brought flowers. She thanked me for the gardenias we'd sent the previous week, gesturing to the glass vase on the window ledge. "Fancy you remember one small time I said I loved gardenias! The fragrance was delightful and picked me up. Tell Rich thanks, too."

Her voice was energetic, without the affect of someone who was, likely, near death. When my adoptive father had been in the nursing home, I saw elderly people languishing and drugged into stupors. Not Karen. Her spirit shone in her eyes and sang in her words, undimmed by her body's weakness. I could well imagine she was staying alive by choice, her life force kindled by some inner fire that cancer couldn't quench.

"I have something else for you," I told her, reaching into my backpack, pulling out a small oil painting, and passing it to her. "It's a rose from the beautiful bush you sent me for Mother's Day!"

She gazed at it. "Lovely! Thank you, darling! Let's set it on the sill," she said, handing it back and pointing where to put it.

When Stephen came in, her liveliness drained away, revealing the discomfort she'd been suppressing. She reached for his hand, telling him she needed a certain vitamin. He found the empty bottle.

"Diane, can you run down the block to Whole Foods for this?" He handed me the container and his credit card.

"Sure," I said, and headed back out of the room, trying not to be upset. It felt good to walk in the open air, and as I entered the store's doorway, the earthy fragrance of live plants rejuvenated me. After finding the vitamins, I grabbed a few more energy bars. These had sufficed as meals all day.

I walked into Karen's room to find my brother Hunter, whose face lit up at seeing me. Mom's face shone with love for him. She brightened whenever they were together.

Moments later the door opened, the curtain swayed, and Lee Purcell walked straight up to Karen and bent close for a kiss, her amber hair swinging. She placed a small bag of goodies on the sheets. Mom was all smiles. Then Lee hugged me, greeted Hunter, and spoke in low tones to Stephen, learning how the day had gone. She came by often and stayed long.

Mom, munching on something that looked like white fudge, said she craved fruit and cheese. She gazed up at Hunter with pleading eyes and beseeched him to get her some.

"Sure, we can go pick it up." Hunter glanced at me as he spoke. I nodded, glad he asked me to join him. Stephen added a stop at a drugstore for a prescription. He declared that Mom needed to rest again and set Lee as the gatekeeper in the hall. My brother and I headed downstairs.

"I can't find a place for my family to stay tonight," he said, as soon as we hit the pavement. "I need to keep trying. I'm not ignoring you." He placed a headset over his ears. With his right hand, he punched numbers into his phone; with his left, he pulled me close with a firm grip on my arm, and we fell in step. I've always had a long gait, and my brother matched me stride for stride. I relished our rhythm. After striking out at several hotel switchboards, he called his wife, Elyse. She was at the airport in Houston, waiting to fly here with their little girl, Jane.

Hunter told her, "My mom has enslaved us again, as she does." He winked at me. It was good to know this was Mom's way, even with her favorite son. They hadn't singled me out as an errand runner and gatekeeper. By the time we returned with her food and medicine, he still hadn't found a room. He was getting nervous.

We stepped off the elevator into a full foyer. Our sister, Celine, was there with a few of mom's friends on couches. We joined them, waiting for Karen to wake up again. After a while, a familiar-looking young woman walked past us. She seemed lost. I was trying to place her when Hunter stood up.

"Juliet!" He said. She turned to him. "Hunter!" They hugged, then stepped back to study each other. She was the actor Juliet Lewis. Years ago, they had played the kids in the pilot of Married with Children. Mom had told me Juliet was like a member of the family; I'd seen her photo in their hallway. This was one of the few times shyness overcame me, and I hung back, starstruck. She had wavy russet hair and eyes that gripped me, then registered surprise as Hunter introduced us.

"Nice to meet you. Your mother's been like my second mom. She inspired me to go into acting, saw something in me I didn't know was there."

While we spoke, Lee came around the corner and announced Karen was awake. Then she led Juliet, with Hunter and Celine, to the room, and the rest of us sat down to wait. I watched them go, feeling left out. There was no question whether I should tag along: I was a daughter but a guest; a sibling but a stranger. Such a unique situation, observing a life I might have lived. They had layers of time together I did not share. Who was I to them? Would I still be family after our mom passed away?

Fifteen minutes later, Juliet trudged past, head down, brow furrowed. I guessed she had said goodbye to Karen, and I fought back tears. I'd have to do that soon, too. The elevator door opened, and Karyn Rachtman stepped out, her curly dark hair pulled back. She hugged and spoke to Juliet, then walked over to where we sat. The tears in her eyes did me in—mine streamed out. I stood to embrace her. We both wiped our faces and smiled. My mom had helped raise Karyn for three years, and they had a mother-daughter bond, too.

Soon we all gathered around our Karen, propped in bed, as she greeted each person in her glowing way. A playful conversation cropped up.

"What was your least favorite role ever?" Lee asked her.

"Hands down, it was Dinosaur Valley Girls," Mom answered without hesitation.

"I've never heard of that one!" Lee said, "You must've hated it."

"Regale us," someone asked. Karen launched into a riotous impression of a cave girl with an LA accent. Laughter rang around the bed. This is what I loved, this creative banter, where ideas and identities were greeted with lighthearted acceptance. I'd never been part of such imaginative conversation until I found my birth mom. Tears rimmed my eyes out of deep relief in the unexpected joy of the moment.

Karen was entranced, fully present, listening and laughing aloud. This was the first time I'd seen her in a group without her makeup; she didn't even have her bridge in, yet her smile was unselfconscious. Supportive, loving people surrounded her, and it did my heart good to see her so well cared for.

Hunter asked the group if anyone could suggest a place for his family to stay because everywhere he tried was full. To his great surprise and relief, Karyn Rachtman offered her home. He thanked her and called Elyse.

One small moment that evening made a big impact on me. Mom asked Hunter for a washcloth. He quietly told Celine; Celine called the request over to Stephen, who was by the sink. Stephen got a cloth down from a shelf, wet it, and tossed it to Hunter who wiped Mom's face. She smiled up at him. What a contrast to the family I grew up in, where Mom voiced demands and the rest of us cowered to her will. I hoped my own children would form this kind of circle of support around me when my time came.

I was standing at the foot of the bed with Lee and told her, "I haven't been part of a family like this before, where everybody takes care of each other with such love."

Lee said, "You are now." She hooked her arm around mine. "And that won't change." She had no way of knowing how much I needed that reassurance that I would continue to be a part of their lives.

Late that night, Hunter left to get Elyse and Jane from the airport. Stephen said I should stay at their house since he was staying at the hospital, and their friend Don Moss drove me home.

When we pulled up at Karen's near midnight, I dragged myself inside, exhausted. Too tired to type notes before sleep took me, I had a sudden inspiration to video it instead. And I couldn't believe I'd lived my whole life without doing this. So, I opened my computer and recorded my first-ever video journal to chronicle that eighteen-hour day.

CHAPTER 25

Wednesday, June 12

I AWOKE IN THE DARK with a pounding headache from sleeping with the little black cat again. This time her fur was coming out in clumps, making me even more allergic to her. I grabbed my pillow and padded across the hall into Karen and Stephen's empty bedroom.

A nightlight shone from the bathroom, illuminating the unmade four-poster bed, the messy nightstands and antique furniture. My mom's bookshelf was a volcano that had spewed half its contents onto the floor. I smiled and crawled in under the covers and was soon asleep.

When morning light peeped beneath the shades, my headache was much better. Drowsily, I breathed in a pleasant fragrance, flowery and soft. I rolled over and sniffed my mom's pillow. It was her scent! Most children grow up knowing their parents' smell, but that was another missing part of my life. Now I had experienced it. I hoped to remember, but of course, scent photos did not exist.

The house was quiet as I made coffee. I supposed Celine was at school, at work or at the hospital. I showered, dressed and brushed my wet hair by nine o'clock when Stephen texted me that Karyn Rachtman was coming to pick up photos for my mom. Karyn arrived within a few minutes. As I helped her search through family snapshots, I enjoyed her lighthearted ease.

After we found the pictures, we hopped in her convertible and rode to the hospital with the top down, sun shining in, and wind whipping our hair. We had a wonderful talk while she drove under the open sky, speaking of life and faith and grief. We cried over our Karen. It was cathartic.

I was upbeat as we neared Karen's room. Stephen was outside the door and drew Karyn aside to flip through the photos. He told me our patient was sleeping, but I could go be with her.

Surprised and pleased, I entered in silence and sneaked over to a narrow bed under the window. As I lowered myself to sit, mom stirred and reached for me. I sheltered her hand in mine, and she fell back asleep. We stayed that way for long minutes. As I studied her pointed cheekbones and pallid skin, reality seeped into my soul. I prayed for her to fight through and live. How would I live through losing her? My mind saw her death as sure, but my heart yearned for a miracle.

I didn't say much that day, just let the changing scene wash over me, trying to store up these precious moments. Even little things like Mom asking for water and the awkward way she had to drink through the straw I bent for her. We held hands a bunch, and hers were cool and smooth despite the prominent bones. I just kept breathing.

She woke again when Linda Kandel walked in, a writer who'd been working on a book with her. Mom brightened. They huddled and Linda got out a notebook. I headed out for a break.

Downstairs in the cafeteria, I grabbed a raspberry bar and mulled over my mom's waning strength, pushing aside the dawning truth my heart saw coming. The openness of the three-story atrium, the amber wood of the walls and brightness of the slanted sunlight helped me push the dark musing aside. I determined to be strong and present for Karen. Then I rode an escalator through the airy space and walked a long, windowed hallway to the fourth-floor lobby.

At the moment I turned the corner, Hunter and his family stepped out of the elevator. "What great timing!" I said, spreading my arms to hug Elyse, charmed by her frank expression of joy as she gathered me in. She had an approachable demeanor and an athletic build. Hunter held Jane, who tucked her blonde head into his shoulder. One big blue eye peeked out at me.

"She's shy," he said. "Janey, this is your Aunt Diane."

"Hunter's told me so much about you!" Elyse said, appraising me. "You do favor Karen. Except for the hair." The sparkle in her green eyes told me she loved the moment. It reminded me of Joan Benedetti's reaction when we met in San Diego.

Hunter put Jane on the floor, and I squatted next to her. She was adorable in her pink overalls. She blinked at me and reached for her mom's hand, but she didn't turn away. I was sure we'd be friends.

I stood up and asked Elyse about her flight the previous day. While she filled me in on her long hours of travel, Hunter checked on Mom and came back saying we needed to give her a minute, so we went down to the cafeteria to grab them a snack.

At the table, Janey smiled and giggled, peeking through Mr. Potato Head glasses. Hunter and Elyse treated her with sweetness and patience. I enjoyed being with them and watching this little human who shared my genes.

On the way to our mom's room, Elyse chased her daughter along the hall, teasing "I'm gonna getcha," while Janey wiggled and wobbled on her toddler legs. It was a delight, and it boosted my mood so much I was all smiles, inside and out, when we arrived at Karen's room. Hunter and I walked in first.

Stephen and Celine exchanged knowing glances with my brother. Karen stretched her arms up off the sheets to get a hug from him.

"Are you ready for a surprise, Mom?" He said, holding her hands. She looked up with lifted brows and hopeful eyes.

Elyse walked in with Janey in her arms. Mom hooted and grinned, reaching for her grandbaby. Janey shied away, but Elyse reached into a bag and handed her toddler two plastic crowns.

"Give one to Grandma Karen," she encouraged. Janey leaned toward Karen, who took the tiara with a delighted thank you, and placed it on her forehead. Janey put her crown on upside-down, so grandma turned hers over. They smiled and played peek-a-boo together for several minutes. But then Jane tucked her head into Elyse's shoulder. The moment was over, but Mom's glow remained.

More people came to visit, surrounding her with camaraderie. Before long, evening sunlight slanted in the window. Hunter pulled me aside.

"Hey, sis, we're leaving. We gotta get Jane to bed. You want us to give you a ride back to Mom's?"

I wasn't sure. It seemed early to leave. I waited while my tired mother said goodbye to Janey, then I bent over her and put my hand on her shoulder.

"Mom, Hunter's asking if I want a ride. I'd like to stay, but it would be nice to go with them. What do you think?"

She said, "You should go." So, I grabbed my backpack and followed my brother's family out the door.

The gridlock was real as Hunter threaded through the network of Santa Monica streets trying to make headway. We'd drive four blocks south to find a street that was open enough to go one block east. The eleven miles from St. John's to Karyn Rachtman's Hollywood Hills home took us an hour and forty-five minutes.

In the sedan, I sat next to my brother, with Elyse and Janey in the back. For the first half of the trip we didn't talk much, as Hunter, in irritated concentration, wound his way toward our destination. His wife fed Janey and changed a diaper.

After a while, the baby drifted into a doze, and I twisted around to chat with Elyse. "She's been such a trooper," I said.

"She's a good baby. We've been blessed," said Elyse.

Blessed was typically a Christian word. "I notice the word blessed, are you religious at all?"

"Yes, we're Catholic," she replied. "Hunter was already, but we both went to church after we had Jane. We want to raise her with faith." Hunter nodded his agreement.

"If you don't mind me asking, how did you become Catholic? Did Mom raise you in Scientology?"

"Yes, but it was always up to me. Scientology didn't help me, and they were okay with that. But my dad was Catholic. Religious belief is the best thing we humans have going."

"I agree." I said.

Now I was curious about his relationship with his father. Our Mom had told me that Hunter's dad, Kit Carson, had stolen him away when he was eleven. I wanted to hear more of my brother's side of the story.

Janey was asleep when we pulled up at Karyn Rachtman's house, and Hunter gathered her in his arms and unlocked the front door. I unscrunched myself, stepped out to look around, and decided the long ride had been worth it. The home was at the top of a steep hillside, with a lower level in a cliff, facing west. It had a grand view. This was a glimpse into how my mom had lived when she'd been famous.

Elyse gathered Janey's stuff from the trunk. She asked me to stay there with them for the night so Hunter didn't have to brave the traffic to Sherman Oaks to drop me at Mom's.

"Oh, that would be dreadful," I joked.

She grinned. "This place is amazing." They had spent the previous night there.

We entered a foyer and then an expansive great room. An island separated the kitchen from the living area where the whole west wall was one long window. A white leather sectional faced a fireplace with a theater-size screen retracted above it. Vintage movie posters lined the walls around a grand piano, and the requisite telescope looked outward toward the setting sun.

Hunter was busy prepping a simple dinner. "Was Mom still rich when you were a kid?" I asked.

"Yeah, our house was twice as big as this—4500 square feet or some crazy thing."

In the quaint post-war neighborhood of my youth, the houses were 1200 square feet. My eyes swept the room, imagining the boy Hunter running through such a vast wonderland. I reached for a glass-framed photo of this home, an old Polaroid of new construction.

"Karyn's lived here a long time," my brother said, seeing my interest. "Since the '90s when she was working with Tarantino. Did Mom tell you she did the music for Paris, Texas?"

"Yeah! And Pulp Fiction, even. But she's so easy to talk to, so real. Everyone here is brilliant and creative, but regular people."

"Mostly." He nodded.

What struck me about Karen and her friends was their unintimidating quality. I didn't feel surrounded by my betters. Instead, they were accessible and friendly with an added spark of genius. Non-judgmental, open to new perspectives—even mine—easily expressing emotions, sharing in my grief. No masks.

I turned back to Hunter. "Can I help with dinner?" I asked.

He shook his head. "Nah, I got this. Look around! There's a patio on the roof." He smiled and pointed to a sliding door in the wall of windows that led to an open-air spiral staircase.

Eyes wide, I explored, bounding up the curved steps. A vista met me. Wispy clouds trailed through the sky. To the south, the city skyline was Hollywood—we had seen the famous sign on our way here. To the north and east was this neighborhood, layering the steep hill. At the top wound Mulholland Drive. To the west, pink and gold sunlight streaked my vision, casting fairy light on a landscape that rolled out into the distance. Below, headlights dotted a winding road. Traffic was a distant hum. I stayed for long minutes as the sun set.

Inside, I found Elyse seated on the sectional, with two plates on a square glass coffee table.

"Eat," she said, and I sat and did so.

Hunter jingled the car keys. "Wine?" He asked. "Red?" He took off into the twilight.

We girls sank back into the soft leather and relaxed, gazing out over the rose-colored valley.

"So how did you and Hunter meet?" I asked.

Elyse told me they'd been friends before they dated. Their dogs had brought them together because they belonged to a group that hung out at a local dog park. She asked how Rich and I got together, and I told the story of meeting him while we worked at McDonald's as teens. We talked about kids, and she said they wanted more of them. I explained we had two-and-a-half grandkids; Matt's two boys in Seattle, plus the baby that Mike's girlfriend was expecting in October. We'd have a grandchild living near us.

"Wow, the baby won't be much younger than Jane," she commented. "We'll have to get them together."

There it was again, evidence of my lasting connection to these people. I would be family, even after Karen passed.

Three bottles of red wine came back with my brother. He opened one, grabbed glasses, and we headed onto the balcony outside the windows. We sat around a wrought iron table under a purple sky.

He poured us each a glass and lifted his. "To family," he toasted, and we clinked.

He and Elyse both lit cigarettes.

"You smoke?" I asked, never having seen it before now.

"Only while we're drinking," answered Elyse.

We chatted as the stars and city lights winked on around us. A warm breeze caressed my skin. Sometime into my third glass of a delicious red blend, I asked Hunter the question on my mind.

"Hunter, at some point can you tell me more of the story of why you left Mom when you were eleven?"

He said okay and started right in.

"Wait a sec," I said, and scrambled over into the chair next to him. "I need to be closer for my old ears," I confessed.

"How old are you?" He asked.

"Fifty-four."

"You look great!" They both said.

"It's the Ziegler skin, I now know." I smiled, patting my cheek. "Anyway, go on, bro."

Hunter had wanted to live with his father. Mom blamed Kit Carson for taking him away, but Hunter had made up his own mind. He didn't want to be an actor, yet Stephen and Mom wouldn't hear him.

"When Mom told me the story," I interjected, "she said you were a great actor, and your dad ripped you away from your future."

"I know she believes that, but I did not want that future, and I couldn't make them see it. They wouldn't listen."

He took a deep breath and lit another cigarette. "There was a Christmas I was supposed to go to my dad's, but I didn't want to. I begged Mom to let me stay, but she was working and made me go. My dad listened to me, and I had a great time."

My mother loved Hunter like crazy. She told me he was her life. Why couldn't she have listened to him and told him it was okay, he didn't have to be an actor? Why couldn't she have put his needs before her career?

"When I lived with my dad, he took me to visit the Jesuit high school he attended, and I dug it. He and my stepmom told me if I passed the tough entry test, they'd move to Dallas, so I could go there. I barely made it, by one question. So, we moved, and those years were close to perfect for me. Even though my dad wasn't perfect, at that point in his life he changed enough to focus on me, to raise me."

As Hunter spoke, my view of my birth mother became balanced. She was fallible and fraught with shortcomings, same as everyone. I'd seen her temper back in March when she and Celine argued, but now I saw it as the offset to her energy and drive, and I knew I would have dealt with it if she'd raised me. For the first time since my journey began, I was almost content she had left me behind. My childhood had been bearable, my marriage was long-lasting, my experiences were wide-ranging. My life had been good, even without Karen.

The three of us talked late into the night and emptied the bottles of wine together. The evening was pivotal and bonding and sweet, one of my favorite memories, right up there with the magical day back in September when I painted a mural with my mom.

CHAPTER 26

Thursday, June 13

ELYSE AND I SAT ON THE HARDWOOD FLOOR in the morning light. Janey played between us. My eyes were heavy, my stomach queasy, and my hands steadied me while the baby babbled sleepily. I hadn't drunk a whole bottle of wine since… well, since never.

At six we piled into the car to beat traffic on the 405. As the sedan crested a hill before the Sherman Oaks exit, red taillights stacked up for miles after the ramp. We coasted down onto Ventura Boulevard and stopped at a diner Hunter liked. The good food and hot coffee eased my hangover. After breakfast we drove a few blocks to our mom's home so Janey could nap.

We arrived late morning at the hospital and found Stephen and Celine at Karen's bedside with her sister, Gail. I recognized my Aunt Gail from photos.

"Oh, Hunter! Elyse! So good to see you!" She cried, opening her thin arms wide. She sounded and looked like Karen, but her hair was kinky blonde. Her enthusiastic gestures reminded me of my mom back in September, whole and full of life.

Then she took my hands and looked at me, beaming. She told Karen, "She does look like you and Beny."

Mom got to play with Jane again. Today they shared stickers, putting them on their faces and laughing. We had a perfect hour together. At one point I stood beside my aunt, holding her hand and Karen's. They felt identical: cool and angular yet sturdy. That moment stuck with me; I was in a story that swept here from the past and traveled into the future with me in tow.

Gail asked to hear how we had found each other. Karen recounted while Stephen videoed. As she spoke, she looked fragile and insignificant, her sallow features framed by her pillow in the pale natural light. But at the same time, she was bold and free, speaking with passion, with a sticker on her forehead and a gap in her front teeth like a child.

"I was at our house doing a reading when Stephen spoke in a voice that says the world has turned: 'Karen. Karen. Read this.' And it was a message that said, 'I was born March 4th, 1959, to a woman named Karen Black. Are you my mother?' And I said, 'Yes I am.'"

I interjected, "It was the most wonderful message I ever got in my life."

She smiled up at me. "But I don't remember what else I said. Something about how I would embrace you, and you would be part of our family. I was completely open to it." Then she turned to Gail, "And soon after that, she stayed with us for a week. She is a fantastic, talented, gifted artist, and so beautiful."

She touched my arm. "Can you show them that one painting you sent me? The one of people outside in the sunlight: so brilliant, like Sicily modernized."

"I can find it on my laptop later," I said, not wanting to brag.

"They won't be here later! You should find it now, dear," she insisted. But as I reached in my bag for my computer, her friend Harriet Schock came in and greeted her. The moment passed, and I didn't have to show my work, only let my mom's enthusiasm settle into my heart.

While Karen played with Jane again, I introduced myself to Harriet. She was the songwriter Mom had told me about in September when she had listened to my son Ricky's song. An aging beauty with natural aplomb, Harriet took my hand in both of hers and expressed, as others had, how significant my presence was for Karen right now.

Soon my mom's eyelids drooped as sleep crept over her. Stephen ushered us out, and Gail and Celine left for the afternoon. Hunter asked me to go to the pier with him and his family.

I'd hoped to see the ocean again, but I wasn't expecting an amusement park over the water. Santa Monica Pier had a huge Ferris wheel, a roller coaster, and restaurants. We spent midday in a milling, sunlit crowd. We ate on a patio in the sea breeze and took Janey to an arcade that had rides for little ones. As we sauntered along, I loved everything about my brother; the way his shoulder-length brown hair curled up at the ends; his unassuming gray Henley shirt; that he walked like me and his nose was so like mine. Stephen had called our noses Bohemian. I liked that, too.

After a couple hours, we dropped Elyse and Jane off at their new hotel and headed back to St. John's. When we entered through the room's open door, Mom was sitting up on the side of the bed with her feet on the floor, a nurse holding her shoulder, another white-smocked man beside her for support. Aunt Gail and Harriet were standing by the window, arms crossed, watching, and Stephen held up a hand for us to be quiet while Mom concentrated. She was trying to walk.

I backed against a wall, watching too, proud of her. She stood, then swayed back against the bed, steadying herself with her hands. Then she pushed off again, and as she did so, her hospital gown swung forward, exposing her entire naked side to my view. Karen was skeletal.

Back in the '90s, I worked for World Relief, a non-profit company that helped people in the poorest countries. I kept the photo archive and cataloged haunting images of starving humans. One in particular came to mind, an emaciated boy from Sudan, lying in the sand near death.

My birth mother was going to die. My heart understood that now.

She walked to the door and back, shaky but satisfied with her effort. The others in the room all focused on Karen, praising her. No one's face reflected the horror in my gut. Maybe my vantage point was the only one open to her side, or no one else recognized what they'd seen. But it shook me to the core.

The day went on, but for me, time stopped. A tsunami of grief engulfed me. To be here, face-to-face with her mortality, was worse than being trapped at home in anxious waiting. Since I'd arrived my emotions had risen and fallen, a twisting mountain road with tall ridges of joy such as last night and deep valleys of grief like this moment. I wanted to run away.

While everyone was engaged with my mom, I stole out into the corridor and rode the elevator downstairs, trying to calm my torn heart, breathing back the heartache that threatened to undo me. There was a courtyard outside and a table to lean on and weep until my tears ran dry. I wiped my face and headed for a curved path through a plot of lavish blooms. The rhythm of walking allayed my distress. As I strolled in the sun, inhaling the garden air, I prayed for comfort, and refocused on the present. Watching bees hover over flowers, listening to the buzz of the city, I practiced seeing like an artist. To compare the tones of nature was a skill I'd learned in my painting workshops: were the colors cool or warm, bright or muted, dark or light? The warm sunlit greens and yellows of foliage and flowers contrasted with the darker, cooler tones of the shade beneath. The darkness of the shadows lent brilliance to the blooms. I let this truth sink in. Our sorrow brought to light the beauty of each gifted moment of life.

I meandered for maybe a quarter hour until I regained my composure and, although shaky, I was ready to socialize again. Harriet met me in the hall, and as we walked, I asked her to tell me a Karen story.

She paused, then related, "This was Sunday evening. We were all standing around her bed and we were singing. All of a sudden Karen howled! We stopped and asked what was wrong. 'I'm sad to be dying and leaving everyone behind!' 'I thought you weren't afraid of dying,' said Lee. And Karen answered, 'I changed my mind!' That was a precious moment."

Harriet's eyes were full of knowing empathy. She'd come to grips with Karen's death; I could see. Grief drew people together, it was a bond hard to break; a deep, inner experience, the kind we often keep from each other. But grief was hard to hide if you were at all honest. It welled up, an ocean inside you that leaked out of your eyes. It resonated between the stricken, and even in the laughter around a bedside, mourning was present. Shared grief hastened friendship, and I'd found a friend in Harriet Schock, as I had in Lee Purcell.

When we walked back in the room, Karyn Rachtman and our Karen were scrutinizing the large prints of the family photos we'd found. They were part of the plans for her funeral. Mom was commenting while enjoying a piece of chocolate cake, widening her eyes at the delicious taste. I took my place at the bedside next to Hunter, content to give my attention to my mother.

Into this scene walked Toni Basil. Karen had worked with her in Easy Rider and Five Easy Pieces, and they were still pals. Toni was an exotic beauty, with her long dark hair twisted up in a striped scarf. Mom asked her what she'd been up to, and with zest she described street dancing, her arms moving with grace as she spoke. She judged competitions and loved working with young dancers.

When she asked what Karen had been doing, Mom said, "I'm brilliant in this movie that opened on Sunday."

"What's the name of it?"

"*She Loves Me Not*, with Cary Elwes, and I play a crazy housewife."

They continued talking in low tones together, enjoying each other's company. Later, in the hall, I got up my courage and asked Toni to tell me a Karen story.

She answered, "We were on the set of *Easy Rider*, and I watched Karen, in character, stand up and walk with Dennis, and I knew—just from that simple movement—wow, here was a most gifted actress."

I asked, "Is it because she became that character?"

And Toni said, "Yes, but more. She had a charisma that drew you in. I'll never forget that."

Late that evening, the doctor came by to discuss a CT scan. The last one had depleted Karen for three days, and I hoped they wouldn't do another. Why know if the tumors were growing? More chemo might kill her. They should just let her be happy. I wished Hunter was still there, but he'd gone to join his family at the hotel.

She smiled up at the doctor with sleepy eyes. "So, here's what happened: I begged the nurse, Sharon, to get the therapist in here so I could walk. And they came."

"Did you walk?" The doctor asked.

She nodded. "I stood up and walked to the door. I was so weak, but I did it. And I have this hope in me, to walk every day."

"You're much better now than you were the other day," he said. "What do you want to do about the scan?"

And mom answered, "The thing I *don't* want to do is plan my future based on what one picture tells me."

I was glad to hear her say that. "And Gail made a good point too," I said, nodding at my aunt.

Gail took up the argument. "CT scans are high in radiation, and she's already had so much chemo. Why does she need another one?"

The doctor answered, "To help us decide if the chemotherapy has helped her."

Stephen and Karen talked more, and they decided to schedule the scan despite our misgivings.

By the time I got back to their house, my energy reserve had run dry. I wanted to flee the emotional upheaval. I called Rich. His family was visiting from Chicago; they were boating and swimming, and I was missing the fun and wanted to get home. The first affordable flight wasn't until Wednesday, too late to see his relatives. I told Rich to send me pictures, and he promised. I purchased my ticket.

Before I let myself sleep, I made my video journal of the day. When I spoke of the doctor's visit, I expressed my helplessness:

"I'm like a fly on the wall. They've screened me out of major decisions because I have no history with them. The reality is there are no layers—those years and shared times that create a family relationship where you talk about important things, and life is woven together. And I don't have that with my mom. And I will never have it."

But being with Hunter and Elyse the last couple days began a new story, one in which I belonged. And with my dad and his kids, I'd become part of the Benedetti story, too. Karen had given me much more than herself when she answered my Facebook message. She'd introduced me to my natural families. With this gift, and with her love, she'd endowed me with the confidence in myself I needed in this turbulent time.

While I was contemplating this, a group of photos caught my eye. On their roll top desk, Mom had placed family pictures, and two photos of me were among them. She was counting me family. She'd said so today, also. Our short time together had bonded us, and I needed to rest in the fullness I had found.

Chapter 27

Friday–Sunday, June 14–16

My eyes and limbs were groggy and heavy the next morning. It took a half hour to get out of bed. As I wandered into the empty kitchen, trying to remember how to make coffee, I realized through my mental haze I hadn't eaten since breakfast yesterday. Under stress, I just didn't eat, but now my belly growled. Was I starving myself? I was under a hundred thirty pounds, not good for my five-eight frame.

In my stupor, I forgot to press the brew button until I went back to fill my mug. When the warm cup was finally in my hands, the aroma revived me. I took it outside under the new tan gazebo cover, listening to birds and cars, drinking in the coffee and the soft scent of jasmine. Our mural was faded from the sun, and I didn't have the energy to enliven it, but it still made me smile. After the good times I'd had in this house, it felt like home. I was glad to be here again.

Angela picked me up later that morning in a red European-looking car. We talked as she drove.

"My friendship with your mom was unlikely. She's a Scientologist, and I'm an atheist. She once sent me a card that had a picture of a large dog and a tiny kitten on the front, and inside it said, *some friendships just can't be explained*." Angela smiled at the memory, so I asked her for a Karen story.

"On a film set, she and her costar wore zippered coveralls to protect them from bees in the scene. The costumes were hot, so they didn't wear clothes underneath them. The bees invaded their coveralls, and the costar ran screaming and jumping off set, patting his suit, giving himself multiple stings. Karen stayed calm, unzipped her gear, stepped out of her costume, and—stark naked—shook the bees to freedom, then serenely put on her suit again. That was your mother. She made the logical choice because she didn't subject herself to the dictates of decorum."

At the hospital, when we opened the door to Mom's room, we found friends and family around the bed in the middle of a conversation. Celine and Aunt Gail were there, and Harriet was holding Karen's hand.

Mom greeted us, and Harriet told the group, "Yesterday I told Karen she was wonderful, and she asked if it meant she was a good actor. I said, 'No, it's because you give so much attention.'"

There was a murmur of consent to Harriet's sentiment. Gail said, "I sent you an email just like that, saying how terrific you are."

Angela added something from our conversation in the car. "I was telling Diane on the way here, that you have an unparalleled ability to observe, and connect, and see everyone's point of view just by touching it. Everybody feels loved because you appreciate them."

"A long time ago I came to understand that all different perspectives are correct," my mother said. "What makes them magnificent is the spirit of the person who has the point of view. It's not what they're saying but that they're saying it."

Harriet added, "You get people, even if nobody's gotten them before. So, they're not alone anymore."

Then someone recommended making it a song. Mom squeezed Harriet's hand, looked into her eyes and said, "You write it."

And Harriet agreed through tears. "I remember I used to tape every message you ever sent me because I thought, 'Oh my god, Karen Black is saying this; I'll save it for my dotage!' And I've lost them now."

"Do you know that Russell made a whole book of my voice mails?" Mom asked us.

Celine said, "Every voice mail she sent! When you read them, it's amazing."

I wished I'd met Karen in time to experience the full measure of the robust soul she'd been. She invested so much of herself in her friends, and their love for her was vibrant.

Into this reminiscence walked Lee, straight over to Karen and handed her a small, white bag.

Karen peeked in. "Oh, you brought me sugar!"

Lee smoothed her hair and kissed her forehead. "Are you on it or off it today?"

"I am it!" Said Mom. Then she told her we were working on a song.

I told Lee, "Karen is the most encouraging person I've ever met, and she's my own mother! She gets into your heart and makes you see yourself. You say, yes, that's right, she's got it!"

Lee agreed. "When most people give you encouragement, you're acknowledged, and that's all. But when Karen encourages you, it makes you strive to do more."

Mom looked at me and spoke to the group. "It's true for me, that Diane is a fabulous artist. There's no taking it away from me, there's no removing it from my point of view, and she can tell that I'm not just being nice."

"Exactly," I said.

Then Karen and Gail exchanged stories about their parents—my grandparents. Gail said, "Mother was great, I don't want to obscure that, but she had a hardness to her, too. I was in a performance when I was young. I had seen ballet dancers float in the air, and I said to her, 'Did it seem like I was floating?' And she just shook her head and said 'no.'"

Gail talked with her whole body, swaying her arms when she floated, dropping them to her sides when her mother said no. We laughed, and Gail's face lit up in a wide smile.

But Karen's expression grew serious. "I tell you, Daddy had no excuse. He was not supportive to us, or to mother."

I asked, "He wasn't encouraging like you are?" This surprised me because of how intrinsic it was to her nature.

She said, "That's right. Mother would write books—they got published, she won awards, she sold short stories all over the country. We were in Mexico once, and Father read her writing, and he rolled his eyes and made fun of it with a sarcastic comment. And it shocked me. I had no idea he was so egotistical."

"But also insecure," Gail added, "His depression came along when they both were getting an education, and he couldn't continue, and that affected his self-esteem. I'm not defending his position with my mother at all. I think it's sad because they both needed what they couldn't each give each other."

Karen said, "I tell you that Daddy had no excuse for not being familiar with me. It hurt me so deeply."

Lee voiced what I wondered. "What do you mean familiar?"

Mom's brow furrowed. "You couldn't be close to Daddy. He would drink too much and get mad at you and punish you for things you didn't do. He would turn on you. I had no friend in my father, and I needed a dad I could be close to. Mother needed it, too."

Gail said, "He was distant with me, too. And Peter, he was very hard on Peter. He couldn't even make a friend of Mother."

"That's a good point. But what I mean is they weren't the best parents. And I don't understand that because building kids up is so important for person-forming," Karen countered.

Her last word resonated. That was how our reunion had affected me. Her acceptance had started me on a path of self-discovery and renewal.

I reached for my mother's hand. "That's what's happening to me now."

She became still. "What?"

"Person-forming."

She let out a soft howl, clasped my hand with both of hers, and smiled at me through tears. Gasps sounded around the bed, followed by cries of amazement. There wasn't a dry eye.

———•••———

That afternoon while Karen slept, I tagged along with Hunter's family to the Third Street Promenade in downtown Santa Monica. Lined with palm trees and upscale shops, the avenue was only for walking. It had a relaxed vibe as two street performers with a guitar and a black hand-drum beat out a rhythmic harmony to the scene.

We strolled into an alcove, up cement stairs and through glass doors into an open space with ocean decor. Half was an eatery and opposite was a playground in the shape of a whale, made of wood and netting. Jane toddled over to it, and I followed, telling Hunter and Elyse to have lunch; I'd watch the baby.

My new niece and I had a super time crawling around together inside the colorful whale. She was not fearful as she climbed, but careful, expressing wonder at her discoveries. On one platform we found vintage knobs to turn. The netting above us filtered sunlight into small spots. Janey noticed these on her arm as she twisted the knobs. "Spot," she said, touching her forearm. "Yes, spots from the sun," I said, pointing up toward the glass ceiling. She looked up and then down at her arms, watching the specks as she moved.

After they'd eaten, Elyse came over and beckoned for her daughter, but Jane shook her head and came snuggling back to Auntie Di.

Back at the hospital, Elyse and Jane said an upbeat goodbye to Karen, not tearful but as if they'd be seeing her soon. We hugged at the elevator, and they left for the airport.

I sat pecking at a chicken salad sandwich in the cafeteria, trying to get calories into my body. Lee walked up and asked if she could join me, and I was glad. Her even-keeled nature was calming.

We shared how difficult it was to watch Karen's slow decline, knowing we'd lose her soon. "I don't have a playbook for this," she admitted. "I'm walking in the dark."

"When my adoptive dad suffered a stroke in 2007, I learned to keep putting one foot in front of the other, forcing myself to walk down the hall to his room. It was how I coped. Sometimes all we can do is walk and breathe."

The next morning no one was available to drive me to St. John's, so I walked from Karen's home in Sherman Oaks to the bus stop at Ventura Blvd., just past Whole Foods. I waited a bit, climbed onto the crowded bus, and found a seat near the back. We followed Sepulveda Boulevard as it hugged the 405 southward, curving through tree-filled neighborhoods before the bus headed west toward Santa Monica.

An elderly woman leaning on her cane took a seat near me. The lines on her face spoke of an interesting past, but she stared at the passing city with a glazed expression. Karen had once told me, "When I'm sitting on a bus, I'll ask the person next to me, 'So you get up in the morning, and then what?'"

I took a breath, leaned over and asked if she took the bus often. I was going to St. John's to see my mother, where was she going today? As she described the grandson she would visit, her kind, dark eyes sparkled. It was another lesson from Karen: when I looked and listened with my full attention, people came alive.

Mom had her CT scan that morning, and it wiped her out, as my Aunt Gail and I had dreaded. Gail said goodbye to her sleepy sister after I arrived, explaining mini exercises to Karen to help keep her blood flowing. "Just moving your foot back and forth can help. Move throughout the day."

Karen followed her big sister's instructions, and Gail leaned over for a long goodbye hug. She clasped Karen's hands as she left and encouraged her to keep fighting.

That afternoon, only Stephen and I kept Karen company. He told me she would move to a nursing home on Monday where he had secured a bed at Canyon Oaks Rehab. While Mom rested, he spoke in low, animated tones describing the excellent facility in a quiet neighborhood. It was closer to their house, too.

We were working at our computers when Harriet entered. Mom had been dozing but opened her eyes and smiled when she saw her friend. They exchanged knowing and expectant glances. Could Harriet have the song done so soon? I stood up and moved to the end of the bed. She held a phone-size device and reached for Karen's hand. Stephen picked up his ever-present video camera.

The audio played. It was a piano piece, and Harriet sang along in a soft, crystal voice. Karen coaxed her on with nods and smiles. Here and there she stopped and backed up to sing a stanza a different way. Privileged to be there, I got to watch this famous songwriter make an idea come alive after I had been part of the conversation that inspired it:

People say you're wonderful, you ask what they mean
How to explain wonderful? One-part angel, one-part queen.
It would take forever, perhaps you'll start to glean
All the ways you're wonderful if I put it in a scene:

Girl sits at a table; you sit by her side.
She pours out her story. You look at her wide-eyed.
And just because you listen with your mind and soul and heart,
She's changed for the better. With you, listening is an art.[5]

There were three more verses. Mom laughed and smiled, squeezing Harriet's hand. To watch that song take shape was a highlight of my visit.

That evening I left early to catch the bus. As I kissed her good night, Karen surprised me with a request. "Can you ask your church people to pray for me to be more present during the day? I don't like feeling out of it. You know I avoid pain pills for that reason. I want to listen well and respond to everyone, and it's all so overwhelming."

I assured her I would.

———

Sunday was Father's Day. Right after breakfast, I sent my birth dad an ecard with this message:

Beny, this is our first Father's Day! Thank you for your natural acceptance of me into your family. You have done many wonderful things in your life, but your big heart impresses me the most!

Out on the patio in the cool morning shade, I spent time on the phone with Rich. He filled me in on the visit with his family, then he texted photos of fun on the lake and a video of Ricky catching a water snake. Our youngest son was unafraid, just like his Grandma Karen. The video made me homesick.

That afternoon I took the bus to St. John's for the last time. In her quiet room, a constant parade of callers came to give their regards to Karen. She awoke and gave each one her full attention. Between visitors, she became listless, only drowsily aware that I sheltered her cool hand in mine. When someone new entered, she engaged with interest once again. She was straining her whole being toward continuing to interact with well-wishers.

As she spoke and listened, I watched her hazel eyes—when had their blue faded? And I loved her so much. She was a deep part of who I was, and now our remaining time was short. All I could do was breathe.

Then a curly-haired stripling of a boy sat down next to Karen. He had come with his mother, who stood back, giving him a supportive glance. Had she coached him on a proper way to say goodbye? He took my mom's hand and related a story about a time when he and Karen had been together, when she was a positive influence on him. She, in turn, told him of remarkable traits she saw in him. Then he thanked her, and soon after, stood up and told her goodbye. The scene brought tears to my eyes. When it was my turn, I should have a story ready, a certain occasion that meant a lot. I had dreaded that final moment so much; I hadn't prepared for it. How would I choose from among the many meaningful ways she had influenced me? How would I let her go?

CHAPTER 28

Monday–Wednesday, June 17–19

THE NEXT DAY, MOM WAS MOVED to the Canyon Oaks nursing home. Stephen picked me up once she settled in. "She'll have great care," he explained. "We're lucky to get a bed; the Screen Actors Guild made it possible." He also let me know the CT had shown the tumors had not grown, which he took as an encouraging sign. I did not share his optimism.

The trip took only a half hour, much less than the trek to St. John's. We pulled up to a sprawling suburban ranch surrounded by pink-flowering bushes and fronted with a railed ramp. Inside, a traditional foyer welcomed us with muted yellow walls and lots of art. The carpeted hallway muffled sounds.

Karen greeted us with smiles from the sole bed in a double-patient room. After a hug, she and Stephen talked logistics. Pleased to see a patio door, I stepped outside into a large courtyard. A white, wood pergola shaded stone pavement, round glass tables, and wrought iron chairs. A tall fountain rippled and pattered, surrounded by greenery. I determined to get my mom out here in the open air.

Stephen made several trips back and forth from home, for laundry, sundries, and his futon mattress. Mom slept, and I read under the pergola with her door ajar in case she woke.

After her nap, I asked if she wanted to go outside. "Oh, no, I don't think so, dear," she said, confounding my plan. "How could we accomplish that, anyway, with me stuck in this awful bed?"

"I'll bet we can move it. You're not hooked up to anything." I scanned the bed, looking for a wheel lock. I pushed a bar near the floor with my toes, and the bed became mobile.

"Let's try to fit through," I suggested, wishing her to catch my sense of adventure. She shook her head with a frown. Arguing with Karen was futile, so I compromised. "Well, what if I angle the bed so you can see the courtyard?"

She agreed, and I urged the heavy bed into a diagonal angle, inclined her upper body, and fixed her pillows. Then I pulled up a chair next to her. With the sliding door wide open, a fresh breeze whispered on our faces, and outdoor sounds embraced us.

She reached her my hand and gave it a squeeze. "Thank you, darling. What will I do once you're gone? Who will take care of me?"

"I know you'll find someone."

We sat in comfortable silence for a time, breathing the fresh air.

"A dear friend of mine is in town," she said, contemplating her next caregiver. "I met her in the nineties. Her husband, Rodion, is a fabulous actor and director in Russia. I was doing one of his films in Moscow, and Natasha and I became fast friends. I cooked an American Thanksgiving dinner for them, at their home. What fun we had, Diane."

Mom smiled with recollection. "She once took me to a small Russian church, exquisite and peaceful. There were dark wood walls, candles everywhere, a statue of Mary in a corner. Natasha prayed, and I sensed her real faith. Like yours, dear."

Tenderness for my birth mom filled me. She had a genuine admiration for people's faith. She could wrap herself in the warm spirit of an Orthodox church and speak of it with affection.

Stephen came back and moved Karen's bed to where it belonged, although he didn't mind what I'd done. On the way to their house later, he asked me to spend the next night, my last night, with Mom. He hadn't slept at home for three weeks, and his face had haggard lines from his long vigil. He had been a solid rock for my mom throughout her protracted illness.

So, that evening, after folding my clothes into my suitcase, I walked around their empty house, touching the family photos, memorizing the rooms. The scents stayed in my memory: spices in the kitchen, antique wood and dust in the dining room, lavender in the bathroom. I would miss this home where so many bright memories happened.

On Tuesday morning, Stephen drove me to the convalescent center. Karen's room overflowed with visitors, and she was vibrant. A longtime friend, Rose Kuo, came at lunchtime. Petite and stunning, she had a lively presence.

"Rose, I'm so glad you get to meet my daughter," Karen said. "Diane, Rose and I have been friends since the nineties. She's been in charge of film festivals in Los Angeles and New York for years. Plus, she's a marvelous cook."

"Your mom used to throw the most outrageous parties. She'd call on a whim and say, I'd like to have a few friends over Saturday—this would be Wednesday, mind you. Then she'd invite 150 people, and we'd shop, and she'd cook for them all. Her kitchen would look like it had exploded!"

"I took such great pleasure in cooking, Diane," Mom said. "And Rose used to bring the best fruit and cheese spreads to my parties. You know, I'd love that right now."

"Are you sure?" Asked Rose, her eyebrows raised.

"Can we?" Asked Mom.

"Why not!" So, Rose and I raided the nearby grocery store and came back with an overflowing bag of assorted goodies. I helped her spread them all out on Karen's rolling tray. There were soft cheeses, jellies, grapes and apple pieces, tiny French bread slices, a fancy cheese roll with nuts and berries. Karen's eyes were wide with joy. We nibbled as they swapped more stories, forming an image of Karen charging headlong into each day, full of wonder.

That evening, after my mom's nap, the mood mellowed. Stephen had gone home. Lee sat next to Mom; Cary Kozlov, Karen's literary agent and friend, had pulled up a chair near Lee; and I relaxed on the bed at my mom's feet. I had opened the patio door; it was June in southern California, and a pleasant breeze ruffled the sheers. Birds were singing as I focused on my mother.

Her friend Russell Brown had come by earlier. He and I had a good talk, and he expressed a truth: "If you just look at Karen's eyes, you'd never know she has cancer."

Those eyes now danced as she shared the wonder of a favorite memory. "There are moments in everyone's life, moments that wake you up. I was sixteen when I was jarred awake to literature. It was a story called "Winter Dreams" by F. Scott Fitzgerald; I don't remember the story now, only the feeling, the realization that this invaluable thing was within my grasp at any hour of the day. I could just get literature. Somehow that day, that book, woke me. And what I want to ask you all, is this: what were watershed moments that changed your lives?"

I knew right away what I'd share and wondered how to start.

Cary spoke up first. "I managed a comedy club, and one night I survived a takeover armed robbery. It was right after closing time. I was closing the bar and looked up into the barrel of a pointed gun. A man in a ski mask had his finger on the trigger and said in a low growl, 'Get down on the floor.' I obeyed. He asked who was in charge. When I said I was, he hauled me up and told me to give him all the cash we had. I stood at a desk and emptied the drawer, then sat on the floor and opened the top portion of the safe, filling his bag.

"Then he ordered me to open the bottom of the safe. This was impossible; I didn't have the key. I told him so, but he said I had till the count of three. As his quiet voice counted, my life force drained out of me from my head to my feet. I remember thinking, this isn't right, this shouldn't be the way life ends. Before he said three, I looked straight up into his eyes and said evenly, 'I have given you all I can.' Then I waited for the muzzle to explode.

"At that moment another masked man came in and said, 'We have enough. Let's go.' The gunman lowered his weapon, they pulled me up and walked me into the kitchen, pushed me down, and tied me up with the rest of the staff. I thought they would kill us, but they left, and we breathed again. On that cold, damp floor, I examined my life. I'd been dragging my feet about accomplishing things. When I answered that gunman, I found something inside me I didn't know was there. I determined to do what I came to California to do."

We looked at each other with wide eyes as he told this heart-pulsing story. Karen said, "That small act of courage changed your life."

"Yes, it changed my opinion of myself. I was stronger than I knew."

"That's fantastic. And you're a successful literary agent, one of the best."

Cary gave a bashful smile.

"Mine is about showing up dirty for an audition," said Lee. "A commercial agent had put me up for a role, and I made it through the first two rounds of auditions. It was a Saturday morning, and I was working in my garden. It was hot, and I was sweaty when the phone rang. It was the agent. He said, 'Can you come here right now?' 'I've been working in the yard. Can I shower?' I asked. 'No, come right now if you want the part. You have ten minutes.'

"So, I showed up. And the first person I saw when I walked in the studio door was Steve McQueen. I was embarrassed, aware of how grimy I looked. But he was impressed that I had the guts to show up, and I got the part. He was my mentor from then on, and it changed my life."

"What a serendipitous meeting," I commented.

Mom gave Lee a recollecting nod. Then she turned to me. "What about you, daughter-of-mine?"

I took a deep breath and began. "My story is different; the circumstances were not distinctive. Last October, Stephen posted a video of you singing, Mom, at a piano. The song was Gershwin's "Summertime." And the moment I heard you sing, something happened to my heart, something powerful. It burst open as if an underground spring had broken through the earth. Out poured abandonment I never felt before, all tangled up with warmth and peace, like I remembered the loveliness of your womb and the struggle of being torn from you."

"Oh!" Mom exclaimed, "I never knew!"

"Neither did I, Mom. But it's okay now," I assured her, as tears rimmed her eyes. "I am past it—"

She interrupted with passion. "I couldn't help it, it's what I had to do. I could not keep you; don't you see? I would have become a secretary or something. I never planned on keeping you."

"You did what you thought was best for me."

She winced, "No, I didn't. It was selfish; I wanted my career. How can you get past that?"

I was over to her in a flash, gathering her frailness into my arms. I needed to explain what a gift that moment had been. "I love you no matter what, Mom. I forgive you." I whispered into her hair and held her. Then I sat up and took her hands in mine. Her doleful expression softened.

"Remember, on the day we made our mural, I described a sweet melancholy place inside me? My reaction to your song showed me—it was my memory of you. All my life, you were always with me in my heart." I touched my chest.

She stared at me wide-eyed, pain seeming to melt into love.

"Thank you, darling. What an amazing person you are! The universe has given me such a gift!"

"The gift is for both of us," I said, grateful down to my toes for the time I'd had with my birth mother.

When I opened my eyes to morning light, I rolled off the futon, careful not to rouse my mom, and padded into the hall to search for coffee. Dishes clattered behind a door. Hesitant, I pushed inward to peek through; it was, indeed, a kitchen.

A worker in scrubs came over to me. "May I help you?" He asked, crinkling his forehead.

"I'm looking for coffee?"

"Oh, okay. If you wait a minute, I'll bring some."

He brought hot coffee in a Styrofoam cup, with sugar and creamer packets.

Tiptoeing through Mom's room and out the sliding door, I relaxed on a cool wrought iron chair, propped my feet up, and stirred my drink. Birds chirped; cars hummed on the suburban street. I rehearsed what I might say later that morning when our goodbye came.

With my hands clasped behind my head, I leaned back in my chair. Karen was big on specifics; I wanted to point out distinct ways she'd made me a better person. I was learning to be present and to explore my artistic side; those were big. There were small ways, too: the time she tried on my glasses and became a parochial schoolteacher taught me how to size up my look in a mirror. This was something a young girl might learn from her mother, but I soaked it in now, in my fifties, and how could I express that? She was adding building stones that had been missing from my foundation.

There were my favorite times: the patio mural we painted, the dinner party with her friends, my birthday at her house. Could I pick one of those memories?

I was still considering when Stephen came out of Karen's door. "You hungry?"

We walked a block to a taqueria that served breakfast, and we chatted in a yellow booth surrounded by bright blue walls. My hunger was acute, and I opted for a last taste of real SoCal street tacos.

We had set my airport shuttle to pick me up at eleven. Since we had returned to the nursing home before ten, I stayed outside and gave

Rich a quick call while Stephen stepped into Karen's room. I'd just hung up when he came back out.

"Diane, your shuttle will be here in a few minutes, it's running early."

My eyes widened. "I have an hour…." But he shook his head. I melted. The time had come, and I hadn't decided what to say. I hurried inside and gathered my things, stuffing them into my red suitcase and tan backpack. Karen watched from her bed, cool light from the courtyard glowing around her.

"Stephen told you I have to leave right now because my shuttle's here?"

She nodded and gave me a radiant smile as I bent over and hugged her. My eyes were wet, my mind was blank. I yearned to express my best memories with her to make this a real goodbye as I'd seen so many people do. But now I had only a minute. None of the uplifting words I'd thought of sprang to mind. What tumbled from of my mouth was the depth of my heart.

"I'll miss you forever, Mommy."

She reached up and touched my cheek with her fingertips. "Affinity lasts forever, dear one."

She reassured me when I wanted to encourage her. I nodded, and my face softened into a small smile as I looked into her sparkling eyes. I smoothed her hair away from her forehead and kissed her cheek. "Yes, affinity lasts forever."

With my backpack and suitcase, I paused at the door, turned and took her in one last time. One last breath. Then I walked down the hall, out into the sunlight and my waiting airport shuttle.

CHAPTER 29

July 2013

KAREN'S 74TH BIRTHDAY arrived on July 1, and her friends threw a huge celebration for her, in the dining room at Canyon Oaks. Aunt Lee—I called her my aunt now—video-phoned me in the midst of the revelry.

"Diane?" Lee spoke over music and talkative voices.

"Hi, Aunt Lee! Sounds like fun there."

She panned her cell to show me the milling crowd. Balloons floated above Karen's bed in the middle of the spacious room. Streamers twirled from the ceiling. Celine waved as Lee carried the phone through the party and brought it near my mom's face.

"Happy Birthday, Mom!" I said, careful to enunciate and speak with force because of the noise.

"Thank you, darling!" Karen answered. "Do you see what my friends have done for me? They wheeled my bed in here, and what a surprise! So many lovely people!"

Someone outside my field of vision squeezed her hand. "I'm talking to my daughter," said my mother, looking up with a smile.

She turned back to Lee's phone. "My day's complete now that I've seen you, darling! But I have to let you go—it's hard for me to talk with you this way. So much going on here."

"Okay, Mom, I'm glad I had the chance to see your party."

"Give my love to Rich."

"I will. Love you very much."

"Love you." She smacked her lips several times.

Lee swung the phone back to herself. "Sorry it was short, but she's overwhelmed."

"That's fine. Thanks for including me!"

"Wouldn't want you to miss it. Take care."

"You too."

I hung up and cried. So many emotions whirled. Sadness because I was two thousand miles away; happiness that my mom had such good friends; thankfulness that Lee had included me. And, woven through it all, grief.

The next morning, I sat with my breakfast in my home office. I opened Gmail and found a message from Beny:

Stephen just emailed asking me to come and visit if I was in LA soon. Here is my response—I'd appreciate your reactions to it.

His honesty and sensitivity impressed me. He expressed his hesitance to go, wondered if Karen would want him to see her in her condition, if his visit would intrude on their family, and if he himself had the emotional stamina to do it.

I assured him my mom would love to see him because she'd expressed it; she and I had imagined being all together someday. Last fall we'd envisioned the two of us visiting Beny and Joan in Santa Fe when Karen recovered.

I told him my mom was letting people see her without makeup, even without her bridge. And that Stephen was asking everyone who'd been close to her. My email included a picture of Karen in her hospital bed, surrounded by family, to help him decide if he wanted to brave a visit. I knew well the emotional toll it might take.

He said he'd think it over, and hours later he emailed that he would go. As I replied, I typed an idea as it occurred to me: Maybe I can join you two on Skype... And we set it up in another message.

Twilight darkened the sky outside the patio door when my phone dinged to a text from Stephen. A week had gone by, and Beny was at the nursing home. Rich put my computer on his desk in the kitchen, and I pulled up a chair next to him. Denise stood near, and Mike stayed behind us with the video camera. The Skype ringtone sounded, my throat closed tight, and my heart thumped against my ribs.

Then my birth father and mother appeared on the screen. I was wonder-struck to see them together. Beny was beside Karen's bed in the room where I'd last seen her. It was still daylight there in California. She had her makeup on and a violet headband in her hair. Her smile was wide and genuine, schoolgirl-ish, like she was with her beau. They held hands. Beny was smiling, too, but his was sober, tender. They looked up at my image in a computer.

Mom was telling a story of a professor at Northwestern who noticed Beny's interest in her and encouraged her to date him.

"I'm sure glad he got the two of you together," I managed to say. My mind buzzed like a radio between stations.

Rich said, "So am I." We laughed.

Mom asked me, "Do you see anything alike between you and Beny?"

"I have his eyes."

My father said, "Everybody on my side of the family says that you look a lot like my mother."

"I've noticed that in pictures I look like both of your mothers."

"Okay," said my mother, taking charge, "You're both awfully smart, you both have great vocabularies. And ways of carrying your language around with you and expressing yourselves. You're both— more than I—gentle and softhearted."

Beny added, "We have the same naïveté, a childlikeness. We are surprised by things in the same way."

Mom said, "That's great."

"Thank you." I nodded. She wanted us to dig deep, beneath surface ideas. But my mind blanked. All I could do was stare at their image, watch Beny cradle her hand, and savor their smiles. I wrenched my eyes from the screen to my family, who were meeting my parents for the first time.

"Our second boy, Mike, is here taking a video of this," I gestured behind me as they greeted him. "And Denise is over there."

My mom and dad both said, "Hi, Denise," and waved. She waved back.

Then Mom said, "I wish Matt was there for me to see. Beny said Matt has my eyes. He thinks you have the same eyes, too."

"I know, that's cool. I'm glad." Where was my great vocabulary?

Rich saved me. "Diane has been waiting for this day for a long, long time. It's been a wild journey since she found you two. Just spectacular."

Beny added, "I wouldn't have gotten up the gumption to make this trip without Diane prodding me." They both thanked me.

"We three loved each other all these years," Mom added.

"Absolutely, I feel that's true." I agreed. Our reunions were actual homecomings.

"I've known your daughter since she was sixteen," said Rich. "And she has always, her whole life, wondered who her mother and father were. I can't even talk about it without crying." His tears glinted in the light of the screen.

"Somehow it entered my life with ease," commented Karen. "The way we are in each other's hearts is rather cozy. It's not wearing a red bandanna and flying a flag."

"And it's wonderful that you've assimilated so well into my family," added Beny. "And Nina has gotten to be good friends with Matt and Becca. They live near each other and spent Thanksgiving together."

Mike said, "That's the startling coincidence to me, how they ended up living a half hour apart."

Karen's voice was fading. "I have to go now. I'm tired."

"Okay, Mom. Thank you for including me, you two. It was amazing to see you together."

We all said goodbye, and then the connection ended.

I sat back, and a sense of warmth filled my chest. The Skype call had fulfilled a dream—the three of us had been together as a family.

A week later I got up at dawn, walked out into the dew with my plein air supplies, and painted a nearby barn in the early morning light. I took the wet painting to our Art Guild meeting in the bright conference room at the library. Doreen was admiring it and asking questions about my process when my phone dinged. I glanced at an email notification, from my new stepsister Kirsten. The subject line said, Dad is in the ER. I gasped.

Doreen looked at me, alarmed. "What's wrong? Something with Karen?"

"No. It's my new dad." Rooted to the tile floor, I read the message as a wave of nausea threatened to knock me over. "They rushed him to the ER after a brain CT scan… going to surgery this afternoon… Kirsten apologizes for saying this in an email, but she didn't have my phone number. She gave me hers."

"Do you need to leave?"

"One of us can bring Denise home," Mary added.

"No, no, I can't help. They're in New Mexico. Kirsten and Susan live near them, so they'll help. I'm just… shocked, that's all. This came out of left field. I better call Kirsten."

I walked over to the corner window and stood in the sunlight as I talked with my stepsister. Her voice was strong, and although I heard a tremble of worry, she projected a solid, trustworthy, we'll-get-through-this attitude. She was on her way to join them at the hospital and assured me she'd keep me posted.

I sat back down to work, but inspiration fled. I could only sit still, breathe, and pray that God wouldn't take both my parents. The ladies offered supportive comments, and Denise asked me what was wrong.

"My birth father is having brain surgery."

"I know what that's like," she said.

"Yes, I guess you do." Her show of concern lightened my heart.

Later, at home, I received an email from Joan to the whole family, explaining the situation. I read it at my desk.

Beny had been having headaches for months and hadn't been himself. Doctors gave him several diagnoses, but never did a CT scan of his head. Finally, he insisted, and they began the scan. But they stopped mid-test and sent him straight to the ER—right across the street. Within ninety minutes they were shaving his hair in the surgical unit. A neurosurgeon drilled two holes in his head, one on each side, and drained two massive subdural hematomas. The prognosis is good, and he's resting in the ICU. It was a frightening close call.

Nearly losing my new dad put me over an emotional edge. I was in actual, physical pain, like my heart was literally breaking. Thankful beyond words to hear he was okay; I broke down into gulping sobs for a long while.

As Beny recuperated, Karen worsened. Her lungs filled with fluid, so much of it that breathing became a chore. She told me in one of her few texts:

Nina, it is so difficult for me to communicate just now. I spend every moment on rehabilitation! My lungs got worse from exhaustion and that is very scary.

I continued to send her phone pics of my new paintings, and she responded to them with praise. She'd use interesting words in comments such as: I love your style, it's not rococo or fussy.

One afternoon late in July we had a beautiful thunderstorm. The light was a rich storm-yellow, the air carried a soft rain scent. Distant booming came close in rolling echoes. As I listened to the downpour and watched the silvery green leaves shining with rain toss in the wind, I wanted to capture the weather in paint. My plein-air easel and paints were handy; I set up on our porch under the dripping eaves and began. As I worked, letting my brushstrokes follow the sway of the branches, the moment entranced me. When the raindrops went from shower to sprinkle, the sky glowed with rose tones, and the painting was complete. Right away I sent Karen a photo, snapping the picture as I held the little canvas in front of the trees I had painted.

Her reply was classic: *I can't believe what I am seeing! I have birthed a genius!!!*

It would be my last communication from her.

CHAPTER 30

August 8, 2013

Dangling off this precipice
my hands strangle a sapling
its roots slowly rip away
dirt clods loosen
dust falls silent
down
down
I look up
and know His Hands will catch me
but still I fear the falling
this
next
moment…

ONE YEAR TO THE DAY from Karen's first Facebook reply, I woke up alone. That wasn't unusual; Rich's fishing trips started early. But this morning, I missed him. I hadn't heard from my mom in two weeks. Worry engulfed me, although Hunter's texts assured me her condition was stable.

I kept imagining her gurgling breath. I prayed continuously, for her and for me. There were musings of the hoped-for future that rolled in my mind like music—we would play in the ocean together; she would meet Rich, our kids, our grandkids. Those dreams had to fall away like leaves in the wind. Although she continued to live, I had to let her go, get back to my life, and stop brooding—to embrace everything she'd taught me, and all the love she'd given me, open my hands and let her fly away.

I cried as I rolled out of bed, as I fed my dogs, as I made my coffee. Just let the tears roll down and drip off my chin. When I finished my morning routine, I sat back on my bed and leaned against the wall, breathing. I could video a proper goodbye. For myself, if nothing else.

With my computer on my lap, I practiced, crying through much of it, expressing what I had to say. Then I got up, washed my face, brushed my hair, put on makeup and a purple top. Out in the porch air, I positioned the screen so our Rose of Sharon bush was behind me. I was ready to begin.

Hi, Mom. It was one year ago today, on this very spot, that I opened this computer and found your reply on Facebook. It has been the most amazing year of my life. I don't think you can know how much you've given me.

Just by accepting me, by loving me, you gave me my roots. Knowing my genealogy from Uncle Peter. Reading Grandma's autobiography. Connecting with Beny. All because you let me in.

I mentioned the day we spent on the mural, the parties she gave in my honor, the life lessons she'd taught me. Small things like doing her makeup and important ones such as being present.

Thank you for letting me help you after your ablation. I got to be a daughter to you… and you've been a mom to me. And that has healed my heart.

I never said a proper goodbye, so I'm doing it now. I'm letting you go. It's been a wonderful, healing time. I'm very thankful you've been in my life. I will always, always love you. Goodbye, Mommy.

I held myself together and didn't cry until I switched off the camera. After the video processed in my software, I posted it privately on YouTube. Should I let Karen see it? I called and asked our pastor, and he said yes. When we lose someone over a period of time we can grieve before they die. His assurance gave me confidence.

I texted Stephen, telling him where to find the video. But he'd just left the nursing home and said he would show Karen when he got back.

Rich and I walked into the kitchen door that afternoon. As I put away groceries, he sat down at his desk to check Facebook.

"Oh my God, Di!" He cried. My heart pounded. "Stephen just posted that Karen died!"

A pause in the universe, a second of nothingness.

Then anger. "How could he do that?" I wailed. "Why wouldn't he call first?" My face wrinkled into sobs as grief took me. "I wonder if Hunter knows yet." Rich stood up and held me as I wept and shook.

My cell rang. I ran to pick it up, expecting Hunter or Stephen. It was Harriet.

"Hello?" I said, through my pain.

"Diane? It's Harriet. You saw Stephen's post?"

"Uh-huh." I tottered outside with the phone and leaned against the house.

"I thought so," she said, "and I wanted to call right away. That was not a good way to find out."

"No, it wasn't."

"I was with her, Diane. Stephen had gone out; he wasn't there when she passed. I called him and saw his post a minute later. I didn't want you to be alone right now."

"Thank you so much, Harriet. It's good to hear your voice. He should have phoned me before he posted."

"Yes. But that's Stephen. I'm sure he'll feel awful when he realizes what he did."

I nodded, hugging myself. "So, was she in pain?"

"No, no, she was asleep, thank God. She took a Norco, drifted off, and she was gone."

Relief made me lighter. I had been so worried that she'd be in terrible agony, that she would struggle for breath or something miserable. Hearing Harriet's calm voice say she died peacefully took the edge off my angst.

"Does Hunter know?" I asked.

"I'm not sure. I'll call him next."

"Okay. Love you."

"Love you, too."

Back inside, I stood behind Rich's chair and we watched Facebook. Condolences were nonstop on Karen's fan page. Sobs shook my shoulders again. Rich swiveled around and gathered me onto his lap and let me cry.

Stephen called a while later, his voice thick with sadness, apologetic for not calling first. Was I angry? Well, yes—but it was okay, I forgave him.

He said, "She was beginning to understand that it didn't matter if her tumors were getting better if she couldn't breathe. She was gurgling the past couple days. It was good she passed in her sleep."

"Did she see my video?"

"No, I'm sorry. She was gone before I got back."

How was it possible she died on this day? We had exactly one calendar year together—we celebrated the day I was born, we had one Mother's Day, one chance to share all of life's seasons. And even though she didn't see my goodbye, I had found closure and peace by recording it.

That evening, there were many posts, comments, and expressions of sympathy. I broke my imposed Facebook silence, shared her name and posted photos of the two of us. Hunter wrote a touching farewell.

Elyse shared my picture, acknowledging me as Karen's daughter and Hunter's older sister. Rich's mom called. I leaned into all their support and let it comfort me.

One evening a week later, I hung up the phone and sat next to Rich on the couch, curling up to face him. "Stephen says the family funeral is the 19th. There's a Hollywood memorial that will be later, a show where famous people get up on stage to talk about Karen."

He raised his brow. "Do you hope to go to both?"

He was thinking of the expense, but I'd feel out of place at a big production like the memorial.

"No. But the funeral for sure. That's important." I touched his arm and caught his gaze. "Rich, I want you to go with me."

He frowned. "I'd like to, but how could we swing it?"

"Maybe people will help us? We can ask at church; they've prayed this whole time."

"I could ask my buddies, too. They might have extra airline points. What about Denise?"

"Maybe someone will stay with her?"

Within a week, several ladies contributed, and Rich's friends gave miles and money. We received enough to cover our flights and found a fantastic friend to stay with Denise while we were gone.

———

A night before our flight, I dreamed. In the dream, I was driving a lonely desert road, evening sun low and bright, casting long shadows. Suddenly there was a wooden barricade before me—the kind that warns of construction. I stepped out of the car and around this barrier. Men in hard hats and orange vests worked on a stretch of white cement, building the road by hand. Here and there, one poured a manual cement mixer, one troweled on his knees. The road went on for a hundred yards or so until it ended in exposed rebar and gravel. After that, a faded path in the sand curved to a distant red rock horizon.

There was a man beside me, bending to his work. He had a red bandanna around his tanned forehead.

"What is this?" I asked him.

He looked up at me. "It is the beginning."

"What do I do now?" I asked.

"Walk on," he answered, gesturing to the distance, toward the long, unfinished road ahead.

CHAPTER 31

August 19, 2013

THE SOUTHERN CALIFORNIA SUN shone with warm light. Rich was driving our rental car, following Hunter to Eternal Hills Cemetery in Oceanside, north of San Diego near Uncle Peter's home. I gazed out the window as the rolling, grass-covered landscape swept by, immersed in mixed emotions and detached. The world was surreal. Rich held my hand, and his touch anchored me to the moment so I didn't drift away on the wind.

Eucalyptus trees lined the driveway of the funeral home. Car doors thudded closed as we stepped out in the parking lot. The breeze carried a light menthol scent, reminding me of the pines in Wisconsin. Elyse lifted Janey out of her car seat and then we all walked together. On the sidewalk leading to the canopied entrance, I reached for Hunter. We stepped hand in hand toward our reflection in the glass front door, both in somber black.

Inside was a well-lit foyer. Stephen had set up a long table, and he was busy taking photos out of boxes to display. Four of his brothers—tall, dark, imposing men—shook our hands while they introduced themselves: Riggs, Nicholas, Alex, and Anthony with his wife, Lore, an artist. We chatted with them, but I drifted alone, a spectator. People flowed in, shaking my hand, all with a story of how they knew my mom. I seemed to stand inside the doorway forever.

Then someone—it was Lee—led me into a hallway from the lobby. She stopped at a door on the right where organ music played.

"She's in here, Diane. I want you to be prepared, she doesn't look good. You don't have to approach the casket."

"No, I want to. That poem I showed you," I fumbled in my purse and pulled out a folded paper, "I want to put it in there with her." It was *I Am New*, the one I had written that winter.

"That was the most beautiful poem I ever read. How appropriate," said Lee.

I inhaled a long breath and let it out as I stepped into the room. On my left a charming lady played the organ. She smiled at me. I walked up to the casket. Lee was right, my mom's face wasn't pretty. I shifted my gaze to her hands, which were as I remembered them. Placing my poem beside her, I bowed my head and prayed for her soul.

Lee and I rejoined the crowd in the foyer. I looked for Rich and found him by Stephen, who was setting up to record the service in the chapel. A dozen rows of cushioned chairs flanked a center aisle. Three large, arched windows let light in from a garden.

"I went to see Karen," I said.

"Without me?" Asked Rich, concerned surprise in his eyes.

"Lee took me. Do you want to go, too?"

"Yes, I thought we'd do it together."

"We still can. Come on." We left Stephen to his work.

I brought Rich to the casket room, and we stood over Karen. "She doesn't look like herself," I whispered. He nodded and squeezed my hand while he said a quiet prayer, for Karen, for me, for my new families.

Lee met us as we came out of the hallway. "We're getting ready for the service to start soon. Diane, you'll be in the first row with the family. You're speaking fourth after Gail."

Lee had called a couple weeks ago and asked if I wanted to talk, so I had a page of notes prepared. As the congregation found seats, a montage video of Karen's life played, set to the upbeat song "I Go to Rio."

A Scientology minister began the service, letting us know how it would progress and saying a few words.

Then Stephen took the podium. "I edited that video all weekend and cried the whole time because Karen loved that song. Sometimes she would belt it out for no reason." He paused for audience chuckles. "Today is a memorial for you guys, Karen's family and friends. Karen wanted people to tell stories about her here. So, going through all the pictures for this video, Celine came across a press clipping from 1996, a short-answer interview. And the last question was, what are three words that best describe you? Karen's answers: *light, present, and non-derivative.*

"On the subject of *light,* she was to her core, a happy person. She worked really hard, and she put as much energy into having fun as she did into her work. All of you know, her parties were legendary." Laughter and applause.

"As far as the word *present,* what she meant by that was being present. She engaged life right until the very end, which astounded doctors. They never saw anything like it. She once took morphine, and she said, 'I can't stand the way I feel. I don't feel like I'm there.' She chose being there over anything else.

"The last one, *non-derivative.* Karen had her own conclusions and ideas about everything. She was superstitious about numbers. I mean lots of people are. But rather than picking a system, she made up her own." More laughter from the crowd. "Harriet and I did the whole math to figure out which day to have the funeral. Today is a five day, it's a lucky day.

"Karen was completely original when it came to her work, acting. She combined an insane amount of preparation with an entirely in-the-moment expression. Complete control and complete lack of control at the same time. It's a trick that few people are capable of doing.

"The last thing I want to talk about is help. Endless stories of how she helped people. She helped me. I was introverted when I first met her, reading books all the time. She made it okay for me to engage life, and she led by example. It was a joyous charge at existence. I believe Karen must have loved an awful lot of people because she helped everyone who had the fortune to cross her path. Thank you." The applause lasted a long time.

Hunter was next. As he walked on the stage, Janey said into the silence, "Uh-oh! Daddy now."

"That's my daughter," he said, and chuckled with us. "My mom always broke into spontaneous song. And that's what I want to do, sing a hymn." He began "Swing Low Sweet Chariot," singing accappella. Janey toddled up the stairs to him. He picked her up and held her as he swayed, crooning the chorus several times. The whole congregation joined in on the third repetition. I doubt there was a dry eye. He concluded, "I love you, Mom. She loved all of you. Thank you for being here."

Celine cried through her turn, telling anecdotes of her childhood. She said Karen made everything magical. "When I was a little girl, she'd play this game with me. She'd be in the kitchen, and I'd be in the bedroom. I'd get on the edge of the bed, and I'd scream 'I'm falling off the bed! Come save me!' And she would run as fast she could, no matter what she was doing, to get to me in time. And if she didn't, I'd hit the floor. And she'd get there almost every time."

The audience laughed. Celine finished by saying, "Even the last few days she was still herself. Still the same magical, happy person singing and doing people's colors, still trying. Her body gave up on her, but she fought till the end with a smile on her face. So, remember her with that smile."

Karen's sister, Gail, looked small behind the podium, hands grasping both edges, her blonde frizz framing a face so like my mom's.

She spoke in a quiet voice, telling stories. "One night we were in our backyard looking at the moon. Karen said, 'The moon follows me,' and I said, 'No, it follows me!' So we decided to see who was right. She went around the house one way, and I went the other. When we met, we both said the moon had followed us again. So that argument was never resolved." Her remembrances had us all chuckling.

Gail concluded, "I was having trouble deciding what to say, so I said, 'Karen you have to help me; what do you want me to say to these people?' And she replied, 'I want you to tell them: thank you for loving me, and thank you for sharing your life with me.'"

There was applause, and as Gail descended, I stood up, straightened my dress, took a gulp of air, and mounted the stairs. Once I faced the audience, my jitters stopped. These people loved my mother. Scanning the crowd for familiar faces, I put on my reading glasses and began.

"Hi. Some of you know me, some of you don't. My name is Diane Bay. I'm Karen's daughter from a teenage relationship." Gasps scattered through the chapel. "She lovingly gave me up for adoption because she was too young to raise me. And in Illinois, the state law prevented us from ever finding each other until just last year." The audience groaned. "They changed the law, and I got my original birth certificate with Karen's name on it. And after that it took about two minutes to find her on the internet." Lots of laughter made me smile, too. My shoulders relaxed.

"I sent her a message on Facebook and asked if she was my mother. And the morning of August 8, 2012, Rich and I were sitting on our front porch, and I opened my Facebook to check, and there was this message from Karen. She told me very simply, 'Yes, I am your mother.'" The page on the podium blurred as I fought to keep reading.

"And she just accepted me, welcomed me, right back into her life. So, for exactly one year, it has been my privilege and delight to call her Mom. And I found, as you did, she was amazingly interested in the real me and somehow able to help me bring out the best in myself."

I told my favorite memory, the day we played together painting the mural. I ended by saying, "My mom was the bravest and most encouraging person I've ever met. She was a gifted listener, full of the zest of life. Her love has filled me to overflowing. I am whole; I am complete now. I am honored and awed to be her daughter."

As I stepped off the platform to a long and hearty applause, Celine looked up with tears on her face. I bent and hugged her before taking my seat next to Lee. She squeezed my hand and nodded that I'd done well.

After me, Stephen's brothers spoke, and they had hilarious anecdotes to tell. Then, Harriet sat at an electric keyboard. She told the story of the night around Karen's hospital bed when her song had evolved. Then she sang and played the music she'd written, "All the Ways You're Wonderful." Joy seeped into my bones listening to her voice, realizing anew that I had become a part of this tremendous story.

When the service was over, we left for the graveside. A breeze wafted through the open car windows as we caravanned around grassy slopes and curving cemetery lanes. A green canopy was atop one knoll. There were white roses for us each to take as we found our seats. Hunter and I sat side by side in the front row.

The minister recited a few words at a wood lectern next to the grave. Karen's casket lowered. Then we stood and filed past, tossing our flowers down until a snow of white covered her. Stephen found me and beckoned me to follow him. We walked a few yards. "Karen wanted to be buried near her mother," he said, pointing to a polished red marker, my grandmother's gravestone. I stood silent with hands clasped, the sun warming my shoulders. He left me to my reverie. My mind flitted through imaginations of Manitowoc summers long ago, Chicago streets in the 1920s, and a white house with a screen porch in Park Ridge.

Rich found me, and after I showed him the grave, he took my hand and turned me. A mic was keying up. A woman I didn't recognize stood before the milling crowd. Hunter walked near, and leaned in to whisper, "That's Ronee Blakley. She acted with Mom in *Nashville*."

Ronee sang, her pure voice rolling over us. The breeze cooled tears that dripped from my face unabated as "Amazing Grace" resonated over the hillside. What a perfect tribute to the great heart of my birth mother.

The funeral took on a celebratory vibe when we gathered in a dining room where Stephen set up another mic for people's remembrances. Themes repeated: Karen's encouragement that led to life-changing action, her overflowing kindness, her courageous brilliance.

Contented to listen, I sat in back as dozens of friends took the mic. Nostalgic or hilarious, raunchy or sweet, all the stories were told with fondness. The fairytale wonder of our first shared weeks filled me again. Karen would have loved it, and I hoped she was watching.

On the evening after the funeral, we drove through Encinitas to a parking lot on a coastal dune overlooking the ocean. The view was vast. Luminous clouds broke the setting sun into a hundred rays, painting the ocean liquid silver. The beach below was where Ziegler family reunions had taken place in years past. I needed to walk down to the shore, so I kissed Rich, and he stayed in the car as I wound my way downhill through twilit shadows.

A warm salt breeze and expansive quietude enveloped me. I rounded a grassy knoll into the light and heard the gentle rhythm of waves. Gulls cried. A few clutches of beach-goers milled around small fires. Walking beyond them, I was alone with the sea.

The world glowed golden as I slipped off my sandals and stepped onto the wet sand, my toes sinking in, the cool water washing up my ankles as each wave passed. I strolled, enjoying the tactile connection to the infinite ocean, watching the ripples of amber, silver, rose, and turquoise rolling toward me. A small sailboat drifted into the distance, sailing away from me. Just then a bright ray shot from behind a cloud, and the little boat floated into the oval of heavenly light. I stood still, enthralled.

A prose poem I'd heard at several funerals came to mind. It likened a loved one's soul to a sailing ship on the horizon:

Just at the moment when someone says, "There, she is gone,"
there are other eyes watching her coming, and other voices
ready to take up the glad shout, "Here she comes!"

I whispered, "Goodbye, Mommy!" And tears streamed over my face, wetting my tongue with salt as I keened and sobbed, falling to my knees in the flowing foam, letting the ocean rhythm rock me, heedless of my soaked clothes.

Then I stood and waded to the sand, feeling lighter. Barefoot with my sandals swinging, I meandered up the hill where Rich waited for me. The next day we flew home to Kentucky, back to Denise and our life together.

EPILOGUE

October 24, 2013

IN THE HALLWAY OF ANOTHER HOSPITAL, I stood looking out of a sunny window. There in the glass was my hazy reflection, and I saw my mother's features in my face. I whispered to her. "Mommy, you're about to have another great-grandbaby. Her name is Piper, and she's being born right now! I'll hold her soon, and she'll be a real live connection to you."

A commotion in the hall caught my attention. I took a deep breath and dashed around a corner. There was our son Mike, standing, beaming, hands on the handle of a cart where a small wrapped bundle lay. I joined a flock of relatives gathering around him.

I touched little Piper's cheek and smoothed her silky brown hair. Her dark eyes opened wide to the world, absorbing these first moments of her new life. As I gazed at her tiny enchanting face, my heart sang with Karen's vitality, resounding with the rhythms of life: longing and embracing, dancing and dying, tiptoeing into the universe, small but immense.

So much deeper and richer than my old peaceful melancholy, my mother's fire now lived in me. I intended to pass it on.

References

1. "Karen Black," accessed July 22, 2012,
   https://en.wikipedia.org/wiki/Karen_Black

2. "Neil Armstrong," accessed August 13, 2018,
   https://en.wikiquote.org/wiki/Neil_Armstrong

3. New American Standard Bible. La Habra, CA:
   Foundation Publications, for the Lockman Foundation.
   Zondervan, 1999. Print.

4. Gershwin, George. "Summertime." Porgy and Bess, 1935.
   DuBose Heyward, lyrics.